NEW LEFT REVIEW 61

SECOND SERIES

JANUARY FEBRUARY 2010

PROGRAMME NOTES

SUSAN WATKINS: Shifting Sands

What remains of the neo-liberal order after the implosion of 2008—with what implications for a journal of the left? Notes for a future research agenda, as NLR enters its quinquagenary year.

MIKE DAVIS: Building the Ark

Copenhagen's charades dispel any illusion that world rulers intend to deal with the environmental damage industrialization has caused. Mike Davis argues that green urbanism's twining of social equality and ecological sustainability could offer an alternative starting-point.

TERI REYNOLDS: Ward Notes

Dispatches from an Oakland Emergency Department, testifying to the stark inequalities between public and private, insured and unprotected, that Democrat proposals will enshrine.

PERRY ANDERSON: Two Revolutions

How to explain the opposed outcomes for communism in Russia and China, after 1989? Classes and leaders, *anciens régimes* and external settings, examined in comparative perspective.

TARIQ ALI: President of Cant

From declamations in Cairo to silence over Gaza, occupation of Iraq and escalation in Afghanistan and Pakistan, Tariq Ali asks what has changed in US foreign policy since the departure of Bush.

FRANCO MORETTI: The Grey Area

Flexible morality and capitalist imperatives of the bourgeois fin-de-siècle, as captured in the obscure misdeeds of Ibsen's protagonists.

ERIC HOBSBAWM: World Distempers

The author of *Age of Extremes* discusses the major developments since the end of the Cold War. Amid the turbulence of capital's advance, what larger problems should historians seek to understand?

ROBIN BLACKBURN: State of the Union

The fate of post-bellum attempts to extend egalitarian impulses across race lines and factory floors, amid the sharpening class struggles of the Gilded Age.

STUART HALL: The First New Left

NLR's founding editor recalls the emergence of the British New Left out of the double conjuncture of 1956—Hungary and Suez—and identifies the cross-currents, cultural and political, that nourished its initial cohort.

BOOK REVIEWS

ANDERS STEPHANSON on Susan Buck-Morss, *Hegel, Haiti and Universal History*. Did the *Weltgeist* drop anchor in revolutionary Saint-Domingue?

GOPAL BALAKRISHNAN on Reinhold Niebuhr, *The Irony of American History*. Consoling homilies for today's liberal imperialists, from the theologian of the nuclear era.

AARON BENANAV on Jan Breman, *The Poverty Regime in Village India*. A sociologist explores the mechanisms of inequality shaping the life-world of informal labour.

CONTRIBUTORS

AARON BENANAV: *studies history at* UCLA; *see also* NLR 48

STUART HALL: *founding editor of* NLR; *former director of the Centre for Contemporary Cultural Studies at Birmingham; papers on 'The Multicultural Question' and 'Modernity and Difference' appeared in 2001*

ERIC HOBSBAWM: *author of* Age of Extremes *(1994)*, The New Century *(2000)*, Interesting Times *(2002) and, most recently,* Globalisation, Democracy and Terrorism *(2007)*

FRANCO MORETTI: *teaches literature at Stanford; author of* Graphs, Maps, Trees *(2005) and editor of* The Novel *(2006); see* NLR 24, 26, 28, 41 *and* 52

TERI REYNOLDS: *emergency physician in the Bay Area*

ANDERS STEPHANSON: *teaches history at Columbia University; author of* Manifest Destiny *(1995); see also* NLR 49

SUSAN WATKINS

Editorial

SHIFTING SANDS

C ORRELATIONS BETWEEN anniversaries and historical conjunctures are likely to be ironic. When NLR was launched in
London fifty years ago, in January 1960, it was one of myriad
small harbingers of left renewal. Anti-colonial forces were
registering victories in Africa, Asia and the Arab world; the Communist
movement was emerging from the stranglehold of Stalinist orthodoxy;
in North America, Western Europe and Japan a new generation chafed
at the conformism of Cold War culture. By the mid-60s the Review had
staked out a programme of mapping these three world zones in a series
of comparative studies of national social formations—not least its own.
Strongly oriented towards Continental theory and practice, the journal
played its part in the intensive debates within Marxism that accompanied
the heady days of 68. It helped to pioneer work on women's liberation,
ecology, media, film theory, the state.

By the 1990s, the journal survived within an international landscape that
would have seemed a sci-fi dystopia in 1960: the Kremlin's economic
policy run by Friedmanites, the General Secretary of the CCP lauding
the stock exchange; Yugoslavia, the most pluralist and successful of the
workers' states, decimated by IMF austerity policies and subjected to a
three-month NATO bombing campaign, cheered on by liberal opinion
in the West; social democratic parties competing to privatize national
assets and abolish labour gains. Neo-liberalism reigned supreme,
enshrining a model of unfettered capital flows and financial markets,
deregulated labour and internationally integrated production chains. On
its fortieth anniversary, at the high noon of globalization and American
supremacy, NLR was relaunched by its editorial committee in a spirit of

uncompromising realism: 'the refusal of any accommodation with the ruling system, as of any understatement of its power'.[1]

Ten years on again, the continuation of the neo-liberal era itself has been thrown into question by the eruption of an epic financial crisis at the heart of the system. During the *grandes journées* of September 2008 Fannie Mae and Freddie Mac, the giant US institutions at the centre of the mortgage-backed securities market, were taken into government stewardship after their shares had plunged by 90 per cent. Lehman Brothers went bankrupt, Merrill Lynch was forced into a shotgun marriage with Bank of America, HBOS with LloydsTSB; a tottering Citigroup, whose stock value had fallen from $244bn to $6bn, was shored up by government funds, Washington Mutual pulled from receivership by JPMorganChase. Goldman Sachs, Merrill Lynch, Deutsche Bank and Société Générale were saved by massive Treasury transfusions into their bankrupt insurer, AIG. In the months that followed, world output, trade, equity, credit and investment ground to a halt, while unemployment soared towards double digits across the Northern hemisphere.

Running into trillions of dollars in direct and indirect support, the bailouts of the financial institutions will weigh on domestic economies—above all in the US and UK—for years to come. But did the massive state interventions also signal the end of the neo-liberal model? Ideologically, the wealth-creating prowess of big finance has been one of its central legitimating claims. There was a feeling, not just on the left, that the crisis could not but leave the paradigm itself discredited; it might even have dealt a body-blow to American hegemony. The humbling of the Wall Street giants—US Treasury Secretary Paulson offering to go down on his knees before Congress on their behalf—seemed to suggest that the world stood on the brink of a new era. Since then the financial system has been stabilized, although none of its underlying problems have been resolved. But despite the torrent of literature on the crisis, its historical meaning remains obscure. What ended, and what did not, in September 2008?

I

Any answer will need to begin by setting the crash in comparative perspective. Crises that shake the entire capitalist world have been surprisingly

---

[1] Perry Anderson, 'Renewals', NLR 1, Jan–Feb 2000.

rare, for all the creative-destructive nature of the system; but 2008 could arguably be set against the railroad bust of 1873, the 1929 New York stock-exchange collapse or, as a lower limit-case, the 'great panic' of 1907. Their outcomes differed widely. In 1873, German receipt from Paris of the 1871 Franco-Prussian war indemnity—£90 million, paid in gold—set off frenzied building booms in Berlin and Vienna that sucked back German funds from over-extended American railroad trusts, which in turn helped bring down US banks. Financial contagion spread, and the recessions that ensued initiated a widespread deflationary downturn—'a depression of prices, a depression of interest, a depression of profits'—that persisted, punctuated by occasional rallies and further recessions, until 1896.[2] By contrast, the 'Rich Man's Panic' of 1907, upshot of speculative banking failures in Italy and copper and railroad busts in New York, had little lasting impact on manufacturing and trade; after a short, sharp recession, recovery set in the following year. Different again, the 1929 crash signalled a plunge in trade and output that would usher in the Great Depression.

A precondition for any deeper understanding of the 2008 crisis will be a thorough-going comparative analysis; but an investigation along those lines lies beyond the scope of the present survey. What follows will simply take these earlier crises as markers for a preliminary scanning of the post-2008 landscape, to ask what remains of neo-liberalism, as programme and ideology, and what may be consigned to the past.

Neo?

'Neo-liberal' is a dismal epithet, of course, imprecise and over-used. But some term is needed to describe the macro-economic paradigm that has predominated from the end of the 1970s until—at least—2008. Hayek once said that, while he regarded himself as a classical liberal, the term neo-liberalism was not inappropriate, since liberalism had been so completely abandoned in the West after the 19th century that the return—still incomplete—to its principles merited the prefix.[3] Three features have distinguished the late 20th-century variety from

[2] From Alfred Marshall's *Principles of Economics*, cited in Eric Hobsbawm, *The Age of Empire, 1875–1914*, London 1987, p. 36. See also Charles Kindleberger and Robert Aliber, *Manias, Panics and Crashes: A History of Financial Crises*, 5th edition, Basingstoke 2005, pp. 17, 44, 118–9.
[3] Politically, of course, most neo-liberals, less historically minded than he, have always disliked the term.

earlier free-market avatars. First, its Americanness: from Carter on, the neo-liberal programme has been developed and propagated by US-led institutions, and propounded as international policy by the US state. American multinationals and financial giants have been among its principal beneficiaries and it has been experienced in many parts of the world as the Americanization of economies, cultures and societies. Second, its enemies: the social-democratic post-war settlement, organized labour, state socialism. Whereas Victorian-era laissez-faire tried to hold the line against a coming world of protectionism, the genius of neo-liberalism has lain in the destruction and expropriation of existing structures and goods: privatization of utilities, de-unionization of labour, means-testing of universal benefits, removal of tariffs and capital controls. Its positive constructions have been less charismatic: the WTO, shadow banking, workfare, NAFTA.

A third distinguishing feature of neo-liberalism has been its success. Nineteenth-century liberalism was hemmed in on all sides by pre-capitalist property relations, imperial tariffs and a growing socialist movement. Since the end of the Cold War, by contrast, neo-liberalism's hegemony has been almost universal, virtually every governing party adhering to it; the term globalization had to be coined to denominate the same set of policies at an international level. True that it has never been an ideology in the broadest sense—a shared *Weltanschauung*, capable of interpreting the totality of human experience—but rather something narrower and more specialized: a belief in the superiority of one set of macro-economic policies over others, legitimated by their relative success, delegitimated by their costliness or failures. Neo-liberalism mobilized the enthusiasm of those who could count their gains from it; but as an electoral programme it always needed an admixture of some warmer ideological brew: nationalism (Reagan, Thatcher), Third Way social-liberalism (Clinton, Blair), religion (BJP, AKP), etc. It has been contested from below in Latin America, and unevenly applied in Germany, Japan, Korea and China; but since the 1990s the liberalized American economy, with the Treasury–Wall Street nexus at its heart, has been the paradigm for the world.

Rescue

The official account has it that an unimaginably devastating crisis for this system was averted by the decisive intervention of the US Treasury and Federal Reserve, whose prompt actions—public funds poured into the stricken banks, fiscal and monetary relief rushed to the stalling economies—'saved the world'.[4] One much-noted difference between today and the pre-ww2 crises lies in the degree of American co-ordination of the world economy. Unlike their predecessors, Paulson, Geithner and Bernanke could command a vast and densely integrated global financial system. Through the size of the US market, and Treasury hegemony over other key finance ministries, they could orchestrate international responses in a way that Andrew Mellon or Montagu Norman could not have envisaged. The Treasury bailout of Deutsche Bank and Société Générale via AIG was one aspect of this; the concerted doses of monetary loosening and counter-cyclical spending across the advanced capitalist world—an average 2 per cent of GDP for the G20 economies—another.

The neo-Keynesian emergency packages stand in stark contrast to the liberal purity of Mellon, who as Hoover's Treasury Secretary argued for letting the system purge itself.[5] But the 2008 'rescue', aimed at shoring up the existing order, differs just as much from the Rooseveltian programme of 'relief and reform', embodied in the 1933 Glass–Steagall Act. It has been more like a Treasury-funded version of the banker-led bailouts organized by J. P. Morgan during the 'great panic' of 1907, or by the New York Federal Reserve during the LTCM crisis in 1998. As a result, the great winners of the 2008 crisis have been the banks. With the exception of Lehman Brothers, the Treasury–Wall Street nexus has looked after its own. After a period of frenzied mergers, the surviving banks are famously bigger than ever before and still more essential to the system. They have been funnelled trillions of dollars in forms that have largely avoided public scrutiny—one reason why they could repay the condition-laden TARP funds so soon. They have used the Treasury's largesse in profitable trading on their own accounts, benefiting from the low Federal funds rate while charging usurious levels on loans and credit cards, at the expense of almost everyone else. Geithner's March 2009 financial rescue plan, offering to defer mark-downs on their toxic mortgage-bubble assets in exchange for cosmetic stress tests, signalled

---

[4] The phrase was coined by Paul Krugman to describe Gordon Brown's parallel efforts on behalf of the City of London: 'Gordon Does Good', NYT, 12 October 2008.
[5] For Hoover's famous summary of Mellon's 'leave-it-alone liquidationism' see Kindleberger, *Manias, Panics and Crashes*, p. 178. Kindleberger argues that *Schadenfreude* in Washington at pushy New York bankers' come-uppance helped determine the hands-off Federal response to the railroad bust of 1873.

the turning-point. The banks had got away with it, politically; since then their shares have soared.

Despite these concerted interventions, plunges in output, trade, equity and house prices in the first two quarters after September 2008 were steeper than those of 1929. The EU as a whole saw an annualized drop in output of 10 per cent in the first quarter of 2009; the fall was 12 per cent in Japan. Global panic—spread not least by the Federal Reserve chairman ('there may not be an economy on Monday')—was only one factor in the contagion. German and Japanese banks were implicated in the US subprime market, Chinese funds in the broader housing sector. Countries that had most faithfully copied the American housing bubble faced their own blow-outs, as foreclosures increased and foreign capital fled. Austrian banks exposed in Hungary, or German in the Baltics, clamped down on lending at home. Commodity-producing countries in Africa and Latin America, as manufacturing exporters in Asia, braced themselves for falling American demand.[6]

Prospects

By the summer of 2009, epic fiscal and monetary loosening had started to brake the global contraction. IMF prognoses should no doubt be taken with a pinch of salt, after their sunny forecasts in April 2007; but they suggest that American GDP will steady from –2.7 per cent in 2009 to 1.7 per cent in 2010; the Eurozone from –4.2 to 0.3 per cent, with France and Germany doing slightly better, and Japan stabilizing from –5.4 to 1.7 per cent.[7] This is in stark contrast to the 1930s, when output fell continuously for four years in North America, much of Europe and Latin America, dropping by 29 per cent, peak-to-trough, in the US.[8] But as the crisis enters its second year, the world outlook is notably uneven. Hardest hit among advanced capitalist countries are the core Atlantic economies—the

[6] IMF *World Economic Outlook*, October 2009; Carmen Reinhart and Kenneth Rogoff, *This Time is Different: Eight Centuries of Financial Folly*, Princeton 2009, pp. 248–73.
[7] Figures and prognoses from the IMF *World Economic Outlook*, October 2009, and *Regional Economic Outlooks* for Europe, Western Hemisphere, Africa, Asia and the Middle East, October 2009. According to these estimates, emergency counter-cyclical spending has lifted growth by an average 1.5 per cent of GDP in the advanced capitalist economies.
[8] Reinhart and Rogoff, *This Time is Different*, pp. 234–6; Eric Hobsbawm, *Age of Extremes: The Short Twentieth Century, 1914–1991*, London 1994, pp. 85–108.

US and UK, with disproportionately large financial sectors, but also Spain, Greece and Ireland—where credit booms, real-estate bubbles, household debt and over-leveraged financial institutions have all imploded. Worst off is Russia, in the aftermath of a massive foreign-borrowing binge by its corporations during the years of high oil and gas prices: GDP plunged by nearly 10 per cent in the first half of 2009, domestic demand fell by half and industrial production levels plummeted by 40 per cent. Official unemployment is hovering around 10 per cent in the US and the Eurozone, 18 per cent in Spain; jobs in construction, manufacturing and services have all been hit. Employment regimes are one of the few points of divergence in G20 responses to the crisis: in East Asia, France and Germany firms have retained workers; in the Atlantic economies, jobless rates have leapt up by an average 5 per cent. In the US, Latino and under-25s unemployment levels are running at 13 and 18 per cent respectively. This is punishingly high, though not yet approaching the 1930s figures of over 20 per cent long-term unemployment in much of Europe and the US; but it is qualitatively worse than the post-1907 shock, or that of 'normal' recessions.

For the Atlantic economies the IMF outlook over the next four years is for sluggish recovery at best, with a serious risk of further downturns. Fiscal retrenchment and further credit-tightening loom, with debt and mortgage defaults set to be compounded when interest rates finally rise. Most vulnerable are the dependent peripheries of these zones, with little leeway for deficit spending or job protection. Mexican GDP growth plummeted from 3.3 per cent in 2007 to –7.3 per cent in 2009; the remittance economies of Central America were decimated by the collapse of US construction. Eastern Europe has been left exposed to high levels of debt and scarce social provision; currencies struggle to keep up with the euro. The ex-Soviet Republics have been hit by the fall-off in remittances from Russia. It is above all in these regions that countries have been coming under the tutelage of the IMF: Costa Rica, El Salvador, Guatemala; Latvia, Hungary, Bosnia, Serbia, Romania; Belarus and Ukraine.

Across the East and South, the picture is very different. On the back of massive counter-cyclical spending, China and India have rebounded with barely a dip, to predicted 9 per cent and 6.5 per cent growth rates for 2010 respectively. Outsize fiscal and monetary stimulus—some 5 per cent of GDP each, 3 points above the G20 average—is estimated to have added 2 percentage points to their short-term growth figures, and

PRC infrastructural investment is lifting exports from Indonesia and Australia. (With lower counter-cyclical expenditure, Korea and Taiwan are expecting 4 per cent growth in 2010, after a steep drop at the start of 2009.) The Chinese rebound in industrial production has come largely in electronic goods, worst hit by the post-crash trade crunch; but while volume has picked up, the value of PRC exports in late 2009 was still 30 per cent down. How sustainable these growth levels will prove without US–EU recovery remains to be seen; high-end, capital-intensive sectors will be hardest hit by a continuing export downturn. In the meantime, property values have been escalating in Singapore, Hong Kong, India and China, where house prices had already risen by 40 per cent in 2008.

In Latin America, Brazil—buffered, like India, by a large domestic market—is undergoing a mini-boom with the speculative spike in commodity prices: in 2009 soy, a principal export, leapt by 20 per cent. Commodity-based currencies—the Brazilian *real*, South African rand, Australian dollar—have risen by over 25 per cent. South Africa and Botswana were hit by capital outflows at the start of 2009, and Nigeria is suffering from the collapse of an oil-based credit bubble; but many African countries—Kenya, Uganda, Mozambique, Tanzania, Senegal—suffered more from the high food and oil prices of 2007–08 than from the financial crisis. Across the south, poorer countries, less integrated into the world market, have been relatively unscathed in terms of output, the low-end textiles and garment sector least affected by the early 2009 trade crunch. But crude growth figures here are no measure of the impact of cuts in what is already bare-subsistence income.

These are still early days. But at the start of 2010, the 'recovery' seems patently unstable: a jobless North Atlantic, with a crippled credit system at its heart; a bubbling East, yet to recalibrate to the shrinking market for its goods; a mountain of debt still to be settled; speculative funds at loose in the system, driving commodity-price spikes. Finance is still booby-trapped, while turbulence has shifted east and south.

Regulated liberalism?

Behind the 'rescue' lies a remarkable degree of establishment consensus on the causes of the crisis and solutions to apply. The touchstone for this view is that the American economy itself was fundamentally sound before the crash: the problems were limited to the financial sector, albeit worsened by global imbalances of East Asian savings and American debt. For the US, the solution now is to keep the economy going, regulate the banks and institute an aggressive trade policy. Once these have been set in place and fiscal austerity restored—admittedly, a tough call—there is every hope that a more sober and sustainable version of the same globalized and liberalized world economy will emerge. The main differences are over proportions: insufficient or over-lax counter-cyclical spending; regulatory oversight too timorous or too interfering. At a more analytical level, efficient-market theories and representative-agent models have been criticized for neglecting to take human nature, imperfect information or perverse incentives into account. But again, regulation is the answer.[9] With the exception of a few lone voices calling for a free-market clear-out,[10] establishment convergence around what might be called regulatory liberalism seems all but complete. Proponents of other 'varieties of capitalism' have been muted—perhaps because they are now regulatory liberals, too. This is the outlook that tacitly informs the multitude of blow-by-blow accounts of the crisis, which mainly concentrate on the more glamorous end—Wall Street giants, Mayfair and Connecticut hedge funds.[11] Alternative analyses will no doubt appear in due course. But the present unanimity is in striking contrast to earlier crises, where diagnoses and prescriptions were contested from above and below: after 1873, the bimetallism of Prairie populists, trade and agricultural tariffs, or imperialist expansion to find commercial opportunities overseas; after 1929, Keynes vs Schumpeter and virtues of the Soviet five-year plan.

Ideologically, regulatory liberalism would seem to represent an inflection of the neo-liberal paradigm rather than any rupture with it. The term 'regulation' has the advantage of suggesting fairness and neutrality, but it is in fact a hard-line liberal economic concept, as one of its principal contemporary theorists, Giandomenico Majone, makes clear. Pioneered as a way to manage privately owned US railroads in the 1880s, regulation has always been counterposed to nationalization and public ownership.

---

9 Krugman, 'How did economists get it so wrong?', *NYT*, 6 September 2009; George Akerlof and Robert Shiller, *Animal Spirits: How Human Psychology Drives the Economy, and Why It Matters for Global Capitalism*, Princeton 2009. See also Joseph Stiglitz, 'The Current Economic Crisis and Lessons for Economic Theory', *Eastern Economic Journal*, vol. 35, no. 3, 2009; and Jeff Madrick, 'They Didn't Regulate Enough and Still Don't', *NYRB*, 5 November 2009.
10 James Buchan, 'Is Britain Bust?', *Prospect*, August 2009.
11 For example, Gillian Tett, *Fool's Gold: How Unrestrained Greed Corrupted a Dream, Shattered Global Markets and Unleashed a Catastrophe*, London 2009.

Undertaken by the state, therefore on behalf of the people, the latter may be subject to multiple claims and expectations—economic development, full employment, social equity, etc. In a regulatory regime, by contrast, the state delegates responsibility to a third party, unencumbered by electoral accountability. The logic of regulation is thus 'an increasingly complete severance of expert authority from the popular will'.[12] In practice, of course, the banks themselves are determining the new regulatory requirements. Proponents of such modest reforms as a restored Glass–Steagall Act, utility, 'narrow' or limited-purpose banking confess themselves marginalized: even to get a hearing in face of 'the lobbying clout of the big banks'—'one congressman, five finance lobbyists'—'is an uphill battle'.[13] The resulting sense of continuity-through-adaptation, ideological and pragmatic, was summed up in a *Financial Times* sermon on the twentieth anniversary of capitalism's Cold War triumph. The great virtue of liberal democracy, Martin Wolf reminded readers, was its capacity to learn and adapt, spurning utopian programmes in favour of Popperian bricolage:

> In the case of this crisis, the failure lies not so much with the market system as a whole, but with defects in the world's financial and monetary systems . . . Happily, governments and central banks have learnt the lessons of the 1930s and decided, rightly, to prevent collapses of either the financial system or the economy. That is precisely the right kind of 'piecemeal social engineering'.[14]

Underlying problems

The confidence seems misplaced. In the 1870s as in the 1920s, problems of capital accumulation in the real economy lay behind the equity and housing bubbles, and helped prolong the recessions into global downturns. The crash of 1873 came after two decades of sustained world-economic expansion that saw German and American development catch up with Britain's, putting an end to the UK's advantage as

---

[12] Giandomenico Majone, *Regulating Europe*, London 1996. For a full discussion see Perry Anderson, *The New Old World*, London 2010, pp. 105–16. The quotation, from Anderson, is on p. 107.

[13] John Plender, 'How to tame the animal spirits', FT, 30 September 2009; see also John Kay, 'Narrow Banking: The Reform of Banking Regulation', CSFI pamphlet, London 2009; Niall Ferguson and Laurence Kotlikoff, 'How to take the moral hazard out of banking', FT, 2 December 2009.

[14] Martin Wolf, 'Victory in the Cold War was a start as well as an ending', FT, 11 November 2009.

sole industrialized power and initiating a phase of intensifying competition. With labour markets relatively tight, if fluctuating, and workers combative, rivalry between firms largely took the form of price deflation; although investment and productivity grew between 1873 and 1896, profits and prices fell. Despite severe repression—Pinkertons in the US, Anti-Socialist Laws in Germany—these were years of advance for labour, with the growth of mass working-class organizations, broadening literacy and partial suffrage; wages rose, in part through the masculinization of the work force and 'family wage', while food prices stayed low.[15] In 1929 the situation was more uneven: during World War One and after, the booming American economy powered ahead with Fordist auto production, consumer durables and electrification, while Continental output collapsed after a brief post-war revival; but the US was already beginning to over-reach itself when European production levels started to rise from the mid-20s.[16] American farm prices were flat and wages levelling off by the end of the decade; the housing boom had collapsed in 1926 and the subsequent stock-market bubble, which sucked American funds back from Europe and Latin America, plunging those regions into trouble even before the crash, was fuelled by borrowed money. The role of the American colossus as import destination for a great part of the world's primary commodities—Brazilian coffee, Japanese silk, South Asian rice, Argentine wheat—ensured that the ensuing chain of bank and business failures, stock liquidations, price deflations and further bankruptcies would take on global proportions.[17]

What are the comparable conditions today of capital accumulation, labour supply and world trade? Problems of productive over-capacity were already apparent at the beginning of the 1970s, as the US saw Germany and Japan forge ahead in one key industry after another: textiles, steel, automobiles, machine tools, consumer electronics.[18] Since then, large new production centres in Brazil, South Korea, Taiwan, Thailand and finally China have poured competing goods onto the world market. At the

---

[15] Hobsbawm, *Age of Empire*, pp. 34–62; Giovanni Arrighi, *Adam Smith in Beijing*, London 2007, pp. 101–40, 193–210.
[16] Hoover himself blamed the war-time expansion of production outside Europe—not least in Japan and Canada—for the Depression: capacity 'proved excessive at 1925 prices', as European production began to recover. See Kindleberger, *Manias, Panics and Crashes*, p. 120.
[17] Reinhart and Rogoff, *This Time is Different*, pp. 234–6; Hobsbawm, *Age of Extremes*, pp. 85–108.
[18] Robert Brenner, *The Economics of Global Turbulence*, London 2006, pp. 112–3.

same time, a historic weakening in the position of labour and the share of wages in the world economy has served to depress relative demand. The feminization of the labour force since the 1970s, part and parcel of service-sector expansion, has also brought a lowering of wages across the board. The rustbelt-to-sunbelt shift in manufacturing, away from traditional working-class communities, has broken generational continuity in labour organization. Across the South, hundreds of millions have been thrown into the search for wage labour through the decimation of subsistence farming by the vastly higher productivity of Euro-American agribusiness, a process speeded by IMF programmes. The integration of India and China into the global capitalist economy has brought another 1.5 billion chronically low-paid workers into the labour market, doubling its size and, on one estimate, reducing the capital/labour ratio to 55–60 per cent of its previous level.[19] The mass entry of propertyless workers from kitchen, countryside and collective has compounded problems of over-capacity with those of relative under-consumption—'a systemic shortage of effective demand'.[20]

In these conditions, it would seem that revival of profits in one economy could only come at the expense of others: either by lowering costs, expanding markets or altering the terms of trade. At the very start of the neo-liberal era, the failure of American manufacturing to generate sufficient returns in face of growing competition from Germany and Japan was a principal cause of the 1970s US default on the Bretton Woods dollar–gold peg: Fort Knox was being emptied as much by American corporations' investments in lower-wage economies abroad as by soaring military and social spending.[21] Exchange-rate shocks as by-products of US interest-rate switches have triggered much of the turbulence of the neo-liberal period. In 1979 the Volcker–Carter hike, implemented to tame inflation and discipline labour at home, bankrupted indebted Third World and Comecon countries, bringing industrial-development programmes to a halt. Crisis solutions imposed by the IMF and World Bank in the 1980s ruthlessly furthered programmes for abolition of external capital controls and internal liberalization, offering big

---

[19] Richard Freeman, 'The Challenge of the Growing Globalization of Labour Markets to Economic and Social Policy', in Eva Paus, ed., Global Capitalism Unbound: Winners and Losers from Offshore Outsourcing, New York 2007.
[20] Giovanni Arrighi, 'Winding Paths of Capital', NLR 56, March–April 2009, p. 82.
[21] Richard Duncan, The Dollar Crisis: Causes, Consequences, Cures, Singapore 2003, p. 10.

financial operators a privatization bonanza just as the entry of pension and mutual-fund managers into the field as investment players led to a huge expansion of the US financial sector. In 1985, the Baker–Reagan Plaza Accord lowered the dollar to benefit American exporters, throwing booming Japanese and German firms into recession. Japanese capital surged instead into a record-breaking real-estate bubble. After its burst in 1992 Japanese funds, thwarted by poor returns at home and low interest rates in the US, flooded into Korea, Thailand, Malaysia, Singapore, Taiwan, then China. The East Asian Tigers boomed, producing the new electronic goods of the 1990s. International investors followed suit and local banks became kiosks for foreign credit.

From the early 90s, the take-off in the East developed in a complex symbiosis with the continuing downturn in the core zones, mediated through trade, capital goods and investment flows. Throughout the 1990s and early 2000s growth in Japan and Germany was barely positive, while the US 'new economy' boom of the mid-90s proved short-lived. Clinton's strategy, designed by Goldman Sachs, was premised on the wealth-effect of financial-sector profits compensating for poor capital-investment returns and stagnant wages—systemic capital misallocation turned to a virtue. But when the dollar was raised again from 1995, the competitiveness of US firms was weakened. Poor corporate returns led to the collapse of dot.com shares in 2000. Thereafter successive debt-based bubbles were premised on the cheap credit provided by foreign investors, above all Japan and China.[22] Struggling to keep the US economy afloat, Greenspan slashed interest rates from 6.5 to 1 per cent from 2001 and, over the next four years, fanned house prices up 50 per cent. When they threatened to dip in 2003, as American forces poured into Iraq, he urged on the securitized subprime market. But US growth rates continued to decline: 3.6 in 2004, 3.1 in 2005, 2.7 in 2006, 2.1 in 2007, 0.4 in 2008. Job creation never recovered from the 2000 recession. When Bernanke began raising interest rates in 2006, to steady the dollar and subdue the bubble, the great unravelling began.[23]

[22] For data, see Anton Brender and Florence Pisani, 'Globalized Finance and its Collapse', Brussels 2009.
[23] See Robert Brenner, 'What's Good for Goldman Sachs is Good for America', April 2009, to which this account is greatly indebted. See also R. Taggart Murphy, 'In the Eye of the Storm: Updating *The Economics of Global Turbulence*', *Asia-Pacific Journal: Japan Focus*, 7 December 2009.

Against this stands the astonishing transformation of the Chinese economy, qualitative as well as quantitative: it is now the largest automobile market in the world. Over the next twenty years the Chinese Economic Council is planning to build another 200 cities of a million inhabitants each—around the size of Dallas—with dramatic implications for potential growth in infrastructural investment, services and consumption. How resilient the Chinese economy will prove in face of the cumulative pressures now converging on it—falling US markets, rising commodity prices, excess liquidity from its $600bn stimulus package and $1trn post-2008 credit expansion—remains to be seen. Given its current frenzied rate of production, it is hard to see how the PRC can avoid going through some sort of recessionary crisis in the short term, however temporary that may prove.

Frictions

The prospects for any immediate stabilization and rebalancing of the world economy plainly depend on some ongoing agreement between Washington and Beijing, as well as Berlin and Tokyo. At the time of writing, Obama and Bernanke appear to be implementing a turn to neo-Reaganomics: a second Plaza Accord to lower the dollar, inflate away the debt, regain competitive advantage in world trade and stare down the sovereign menace of a major creditor, accompanied by record-breaking deficits and military expansion abroad. Several factors militate against this strategy. First, every further international credit shock or sovereign default risks pushing the dollar back up, as funds surge into its safe haven. Second, although leaders in the Eurozone and Japan have meekly assented to Washington's demands, for the time being Beijing is determinedly matching US exchange-rate protectionism with its own; Chinese officials have called for the EU and PRC to 'play together' against American monetary policy. American advisors have begun recalling Nixon's 10 per cent import surcharge, which swiftly persuaded Japan and Germany to accept a low dollar in the early 70s. Some are now proposing that the dollar be supplemented by other trading currencies, the euro, yen or yuan, in order to free up US economic policy.[24] But if, as Marcello De Cecco has suggested, the world economy is mutating from a 'collusive' to a 'competitive oligopoly', the scope for national

---

[24] See C. Fred Bergsten, 'The Dollar and the Deficits: How Washington Can Prevent the Next Crisis', *Foreign Affairs*, Nov–Dec 2009.

mercantilist strategies remains conditioned by the interdependence of the major economies. This, too, is a new situation, without parallel in the pre-WW2 world.[25]

Yet it would be a mistake to equate any retraction in US provision of economic goods with a commensurate diminution of American hegemony. Support for Washington's direction of the international political system—determining friends and enemies, making war and peace— and for American macro-economic priorities are not the same thing. But in practice they overlap: the same state leaderships are responsible for lifting capital controls or cutting public spending as for granting basing rights or supporting UN Security Council resolutions. Rewards in one sphere reinforce obedience in the other. The US economy has been shrinking as a proportion of the world total for decades—from nearly 50 per cent in 1945 to 22 per cent in 2008; but by most measures its military, political and cultural reach is greater now than during the 20th century. Nor has the Obama Administration retreated from the strategy of imperial power projection that Washington has advanced, via the First Gulf War, the Balkans, Iraq and Afghanistan, ever since 1990. On the contrary: it has not only extended the Bush doctrine of pre-emptive warfare as a US prerogative but succeeded in naturalizing it. The 2002 National Security Strategy report ruffled many feathers. By 2009, Obama's aides could offhandedly announce the redesignation of the Afghan theatre as AfPak without an eyebrow being raised. For that matter, despite its scathing denunciations of the doctrine of 'humanitarian intervention' as cover for a power-seeking hegemon, or description of American attitudes towards international law as *he ze yong, bu he ze qi*—'use when deemed fit, disregard otherwise'—Beijing's geo-political strategy remains, 'build the Chinese pole within a multipolar world', not 'catch up with and surpass the beautiful empire'. Chinese oil companies in Iraq and mining interests in Afghanistan are dependent upon US armed forces. An immensely powerful world hegemon still exists. The transitional era is not an interregnum.

A principal reason for the continuing strength of American hegemony lies in the victories of the neo-liberal project, which always involved both an ideology and a programme. The first took a series of

---

[25] Marcello De Cecco, 'From Monopoly to Oligopoly: Lessons from the pre-1914 Experience', in Eric Helleiner and Jonathan Kirshner, eds, *The Future of the Dollar*, Ithaca 2009, p. 122.

forms—monetarism, Thatcherism, free-market Third Way, triumphal globalization—now behind us. But the revolutionary effects of the programme remain. Social relations have been reconfigured across the globe: finance capital severed from national industry and integrated into global wealth circuits, decorated with new celebrity-media elites; the white-collar workforce, public or private, subjected to new market norms and compensated with small-scale financial assets; a two-tier working class, with most of its youth in the casualized sector, deprived of organizational reach and political project. Perhaps the most striking feature of the 2008 crisis so far has been its combination of economic turmoil and political stasis. After the bank and currency crashes of 1931, governments toppled across Europe—Britain, France, Spain, Germany; even in 1873, the Grant Administration was paralysed by corruption scandals after the railroad bust, and the Gladstone Ministry fell. The only political casualties of 2008 have been the Haarde regime in Iceland and the Cayman Islands authorities. As unemployment mounts and public-spending cuts are enforced, more determined protests will hopefully emerge; but to date, factory occupations or bossnappings have mostly been limited to demands for due redundancy pay. That neo-liberalism's crisis should be so eerily non-agonistic, in contrast to the bitter battles over its installation, is a sobering measure of its triumph.

In his 'Analysis of Situations', Gramsci famously distinguished between longer-term 'organic' historical developments and shorter-term 'conjunctural' ones: 'The conjuncture can be defined as the set of circumstances which determine the market in a given phase'—'the set of immediate and ephemeral characteristics of the economic situation'. He went on to warn—this was in 1933: 'it may be ruled out that immediate economic crises of themselves produce historical events'. At most, they might create a terrain more favourable to raising certain questions; but the decisive element in every situation was that of the organized forces prepared to intervene.[26] In retrospect, the conjunctures of 1873 and 1929 can be seen as marking the deepening of ongoing, organic movements: the intensification of industrial-capitalist rivalries in the first, which would eventually produce the inter-imperialist collisions of World War I; in 1929, the explosive but uneven growth of the US, the dramatic fortunes of Germany and accelerating decline of Britain, against a backdrop of bitter class contestation.

---

[26] *Selections from the Prison Notebooks*, London 1971, pp. 177–85.

The organic movements underlying the conjuncture of 2008 include, first, the relationship between the long-term slowdown in the most advanced economies and the explosive growth of China; second, the continued extension of the US imperial state; and third, the global deterioration in the position of labour. Politically, the outcome of the crisis has been shaped entirely from above. The Treasury–Wall Street nexus has extended its hold and ensured that the entire cost will be borne by working people. The result is a further worsening of conditions for labour, above all in the core economic zones and their peripheries. Ideologically, the triumphalism of big finance may be muted for now. But if the neo-liberal paradigm is undergoing a mutation towards regulatory liberalism, its principal components remain in place: untrammelled capital movement, private ownership and shareholder value remain the goals.

Meeting no opposition, the neo-liberal programme has actually advanced through the crisis, the bank bailouts effecting a larger expropriation than ever before. Yet the massive transfer of wealth from labour to capital that the 'great moderation' of neo-liberalism has brought may now be starting to undermine the system itself. To shore it up with speculative profits based on perpetual future growth can only be a makeshift solution, yet the Treasury–Wall Street order is politically incapable of conceiving any other. As for labour, it may be several generations away from rebuilding a hegemonic alternative that could tilt or transform the world in favour of its working billions. In the PRC, the West encounters a different *Weltanschauung*; but the Chinese ruling class, or caste, has done very well by globalized neo-liberalism. Claims that the CCP stands for a more equitable world order are undermined by gaping domestic inequalities.

Futures

Does history offer any clues as to what the longer-term outcome of the present crisis might be? After the post-1873 downturn, general profitability finally returned in 1896 without a major slump, although the long agricultural crisis helped loosen labour markets in the cities. Imperial expansion helped find new outlets for goods—virtually all remaining independent states and territories across Africa and the Pacific had been subjected to metropolitan rule by 1896—and industrial-scale rearmament got underway. Domestically, the great finance houses built up huge concentrations of capital. Corporations and cartels intervened directly to halt deflation. The technological and organizational innovations that would shape the Belle Epoque turned out to have been incubating during the high-investment downturn: film, recorded sound, the internal combustion engine and large-scale generation of electricity; the corporation, Taylorism, advertising, the department store and mass-consumer markets. Full recovery after the Great Depression came only with rearmament for the Second World War, first in Germany, then in the US, where massive industrial investment unleashed the conditions for the post-war boom. Again, the breakthroughs that would shape the following era—plastics, cathode-ray tube—had already taken place. At the world-political level, American elites drew the lesson of the 20s and 30s and planned single-mindedly for a hegemonic role, drafting the international architecture of the post-war era.

In a recent contribution, Gopal Balakrishnan has argued that, contrary to expectations of eventual shake-out and recovery in the 2010s, the momentum of growth in the most advanced regions may be petering out altogether.[27] In this view, a conjunctural crisis of accumulation is converging with longer-term slowdowns, caused by greying societies and the shift towards low-productivity service economies. The New Economy's revolution in production proved a myth—IT, containerization, post-Fordist production and supply chains 'failed to show up statistically'—as will notions of a China-centred phase of accumulation, since this offers no new and more advanced organization of productive forces but merely a broader dissemination of existing plant. Drawing on Brenner's diagnosis in *Economics of Global Turbulence* of a long-term decline in rates of return on capital investment, Balakrishnan speculates that 2008 may be 'the end of the line' for growth based on account imbalances, asset bubbles and debt creation. In the absence of a far-reaching Schumpeterian shake-out, the capitalist world seems set to drift towards a 'stationary state'.

Countering such scenarios, Michel Aglietta has stressed the still unrealized potential for Chinese growth, while Nicholas Crafts and Kozo Yamamura have pointed out that waves of technological progress are not necessarily determined by levels of profitability: the 1930s saw many technological breakthroughs. Increased entry may lead, as in the 1870s, to greater investment and innovation.[28] The reasons why IT and

---

[27] Balakrishnan, 'Speculations on the Stationary State', NLR 59, Sept–Oct 2009.
[28] See the symposium on Brenner's *Economics of Global Turbulence*: Crafts, 'Profits of Doom', Aglietta, 'A New Growth Regime', Yamamura, 'More System, Please!' in NLR 54, Nov–Dec 2008.

semi-conductors failed to bring about a productivity revolution in the 1990s are still unclear; Crafts suggests that their weight in the overall economy was too small, due to concentration in low-productivity service industries. But the logic of these arguments suggests the possibility of a non-stationary outcome, albeit after further years of depressive turbulence and bursting bubbles. Visions of a synthetic-silicon breakthrough that would solar-power the global South, revolutionize transport and foster green-gold desalination programmes, to transform rising oceans into spring-water irrigation supplies, are clearly far-fetched. But there is clearly room for low-end consumer-market expansion across the villages of China and India: the hundreds of millions trapped on the margins of the world labour force are by no means outside the circuits of global consumption. Shacks in the Brazilian favelas, with no sewage system nor any family member in employment, boast TVs and microwaves bought at extortionate cost through never-ending installment plans, courtesy of the *Bolsa família*. The state has played a stalwart role throughout the neo-liberal era in fostering social conditions for capital accumulation;[29] there is no doubt more that it could do to entangle populations in the net of the world market. But whether a continuing slowdown or a rebooting of the world economy lies in store, the law of unintended consequences—viz., Japanese capital eventually redirected to the East Asian Tigers and China in the aftermath of the Plaza Accord—will presumably continue to apply as the latest recovery operations get underway.

II

What are the implications of neo-liberalism's crisis for NLR's publishing programme? Its relaunch ten years ago scandalized many by demanding from the left a lucid registration of defeat. 'No collective agency able to match the power of capital is yet on the horizon', Anderson noted; at the level of ideas, 'for the first time since the Reformation, there are no longer any significant oppositions—that is, systematic rival outlooks—within the thought-world of the West.'[30] Those judgements stand. To attend to the development of actually existing capitalism remains a first duty for a journal like NLR. In their different ways, Robert Brenner

[29] For a landmark assessment of the state's role across 23 OECD economies in the first decade of neo-liberalism, see Göran Therborn, 'The Prospects of Labour and the Transformation of Advanced Capitalism', NLR 1/145, May–June 1984.
[30] Anderson, 'Renewals', NLR I, p. 17.

on the faltering of the US economy as world motor, Robin Blackburn and Robert Wade on financial intermediation, Andrew Glyn on global disequilibria have raised fundamental questions for future enquiries. Slavoj Žižek's 'Parallax View' insists that consumption as well as production be held in mind by radical critique. From the viewpoint of the South, Giovanni Arrighi's 'The African Crisis' and Mike Davis's 'Planet of Slums' open vast areas for new research. A priority for the Review in the coming years should be a new typology of development outcomes in the age of global finance. Another is a map of the global proletariat—locations, sectors, differentials—alive to contemporary makings and unmakings of class.

In the past few years Arrighi's 'Hegemony Unravelling' and Anderson's 'Jottings on the Conjuncture' have offered contrasting analyses of the world-political order—for Arrighi, a crisis in recent American attempts to impose a new imperial regime and possible emergence of China as an alternative to US leadership, in East Asia and beyond; for Anderson, a concert of powers, within which different states can jostle for rank, held together by a single, superordinate one. For both, the extent to which the PRC represents a different system is—to differing degrees—in question.[31] These remain central issues for NLR to debate and explore. There is a huge amount of work to be done on the new processes of liberal-capitalist rule, its forms and legitimations: empirical research, which might test Peter Mair's findings on parliamentarism's hollowing in Western Europe against third-wave liberal democracies in Latin America, Africa and Asia; conceptual analyses, like Chico de Oliveira's on the étatization of the PT in Brazil, Cihan Tuğal's on NATO-ization of the Turkish AKP, or Wang Chaohua's incisive typology of nationalisms, not least in China and Taiwan. Tom Nairn and Lutz Niethammer have raised commensurate questions about post-national social identity. Far-reaching theorizations such as Wang Hui's 'Depoliticized Politics', bringing contemporary neutralizations into focus through the lens of China's short revolutionary century, or Luciano Canfora on the 'mixed constitutions' of capitalist oligarchies, demand critical engagement at the same level. Hard-fought debates in political sociology during the 60s and 70s sparked a series of insights about the power elites of the time; analysis of today's famously large and fluid American ruling class—its

---

[31] Arrighi's positive answer in *Adam Smith in Beijing*, London 2009, pp. 351–78, was reconsidered in 'Winding Paths of Capital', NLR 56, pp. 79–80, 84–6, 88–9. For Anderson's analysis, see 'Two Revolutions', below.

reproduction, changing component parts, mediated relations with the imperial state—is another priority.

NLR's record on ecological questions has been erratic, to say the least: isolated if highly original interventions—Hans Magnus Enzensberger's 'Critique of Political Ecology', Alexander Cockburn's 'Meat-Oriented History of the World', André Gorz's 'The New Agenda'—interspersed by long periods of silence. This should change. There are many different registers to explore here: empirical syntheses, programmatic interventions,[32] political analyses—the Green parties, hard-line advocates for NATO's wars, await a critical biography. With the movement's programme dismembered (recycling, GMOs, forestation) and reduced to measures acceptable to world-summitry, perhaps only utopian speculation can reconceive the ecological totality of social, economic and environmental relations. In that spirit Mike Davis revisits Constructivist dreams for greener cities in this number. The journal's record on social issues has been just as uneven, not least on what was once the Woman Question. Again, the rightward shift in most discussion of this issue leaves large areas unexplored. There has been no properly global balance sheet of the historic changes in the division of labour and status between the sexes, nor any satisfactory explanation of how and why these took place. Works by Hester Eisenstein and Nancy Fraser on second-wave feminism's elective affinities with neo-liberal capitalism are vital starting points.[33]

In understanding contemporary capitalist culture as a historical phenomenon, the Review has learnt an enormous amount from Fredric Jameson's work; a series of fields open up from this—the built environment, the reign of the image, possibilities of literary or utopian rupture, readings of specific works. In cultural practice itself, Archimedean points from which a bead can still be drawn on the system as a whole mainly lie on its peripheries: film and documentary makers working outside multinational studio set-ups, writers oriented to an audience, not a market. Roberto Schwarz's interpretations—of Chico Alvim's minimalist poetry, or Paulo Lins's epic of the neo-favela—are outstanding examples of an

---

[32] An example of the first would be Kenneth Pomeranz's survey of Asian water shortages, 'The Great Himalayan Watershed'; of the second, Aubrey Meyer's work on per capita carbon budgets at the Global Commons Institute.
[33] Eisenstein, *Feminism Seduced: How Global Elites Use Women's Labor and Ideas to Exploit the World*, Boulder, CO 2009; Fraser, 'Feminism, Capitalism and the Cunning of History', NLR 56, Mar–Apr 2009.

acute social awareness and high critical intelligence brought to bear on the finest instances of these forms. Future issues will chart the desperate impasses of the Arab world through the unillusioned eyes of its young writers, and momentous social upheavals in China through its outsider films. NLR hopes to publish further explorations of past and future radical worlds—Benedict Anderson's trans-oceanic interconnections between avant-gardes, anarchism and the anti-colonial imagination an astounding examplar—and re-readings from the canon: Eagleton on Beckett, White on Tolstoy, Plaks on Cao Xueqin, Wood on Platonov or Moretti on Ibsen, below.

When the Review was founded, as Stuart Hall vividly evokes in this issue, forging a 'new left' was an immediate practical project; in the second decade of the 21st century, it is one for the *longue durée*. But the journal can still think about how to prefigure the general intellectual culture that an effective—therefore, pluralist and internationalist—left would require. By definition, such a movement would defend the conditions for a broader and richer critical culture, a more engaged political practice, a more conscious economics; would be as hard-headed and determined as the power it confronts. However notionally, this is the horizon to be borne in mind as a younger layer comes to the fore. In its early years, the Review benefited a great deal from the overlap of political generations in the two journals that came together to found it, as a joint project. The editors of the *New Reasoner*, born in the 1920s, fought in the War and mainly acquired their political education through the CPGB. The young writers and critics around *Universities and Left Review* were more attuned to the new cultural currents and social rebellion. Today the generational overlap stretches much farther—the ageing society proving an unexpected boon for the left. Hobsbawm, Hall and others share its pages with writers not yet born in 1960: Malcolm Bull in the fields of aesthetics and philosophy; Gopal Balakrishnan, Dylan Riley or Benno Teschke on political theory; Zhang Yongle on Chinese intellectual history; Tony Wood and Forrest Hylton on Russia and Latin America; Cihan Tuğal and Ece Temelkuran on Turkey; Kasian Tejapira on Thailand, Peter Hallward on Haiti; Sebastian Budgen or Alexander Zevin on France; Tom Mertes and Naomi Klein on new social movements; Sven Lütticken, Julian Stallabrass and Emilie Bickerton on the visual arts.

If anything, the inter-generational contrast is starker now than it was in 1960. The editors who saw the Review through its first few decades came of age in a still strongly delineated national culture and public sphere, in which social classes were tangible realities; they hit their intellectual stride in the mid-60s, a time of intense commitments on the left, with victory seemingly within reach; positions were forged and argued within a highly politicized and internationalist milieu. Today's young writers have grown up within far more depoliticized cultural and intellectual environments, structured by the market and mediated, for better or worse, by electronic forms of sociability. Flares of protest have been ephemeral; every mobilization they have known—alter-globo, climate change, marches against the invasion of Iraq—has ended in defeat. But perhaps the very rarity of a serious left forum in these times makes a journal like NLR more valued. The thought-world of the West is increasingly patterned by Atlantic-centred structures of wealth and power. University disciplines—international relations, economics, law, social sciences, area studies—derive their curricula from the narrowing perspectives of its rulers' needs. A neutralized academic Marxism risks being the unwitting reflection of this trend. NLR stands outside this world, defines its own agenda. Can a left intellectual project hope to thrive in the absence of a political movement? That remains to be seen. But in the meantime it will have plenty on its plate.

NEW FROM VERSO

MIKE DAVIS

WHO WILL BUILD THE ARK?

W HAT FOLLOWS IS rather like the famous courtroom
scene in Orson Welles's *The Lady from Shanghai* (1947).[1]
In that noir allegory of proletarian virtue in the embrace
of ruling-class decadence, Welles plays a leftwing sailor
named Michael O'Hara who rolls in the hay with *femme fatale* Rita
Hayworth, and then gets framed for murder. Her husband, Arthur
Bannister, the most celebrated criminal lawyer in America, played by
Everett Sloane, convinces O'Hara to appoint him as his defence, all
the better to ensure his rival's conviction and execution. At the turning point in the trial, decried by the prosecution as 'yet another of the
great Bannister's famous tricks', Bannister the attorney calls Bannister
the aggrieved husband to the witness stand and interrogates himself
in rapid schizoid volleys, to the mirth of the jury. In the spirit of *Lady
from Shanghai*, this essay is organized as a debate with myself, a mental
tournament between analytic despair and utopian possibility that is personally, and probably objectively, irresolvable.

In the first section, 'Pessimism of the Intellect', I adduce arguments for
believing that we have already lost the first, epochal stage of the battle against global warming. The Kyoto Protocol, in the smug but sadly
accurate words of one of its chief opponents, has done 'nothing meas-
urable' about climate change. Global carbon dioxide emissions rose by
the same amount they were supposed to fall because of it.[2] It is highly
unlikely that greenhouse gas accumulation can be stabilized this side
of the famous 'red line' of 450 ppm by 2020. If this is the case, the
most heroic efforts of our children's generation will be unable to fore-
stall a radical reshaping of ecologies, water resources and agricultural
systems. In a warmer world, moreover, socio-economic inequality will
have a meteorological mandate, and there will be little incentive for
the rich northern hemisphere countries, whose carbon emissions have

destroyed the climate equilibrium of the Holocene, to share resources for adaptation with those poor subtropical countries most vulnerable to droughts and floods.

The second part of the essay, 'Optimism of the Imagination', is my self-rebuttal. I appeal to the paradox that the single most important cause of global warming—the urbanization of humanity—is also potentially the principal solution to the problem of human survival in the later twenty-first century. Left to the dismal politics of the present, of course, cities of poverty will almost certainly become the coffins of hope; but all the more reason that we must start thinking like Noah. Since most of history's giant trees have already been cut down, a new Ark will have to be constructed out of the materials that a desperate humanity finds at hand in insurgent communities, pirate technologies, bootlegged media, rebel science and forgotten utopias.

I. PESSIMISM OF THE INTELLECT

Our old world, the one that we have inhabited for the last 12,000 years, has ended, even if no newspaper has yet printed its scientific obituary. The verdict is that of the Stratigraphy Commission of the Geological Society of London. Founded in 1807, the Society is the world's oldest association of earth scientists, and its Stratigraphy Commission acts as a college of cardinals in the adjudication of the geological time-scale. Stratigraphers slice up Earth's history as preserved in sedimentary strata into a hierarchy of eons, eras, periods and epochs, marked by the 'golden spikes' of mass extinctions, speciation events or abrupt changes in atmospheric chemistry. In geology, as in biology and history, periodization is a complex, controversial art; the most bitter feud in nineteenth-century British science—still known as the 'Great Devonian Controversy'—was fought over competing interpretations of homely Welsh greywackes and English Old Red Sandstone. As a result, Earth science sets extraordinarily rigorous standards for the beatification of any new geological division. Although the idea of an 'Anthropocene' epoch—defined by the emergence of urban-industrial society as a geological force—has long circulated in the literature, stratigraphers have never acknowledged its warrant.

---

[1] This paper was given as a talk at the UCLA Center for Social Theory and Comparative History in January 2009.
[2] The Cato Institute's execrable Patrick Michaels in the *Washington Times*, 12 February 2005.

At least for the London Society, that position has now been revised. To the question, 'Are we now living in the Anthropocene?', the twenty-one members of the Commission have unanimously answered 'yes'. In a 2008 report they marshalled robust evidence to support the hypothesis that the Holocene epoch—the interglacial span of unusually stable climate that allowed the rapid evolution of agriculture and urban civilization—has ended, and that the Earth has now entered 'a stratigraphic interval without close parallel' in the last several million years.[3] In addition to the build-up of greenhouse gases, the stratigraphers cited human landscape transformation, which 'now exceeds [annual] natural sediment production by an order of magnitude', the ominous acidification of the oceans, and the relentless destruction of biota.

This new age, they explained, is defined both by the heating trend—whose closest analogue may be the catastrophe known as the Paleocene Eocene Thermal Maximum, 56 million years ago—and by the radical instability expected of future environments. In sombre prose, they warned:

> The combination of extinctions, global species migrations and the widespread replacement of natural vegetation with agricultural monocultures is producing a distinctive contemporary biostratigraphic signal. These effects are permanent, as future evolution will take place from surviving (and frequently anthropogenically relocated) stocks.[4]

Evolution itself, in other words, has been forced into a new trajectory.

Spontaneous decarbonization?

The Commission's recognition of the Anthropocene coincided with growing scientific controversy over the Fourth Assessment Report issued by the Intergovernmental Panel on Climate Change. The IPCC, of course, is mandated to assess the possible range of climate change and establish appropriate targets for the mitigation of emissions. The most critical baselines include estimates of 'climate sensitivity' to increasing accumulations of greenhouse gas, as well as socio-economic tableaux that configure different futures of energy use and thus of emissions. But an impressive number of senior researchers, including key participants in the IPCC's own working groups, have recently expressed unease or disagreement

---

[3] Jan Zalasiewicz et al., 'Are We Now Living in the Anthropocene?', GSA *Today*, vol. 18, no. 2, February 2008.

[4] Zalasiewicz, 'Are We Now Living in the Anthropocene?'

with the methodology of the four-volume Fourth Assessment, which they charge is unwarrantedly optimistic in its geophysics and social science.[5]

The most celebrated dissenter is James Hansen from NASA's Goddard Institute. The Paul Revere of global warming who first warned Congress of the greenhouse peril in a famous 1988 hearing, he returned to Washington with the troubling message that the IPCC, through its failure to parameterize crucial Earth-system feedbacks, has given far too much leeway to further carbon emissions. Instead of the IPCC's proposed red line of 450 ppm carbon dioxide, his research team found compelling paleoclimatic evidence that the threshold of safety was only 350 ppm or even less. The 'stunning corollary' of this recalibration of climate sensitivity, he testified, is that 'the oft-stated goal of keeping global warming below two degrees Celsius is a recipe for global disaster, not salvation'.[6] Indeed, since the current level is about 385 ppm, we may already be past the notorious 'tipping point'. Hansen has mobilized a Quixotic army of scientists and environmental activists to save the world via an emergency carbon tax, which would reverse greenhouse concentrations to pre-2000 levels by 2015.

I do not have the scientific qualifactions to express an opinion on the Hansen controversy, or the proper setting on the planetary thermostat. Anyone, however, who is engaged with the social sciences or simply pays regular attention to macro-trends should feel less shy about joining the debate over the other controversial cornerstone of the Fourth Assessment: its socio-economic projections and what we might term their 'political unconscious'. The current scenarios were adopted by the IPCC in 2000 to model future global emissions based on different 'storylines' about population growth as well as technological and economic development. The Panel's major scenarios—the A1 family, the B2, and so on—are well known to policymakers and greenhouse activists, but few outside the research community have actually read the fine print, particularly the IPCC's heroic confidence that greater energy efficiency will be an 'automatic' by-product of future economic growth. Indeed all the scenarios, even the 'business as usual' variants, assume that almost 60 per cent of

---

[5] Indeed, three leading contributors to Working Group 1 charged that the Report deliberately understated the risks of sea-level rise and ignored new research on instability in the Greenland and West Antarctic ice sheets. See the debate in 'Letters', *Science* 319, 25 January 2008, pp. 409–10.
[6] James Hansen, 'Global Warming Twenty Years Later: Tipping Point Near', Testimony before Congress, 23 June 2008.

future carbon reduction will occur independently of explicit greenhouse mitigation measures.[7]

The IPCC, in effect, has bet the ranch, or rather the planet, on a market-driven evolution toward a post-carbon world economy: a transition that requires not only international emissions caps and carbon trading, but also voluntary corporate commitments to technologies that hardly exist even in prototype, such as carbon capture, clean coal, hydrogen and advanced transit systems, and cellulosic biofuels. As critics have long pointed out, in many of its 'scenarios' the deployment of non-carbon-emitting energy-supply systems 'exceeds the size of the global energy system in 1990.'[8]

Kyoto-type accords and carbon markets are designed—almost as ana-logues to Keynesian 'pump-priming'—to bridge the shortfall between spontaneous decarbonization and the emissions targets required by each scenario. Although the IPCC never spells it out, its mitigation targets necessarily presume that windfall profits from higher fossil-fuel prices over the next generation will be efficiently recycled into renewable energy technology and not wasted on mile-high skyscrapers, asset bubbles and mega-payouts to shareholders. Overall, the International Energy Agency estimates that it will cost about $45 trillion to halve greenhouse gas out-put by 2050.[9] But without the large quotient of 'automatic' progress in energy efficiency, the bridge will never be built, and IPCC goals will be unachievable; in the worst case—the straightforward extrapolation of cur-rent energy use—carbon emissions could easily triple by mid-century.

Critics have cited the dismal carbon record of the last—lost—decade to demonstrate that the IPCC baseline assumptions about markets and tech-nology are little more than leaps of faith. Despite the EU's much-praised adoption of a cap-and-trade system, European carbon emissions contin-ued to rise, dramatically in some sectors. Likewise there has been scant evidence in recent years of the automatic progress in energy efficiency

---

[7] Scientific Committee on Problems of the Environment (SCOPE), *The Global Carbon Cycle*, Washington, DC 2004, pp. 77–82; and IPCC, *Climate Change 2007: Mitigation of Climate Change: Contribution of Working Group III to the Fourth Assessment Report*, Cambridge 2007, pp. 172 and 218–24.

[8] SCOPE, *The Global Carbon Cycle*, p. 82.

[9] International Energy Agency, *Energy Technology Perspectives: In support of the G8 Plan of Action—Executive Summary*, Paris 2008, p. 3.

that is the *sine qua non* of IPCC scenarios. Much of what the storylines depict as the efficiency of new technology has in fact been the result of the closing down of heavy industries in the United States, Europe and the ex-Soviet bloc. The relocation of energy-intensive production to East Asia burnishes the carbon balance-sheets of some OECD countries but deindustrialization should not be confused with spontaneous decarbonization. Most researchers believe that energy intensity has actually risen since 2000; that is, global carbon dioxide emissions have kept pace with, or even grown marginally faster than, energy use.[10]

Return of King Coal

Moreover the IPCC carbon budget has already been broken. According to the Global Carbon Project, which keeps the accounts, emissions have been rising faster than projected even in the IPCC's worst-case scenario. From 2000 to 2007, carbon dioxide rose by 3.5 per cent annually, compared with the 2.7 per cent in IPCC projections, or the 0.9 per cent recorded during the 1990s.[11] We are already outside the IPCC envelope, in other words, and coal may be largely to blame for this unforeseen acceleration of greenhouse emissions. Coal production has undergone a dramatic renaissance over the last decade, as nightmares of the 19th century return to haunt the 21st. In China 5 million miners toil under dangerous conditions to extract the dirty mineral that reportedly allows Beijing to open a new coal-fuelled power station each week. Coal consumption is also booming in Europe, where 50 new coal-fuelled plants are scheduled to open over the next few years,[12] and North America, where 200 plants are planned. A giant plant under construction in West Virginia will generate carbon equivalent to the exhaust of one million cars.

In a commanding study of *The Future of Coal*, MIT engineers concluded that usage would increase under any foreseeable scenario, even in the face of high carbon taxes. Investment in CCS technology—carbon-capture and sequestration—is, moreover, 'completely inadequate'; even assuming it is actually practical, CCS would not become a utility-scale alternative until

---

[10] Josep Canadell et al., 'Contributions to Accelerating Atmospheric CO_2 Growth', *Proceedings of the National Academy of Sciences* 104, 20 November 2007, pp. 18,866–70.

[11] Global Carbon Project, *Carbon Budget 2007*, p. 10.

[12] Elisabeth Rosenthal, 'Europe Turns Back to Coal, Raising Climate Fears', *New York Times*, 23 April 2008.

2030 or later. In the United States, 'green energy' legislation has only created a 'perverse incentive' for utilities to build more coal-fired plants in the 'expectation that emissions from these plants would potentially be "grandfathered" by the grant of free CO_2 allowances as part of future carbon emission regulations.'[13] Meanwhile a consortium of coal producers, coal-burning utilities and coal-hauling railroads—calling themselves the American Coalition for Clean Coal Electricity—spent $40 million over the 2008 election cycle to ensure that both presidential candidates sang in unison about the virtues of the dirtiest but cheapest fuel.

Largely because of the popularity of coal, a fossil fuel with a proven 200-year supply, the carbon content per unit of energy may actually rise.[14] Before the American economy collapsed, the US Energy Department was projecting an increase of national energy production by at least 20 per cent over the next generation. Globally the total consumption of fossil fuels is predicted to rise by 55 per cent, with international oil exports doubling in volume. The UN Development Programme, which has made its own study of sustainable energy goals, warns that it will require a 50 per cent cut in greenhouse gas emissions worldwide by 2050, against 1990 levels, to keep humanity outside the red zone of runaway warming.[15] Yet the International Energy Agency predicts that, in all likelihood, such emissions will actually increase over the next half-century by nearly 100 per cent—enough greenhouse gas to propel us past several critical tipping points. The IEA also projects that renewable energy, apart from hydropower, will provide only 4 per cent of electricity generation in 2030—up from 1 per cent today.[16]

A green recession?

The current world recession—a non-linear event of the kind that IPCC scenarists ignore in their storylines—may provide a temporary respite, particularly if depressed oil prices delay the opening of the Pandora's box of new mega-carbon reservoirs such as tar sands and oil shales. But the slump is unlikely to slow the destruction of the Amazon rainforest

---

[13] Stephen Ansolabehere et al., *The Future of Coal*, Cambridge, MA 2007, p. xiv.
[14] Pew Center on Global Climate Change, quoted in Matthew Wald, 'Coal, a Tough Habit to Kick', *New York Times*, 25 September 2008.
[15] *UN Human Development Report 2007/2008: Fighting Climate Change: Human Solidarity in a Divided World*, p. 7.
[16] IEA report quoted in *Wall Street Journal*, 7 November 2008.

because Brazilian farmers will rationally seek to defend gross incomes by expanding production. And because electricity demand is less elastic than automobile use, the share of coal in carbon emissions will continue to increase. In the United States, in fact, coal production is one of the few civilian industries that is currently hiring rather than laying off workers. More importantly, falling fossil-fuel prices and tight credit markets are eroding entrepreneurial incentives to develop capital-intensive wind and solar alternatives. On Wall Street, eco-energy stocks have slumped faster than the market as a whole and investment capital has virtually disappeared, leaving some of the most celebrated clean-energy start-ups, like Tesla Motors and Clear Skies Solar, in danger of sudden crib death. Tax credits, as advocated by Obama, are unlikely to reverse this green depression. As one venture capital manager told the *New York Times*, 'natural gas at $6 makes wind look like a questionable idea and solar power unfathomably expensive'.[17]

Thus the economic crisis provides a compelling pretext for the groom once again to leave the bride at the altar, as major companies default on their public commitments to renewable energy. In the United States, Texas billionaire T. Boone Pickens has downscaled a scheme to build the world's largest wind farm, while Royal Dutch Shell has dropped its plan to invest in the London Array. Governments and ruling parties have been equally avid to escape their carbon debts. The Canadian Conservative Party, supported by Western oil and coal interests, defeated the Liberals' 'Green Shift' agenda based on a national carbon tax in 2007, just as Washington scrapped its major carbon-capture technology initiative.

On the supposedly greener side of the Atlantic, the Berlusconi regime—which is in the process of converting Italy's grid from oil to coal—denounced the EU goal of cutting emissions by 20 per cent by 2020 as an 'unaffordable sacrifice'; while the German government, in the words of the *Financial Times*, 'dealt a severe blow to the proposal to force companies to pay for the carbon dioxide they emit' by backing an almost total exemption for industry. 'This crisis changes priorities', explained a sheepish German foreign minister.[18] Pessimism now abounds. Even Yvo de Boer, Director of the UN Framework Convention on Climate Change,

[17] Clifford Krauss, 'Alternative Energy Suddenly Faces Headwinds', *New York Times*, 21 October 2008.
[18] Peggy Hollinger, 'EU Needs Stable Energy Policy, EDF Warns', *Financial Times*, 5 October 2008.

concedes that, as long as the economic crisis persists, 'most sensible governments will be reluctant to impose new costs on [industry] in the form of carbon-emissions caps.' So even if invisible hands and inter-ventionist leaders can restart the engines of economic growth, they are unlikely to be able to turn down the global thermostat in time to prevent runaway climate change. Nor should we expect that the G7 or the G20 will be eager to clean up the mess they have made.[19]

Ecological inequalities

Climate diplomacy based on the Kyoto–Copenhagen template assumes that, once the major actors have accepted the consensus science in the IPCC reports, they will recognize an overriding common interest in gaining control over the greenhouse effect. But global warming is not H. G. Wells's *War of the Worlds*, where invading Martians democratically annihilate humanity without class or ethnic distinction. Climate change, instead, will produce dramatically unequal impacts across regions and social classes, inflicting the greatest damage upon poor countries with the fewest resources for meaningful adaptation. This geographical sepa-ration of emission source from environmental consequence undermines pro-active solidarity. As the UN Development Programme has empha-sized, global warming is above all a threat to the poor and the unborn, the 'two constituencies with little or no political voice'.[20] Coordinated global action on their behalf thus presupposes either their revolution-ary empowerment—a scenario not considered by the IPCC—or the transmutation of the self-interest of rich countries and classes into an enlightened 'solidarity' with little precedent in history.

From a rational-actor perspective, the latter outcome only seems realistic if it can be shown that privileged groups possess no preferential 'exit'

---

[19] The shameful charade in Copenhagen, crowned by Obama's desperate deceit of an agreement, exposed less the political gulf between nations than the moral abyss between governments and humanity. In the meantime, the famous 2°C of additional warming, which president and premier have vowed to prevent, is already working its way through the world ocean: a future that will happen even if all carbon emissions ceased tomorrow. (On 'committed' warming and the underlying illusion of Copenhagen, see the harrowing, if awkwardly titled article by Scripps Institution researchers V. Ramanathan and Y. Feng: 'On Avoiding Dangerous Anthropogenic Interference with the Climate System: Formidable Challenges Ahead', *Proceedings of the National Academy of Science* 105, 23 September 2008, pp. 14,245–50.)
[20] UN *Human Development Report 2007/2008*, p. 6.

option, that internationalist public opinion drives policy-making in key countries and that greenhouse gas mitigation can be achieved without major sacrifices in northern hemispheric standards of living—none of which seem likely. Moreover, there is no shortage of eminent apologists, like Yale economists William Nordhaus and Robert Mendelsohn, ready to explain that it makes more sense to defer abatement until poorer countries become richer and thus more capable of bearing the costs themselves. In other words, instead of galvanizing heroic innovation and international cooperation, growing environmental and socio-economic turbulence may simply drive elite publics into more frenzied attempts to wall themselves off from the rest of humanity. Global mitigation, in this unexplored but not improbable scenario, would be tacitly abandoned—as, to some extent, it already has been—in favour of accelerated investment in selective adaptation for Earth's first-class passengers. The goal would be the creation of green and gated oases of permanent affluence on an otherwise stricken planet.

Of course, there would still be treaties, carbon credits, famine relief, humanitarian acrobatics, and perhaps the full-scale conversion of some European cities and small countries to alternative energy. But worldwide adaptation to climate change, which presupposes trillions of dollars of investment in the urban and rural infrastructures of poor and medium-income countries, as well as the assisted migration of tens of millions of people from Africa and Asia, would necessarily command a revolution of almost mythic magnitude in the redistribution of income and power. Meanwhile we are speeding toward a fateful rendezvous around 2030, or even earlier, when the convergent impacts of climate change, peak oil, peak water, and an additional 1.5 billion people on the planet will produce negative synergies probably beyond our imagination.

The fundamental question is whether rich countries will ever actually mobilize the political will and economic resources to achieve IPCC targets, or help poorer countries adapt to the inevitable, already 'committed' quotient of global warming. More vividly: will the electorates of the wealthy nations shed their current bigotry and walled borders to admit refugees from predicted epicentres of drought and desertification—the Maghreb, Mexico, Ethiopia and Pakistan? Will Americans, the most miserly people when measured by per capita foreign aid, be willing to tax themselves to help relocate the millions likely to be flooded out of densely settled mega-delta regions like Bangladesh? And will North

American agribusiness, the likely beneficiary of global warming, volun-
tarily make world food security, not profit-taking in a seller's market, its
highest priority?

Market-oriented optimists, of course, will point to demonstration-scale
carbon-offset programmes like the Clean Development Mechanism
which, they claim, will ensure green investment in the Third World.
But the impact of CDM is thus far negligible; it subsidizes small-scale
reforestation and the scrubbing of industrial emissions rather than fundamental investment in domestic and urban use of fossil fuels. Moreover,
the standpoint of the developing world is that the North should acknowledge the environmental disaster it has created and take responsibility
for cleaning it up. Poor countries rightly rail against the notion that the
greatest burden of adjustment to the Anthropocene epoch should fall
on those who have contributed least to carbon emissions and drawn the
slightest benefits from two centuries of industrial revolution. A recent
assessment of the environmental costs of economic globalization since
1961—in deforestation, climate change, overfishing, ozone depletion,
mangrove conversion and agricultural expansion—found that the richest
countries had generated 42 per cent of environmental degradation across
the world, while shouldering only 3 per cent of the resulting costs.[21]

The radicals of the South will rightly point to another debt as well. For
thirty years, cities in the developing world have grown at breakneck speed
without counterpart public investments in infrastructure, housing or
public health. In part this has been the result of foreign debts contracted
by dictators, with payments enforced by the IMF, and public spending
downsized or redistributed by the World Bank's 'structural adjustment'
agreements. This planetary deficit of opportunity and social justice is
summarized by the fact that more than one billion people, according to
UN Habitat, currently live in slums and that their number is expected to
double by 2030. An equal number, or more, forage in the so-called informal sector—a first-world euphemism for mass unemployment. Sheer
demographic momentum, meanwhile, will increase the world's urban
population by 3 billion people over the next forty years, 90 per cent of
whom will be in poor cities. No one—not the UN, the World Bank, the
G20: no one—has a clue how a planet of slums with growing food and

[21] U. Srinivasan et al, 'The Debt of Nations and the Distribution of Ecological Impacts from Human Activities', *Proceedings of the National Academy of Science* 105, 5 February 2008, pp. 1,768–73.

energy crises will accommodate their biological survival, much less their aspirations to basic happiness and dignity.

The most sophisticated research to date into the likely impacts of global warming on tropical and semi-tropical agriculture is summarized in William Cline's country-by-country study, which couples climate projections to crop process and neo-Ricardian farm-output models, allowing for various levels of carbon-dioxide fertilization, to look at possible futures for human nutrition. The view is grim. Even in Cline's most optimistic simulations, the agricultural systems of Pakistan (minus 20 per cent of current farm output) and Northwestern India (minus 30 per cent) are likely devastated, along with much of the Middle East, the Maghreb, the Sahel belt, parts of Southern Africa, the Caribbean and Mexico. Twenty-nine developing countries, according to Cline, stand to lose 20 per cent or more of their current farm output to global warming, while agriculture in the already rich North is likely to receive, on average, an 8 per cent boost.[22]

This potential loss of agricultural capacity in the developing world is even more ominous in the context of the UN warning that a doubling of food production will be necessary to sustain the earth's mid-century population. The 2008 food affordability crisis, aggravated by the biofuel boom, is only a modest portent of the chaos that could soon grow from the convergence of resource depletion, intractable inequality and climate change. In face of these dangers, human solidarity itself may fracture like a West Antarctic ice shelf, and shatter into a thousand shards.

2. OPTIMISM OF THE IMAGINATION

Scholarly research has come late in the day to confront the synergistic possibilities of peak population growth, agricultural collapse, abrupt climate change, peak oil and, in some regions, peak water, and the accumulated penalties of urban neglect. If investigations by the German government, Pentagon and CIA into the national-security implications of a multiply determined world crisis in the coming decades have had a Hollywoodish ring, it is hardly surprising. As a recent UN Human Development Report observed: 'There are no obvious historical analogies

---

[22] William Cline, *Global Warming and Agriculture: Impact Estimates by Country*, Washington, DC 2007, pp. 67–71, 77–8.

for the urgency of the climate change problem.'[23] While paleoclimatology can help scientists anticipate the non-linear physics of a warming Earth, there is no historical precedent or vantage point for understanding what will happen in the 2050s when a peak species population of 9 to 11 billion struggles to adapt to climate chaos and depleted fossil energy. Almost any scenario, from the collapse of civilization to a new golden age of fusion power, can be projected on the strange screen of our grandchildren's future.

We can be sure, however, that cities will remain the ground zero of convergence. Although forest clearance and export monocultures have played fundamental roles in the transition to a new geological epoch, the prime mover has been the almost exponential increase in the carbon footprints of urban regions in the northern hemisphere. Heating and cooling the urban built environment alone is responsible for an estimated 35 to 45 per cent of current carbon emissions, while urban industries and transportation contribute another 35 to 40 per cent. In a sense, city life is rapidly destroying the ecological niche—Holocene climate stability—which made its evolution into complexity possible.

Yet there is a striking paradox here. What makes urban areas so environmentally unsustainable are precisely those features, even in the largest megacities, that are most anti-urban or sub-urban. First among these is massive horizontal expansion, which combines the degradation of vital natural services—aquifers, watersheds, truck farms, forests, coastal eco-systems—with the high costs of providing infrastructure to sprawl. The result is grotesquely oversized environmental footprints, with a concomitant growth of traffic and air pollution and, most often, the downstream dumping of waste. Where urban forms are dictated by speculators and developers, bypassing democratic controls over planning and resources, the predictable social outcomes are extreme spatial segregation by income or ethnicity, as well as unsafe environments for children, the elderly and those with special needs; inner-city development is conceived as gentrification through eviction, destroying working-class urban culture in the process. To these we may add the socio-political features of the megapolis under conditions of capitalist globalization: the growth of peripheral slums and informal employment, the privatization of public space, low-intensity warfare between police

---

[23] UN *Human Development Report 2007/2008*, p. 6.

and subsistence criminals, and bunkering of the wealthy in sterilized historical centres or walled suburbs.

By contrast, those qualities that are most 'classically' urban, even on the scale of small cities and towns, combine to generate a more virtuous circle. Where there are well-defined boundaries between city and countryside, urban growth can preserve open space and vital natural systems, while creating environmental economies of scale in transportation and residential construction. Access to city centres from the periphery becomes affordable and traffic can be regulated more effectively. Waste is more easily recycled, not exported downstream. In classic urban visions, public luxury replaces privatized consumption through the socialization of desire and identity within collective urban space. Large domains of public or non-profit housing reproduce ethnic and income heterogeneity at fractal scales throughout the city. Egalitarian public services and cityscapes are designed with children, the elderly and those with special needs in mind. Democratic controls offer powerful capacities for progressive taxation and planning, with high levels of political mobilization and civic participation, the priority of civic memory over proprietary icons and the spatial integration of work, recreation and home life.

The city as its own solution

Such sharp demarcations between 'good' and 'bad' features of city life are redolent of famous twentieth-century attempts to distil a canonical urbanism or anti-urbanism: Lewis Mumford and Jane Jacobs, Frank Lloyd Wright and Walt Disney, Corbusier and the CIAM manifesto, the 'New Urbanism' of Andrés Duany and Peter Calthorpe, and so on. But no one needs urban theorists to have eloquent opinions about the virtues and vices of built environments and the kinds of social interactions they foster or discourage. What often goes unnoticed in such moral inventories, however, is the consistent affinity between social and environmental justice, between the communal ethos and a greener urbanism. Their mutual attraction is magnetic, if not inevitable. The conservation of urban green spaces and waterscapes, for example, serves simultaneously to preserve vital natural elements of the urban metabolism while providing leisure and cultural resources for the popular classes. Reducing suburban gridlock with better planning and more public transit turns traffic sewers back into neighbourhood streets while reducing greenhouse emissions.

There are innumerable examples and they all point toward a single uni-fying principle: namely, that the cornerstone of the low-carbon city, far more than any particular green design or technology, is the priority given to public affluence over private wealth. As we all know, several additional Earths would be required to allow all of humanity to live in a suburban house with two cars and a lawn, and this obvious constraint is some-times evoked to justify the impossibility of reconciling finite resources with rising standards of living. Most contemporary cities, in rich coun-tries or poor, repress the potential environmental efficiencies inherent in human-settlement density. The ecological genius of the city remains a vast, largely hidden power. But there is no planetary shortage of 'carrying capacity' if we are willing to make democratic public space, rather than modular, private consumption, the engine of sustainable equality. Public affluence—represented by great urban parks, free museums, libraries and infinite possibilities for human interaction—represents an alter-native route to a rich standard of life based on Earth-friendly sociality. Although seldom noticed by academic urban theorists, university cam-puses are often little quasi-socialist paradises around rich public spaces for learning, research, performance and human reproduction.

The utopian ecological critique of the modern city was pioneered by socialists and anarchists, beginning with Guild Socialism's dream— influenced by the bio-regionalist ideas of Kropotkin, and later Geddes—of garden cities for re-artisanized English workers, and ending with the bombardment of the Karl Marx-Hof, Red Vienna's great experiment in communal living, during the Austrian Civil War in 1934. In between are the invention of the kibbutz by Russian and Polish socialists, the modernist social housing projects of the Bauhaus, and the extraordinary debate over urbanism conducted in the Soviet Union during the 1920s. This radical urban imagination was a victim of the tragedies of the 1930s and 1940s. Stalinism, on the one hand, veered toward a monumentalism in architecture and art, inhumane in scale and texture, that was little different from the Wagnerian hyperboles of Albert Speer in the Third Reich. Postwar social democracy, on the other hand, abandoned alter-native urbanism for a Keynesian mass-housing policy that emphasized economies of scale in high-rise projects on cheap suburban estates, and thereby uprooted traditional working-class urban identities.

Yet the late nineteenth and early twentieth century conversations about the 'socialist city' provide invaluable starting points for thinking about the current crisis. Consider, for example, the Constructivists. El Lissitzky, Melnikov, Leonidov, Golosov, the Vesnin brothers and other brilliant socialist designers—constrained as they were by early Soviet urban misery and a drastic shortage of public investment—proposed to relieve congested apartment life with splendidly designed workers' clubs, people's theatres and sports complexes. They gave urgent priority to the emancipation of proletarian women through the organization of communal kitchens, day nurseries, public baths and cooperatives of all kinds. Although they envisioned workers' clubs and social centres, linked to vast Fordist factories and eventual high-rise housing, as the 'social condensers' of a new proletarian civilization, they were also elaborating a practical strategy for leveraging poor urban workers' standard of living in otherwise austere circumstances.

In the context of global environmental emergency, this Constructivist project could be translated into the proposition that the egalitarian aspects of city life consistently provide the best sociological and physical supports for resource conservation and carbon mitigation. Indeed, there is little hope of mitigating greenhouse emissions or adapting human habitats to the Anthropocene unless the movement to control global warming converges with the struggle to raise living standards and abolish world poverty. And in real life, beyond the IPCC's simplistic scenarios, this means participating in the struggle for democratic control over urban space, capital flows, resource-sheds and large-scale means of production.

The inner crisis in environmental politics today is precisely the lack of bold concepts that address the challenges of poverty, energy, biodiversity and climate change within an integrated vision of human progress. At a micro-level, of course, there have been enormous strides in developing alternative technologies and passive-energy housing, but demonstration projects in wealthy communities and rich countries will not save the world. The more affluent, to be sure, can now choose from an abundance of designs for eco-living, but what is the ultimate goal: to allow well-meaning celebrities to brag about their zero-carbon lifestyles or to bring solar energy, toilets, pediatric clinics and mass transit to poor urban communities?

Beyond the green zone

Tackling the challenge of sustainable urban design for the whole planet, and not just for a few privileged countries or social groups, requires a vast stage for the imagination, such as the arts and sciences inhabited in the May Days of Vkhutemas and the Bauhaus. It presupposes a radical willingness to think beyond the horizon of neo-liberal capitalism toward a global revolution that reintegrates the labour of the informal working classes, as well as the rural poor, in the sustainable reconstruction of their built environments and livelihoods. Of course, this is an utterly unrealistic scenario, but one either embarks on a journey of hope, believing that collaborations between architects, engineers, ecologists and activists can play small, but essential roles in making an alter-monde more possible, or one submits to a future in which designers are just the hireling imagineers of elite, alternative existences. Planetary 'green zones' may offer pharaonic opportunities for the monumentalization of individual visions, but the moral questions of architecture and planning can only be resolved in the tenements and sprawl of the 'red zones'.

From this perspective, only a return to explicitly utopian thinking can clarify the minimal conditions for the preservation of human solidarity in face of convergent planetary crises. I think I understand what the Italian Marxist architects Tafuri and Dal Co meant when they cautioned against 'a regression to the utopian'; but to raise our imaginations to the challenge of the Anthropocene, we must be able to envision alternative configurations of agents, practices and social relations, and this requires, in turn, that we suspend the politico-economic assumptions that chain us to the present. But utopianism is not necessarily millenarianism, nor is it confined just to the soapbox or pulpit. One of the most encouraging developments in that emergent intellectual space where researchers and activists discuss the impacts of global warming on development has been a new willingness to advocate the Necessary rather than the merely Practical. A growing chorus of expert voices warn that either we fight for 'impossible' solutions to the increasingly entangled crises of urban poverty and climate change, or become ourselves complicit in a *de facto* triage of humanity.

Thus I think we can be cheered by a recent editorial in *Nature*. Explaining that the 'challenges of rampant urbanization demand integrated, multidisciplinary approaches and new thinking', the editors urge the rich countries to finance a zero-carbon revolution in the cities of the developing world. 'It may seem utopian', they write,

> to promote these innovations in emerging and developing-world mega-cities, many of whose inhabitants can barely afford a roof over their

heads. But those countries have already shown a gift for technological fast-forwarding, for example, by leapfrogging the need for landline infra-structure to embrace mobile phones. And many poorer countries have a rich tradition of adapting buildings to local practices, environments and climates—a home-grown approach to integrated design that has been all but lost in the West. They now have an opportunity to combine these tradi-tional approaches with modern technologies.[24]

Similarly, the UN Human Development Report warns that the 'future of human solidarity' depends upon a massive aid programme to help developing countries adapt to climate shocks. The Report calls for removing the 'obstacles to the rapid disbursement of the low-carbon technologies needed to avoid dangerous climate change'—'the world's poor cannot be left to sink or swim with their own resources while rich countries protect their citizens behind climate-defence fortifications.' 'Put bluntly', it continues, 'the world's poor and future generations cannot afford the complacency and prevarication that continue to char-acterize international negotiations on climate change.' The refusal to act decisively on behalf of all humanity would be 'a moral failure on a scale unparalleled in history'.[25] If this sounds like a sentimental call to the bar-ricades, an echo from the classrooms, streets and studios of forty years ago, then so be it; because on the basis of the evidence before us, taking a 'realist' view of the human prospect, like seeing Medusa's head, would simply turn us into stone.

---

[24] 'Turning blight into bloom', *Nature*, 11 September 2008, vol. 455, p. 137.
[25] UN *Human Development Report 2007/2008*, pp. 6, 2.

The MIT Press

http://mitpress.mit.edu

TERI REYNOLDS

DISPATCHES FROM

THE EMERGENCY ROOM

I SPENT MY EARLY childhood in a trailer park in Texas so, until I became an emergency physician in Oakland, I thought I knew something about barriers to healthcare access, and maybe even something about poverty. The Emergency Department at the Oakland county hospital has around 75,000 visits a year—say, 200 a day. It has 43 beds; because of overcrowding, there are 'extra' patient beds in the hallways, which have ended up being designated as official patient-care areas: first came Hallway 1, then, a year later, Hallway 2, and now Hallway 3 as well. At night the ED usually has one supervising physician with a couple of housestaff—trainee doctors—a student or two, and around ten nurses; there is double supervising coverage from the late morning through to about 2 AM, the hours of heaviest traffic.

County hospitals are where those with no insurance go. The elderly and disabled who qualify for Federal Medicare and Medicaid insurance may also go there, but they often take the insurance elsewhere. Those who have no insurance, no money and nowhere else to go, come to the county hospital. Our speciality is the initial management of everything. There are patients who bless me for my time, after they have waited 18 hours to see me for a five-minute prescription refill, and another who regularly greets me with, 'Yo bitch, get me a sandwich.' I did have one patient, born at the county hospital, who lied about his private insurance in order to return to what he called 'my hospital', but many more who feel they have hit bottom when they cannot afford to get care elsewhere.

Around 47 per cent of the patients are African-American, and 32 per cent Hispanic. We call the Mongolian and Eritrean telephone translator-lines on a regular basis. We also see the patients who are not entirely disenfranchised, but fall out of the system when they lose their jobs; most Americans have insurance linked to employment, either their own or a family member's. It is not infrequent to see the primary reason for a visit to the hospital listed as 'Lost Insurance', 'Lost Kaiser' (the main private health maintenance organization in California), 'Lost to Follow Up' and once, just 'Lost', but we all knew what it meant. We see patients every week with decompensated chronic disease who say, 'I was doing fine until I lost my job and couldn't get my meds.'

Some of the visits are for true emergencies—there are 2,500 major trauma cases a year. These are usually shootings, stabbings, falls, assaults and automobile accidents; many, if not most, involve alcohol and drugs. In 2008 there were 124 homicides in Oakland alone, most of them due to gun violence; many victims have been involved in violence before. The Emergency Department gets a stream of teenage gunshot victims, cursing and yelling as they come in, swinging at medics and police with arms scored with gang tattoos; by the next day we see them emerge as the children they are, cowed by the presence of their mothers beside the recovery beds. We also see the bystanders, the teenagers who get shot while walking home from school, the elderly Chinese man hit by a stray bullet as he stepped outside to get the newspaper, the mother shot stepping in front of her son—who claimed not to know the shooters when interviewed by the police, but was overheard by the nurse the next day rallying his 'boys' for a revenge run. This kind of trauma has a way of turning victims into perpetrators. The first 'death notification' I did as an intern was to the mother of three boys. The older two had spent three months on the East Coast with relatives to let a 'neighbourhood situation' cool off. Less than 24 hours after their return to Oakland, they were shot while walking down the street together. The two older boys died. The 18-year-old had a collapsed lung, but survived. At his last trauma clinic follow-up, he was referred to social work for 'clinical evidence of depression', though at the time there was no outpatient social-work clinic available.

Drugs and alcohol increase all kinds of risk, and traverse all social classes, but cocaine is its own special force in this community. Smoking crack cocaine is such a common trigger for asthma exacerbation that we have come to call it 'crasthma' at signout. At first, Emergency Department doctors were startled when small, wiry elderly women coming in for chest pain tested positive for cocaine on the urine screen. It turned out they were social opium smokers from the hills of Southeast Asia, who turned to smoking crack cocaine when their immigrant families moved them to Oakland. It must have seemed somehow similar, though it turned out to be much worse for their hearts. I recently saw a 55-year-old woman who had been found on the floor by her family in the middle of the night. Her CT scan showed a large bleed in her brain. After years of planning she had managed to set things up to move her family back to Mississippi where she thought her teenage grandsons, who had begun flirting with gang activity, would be safer. She had been up all night cleaning the house and packing to leave the next day, and had used the cocaine that had likely caused the brain bleed to help her stay awake.

There are the everyday medical emergencies: septic shock, heart attacks, strokes, deadly lung and skin infections, respiratory and cardiac arrests. These, along with the major traumatic injuries, are the cases the ED was designed for. But most of our patients do not have emergent conditions; they are just ill, and have nowhere else to go. The county system has a wide complement of outpatient clinics, staffed by some of the best doctors I know. But the last time I checked, their next available primary-care appointment was six months away. Sometimes there are no appointments at all, just a clipboard where we scribble a name and medical record number, to put a patient in line for the six-month wait.

Then there are the patients who did have an outpatient clinic appointment, but no telephone, and so were not informed when their clinic visit was rescheduled. There are those who have to take three buses to get to the clinic and miss the last one; those who would like to see their doctors, but forget to come in when they drink too much; and others, especially the elderly, who won't come to late afternoon appointments because they are afraid to travel home after dark. Some patients just need prescriptions—those whose medications are stolen, those who finish a prescription before a refill is available because they feel bad and double their own dose, or those who just want the cough syrup with codeine that has become a popular drug of abuse. There are those who have lives so complicated—by three jobs, or six children—that a 3 AM emergency visit is all they can manage. They come to the county ED because we are always open, and refuse care to no one.

Coming onto a shift, we hit the ground running. There is signout, a 20- or 30-minute verbal handover of all the patients in the Department, with an update on their status and discussion of what still needs to be done.

Most of the shift is spent running around seeing patients and discussing their management plans. But we also negotiate with consultants and admitting doctors, intervene to control ambulance traffic, and troubleshoot staffing issues. There is no official break—we grab food when we can. I carry a portable phone that rings off the hook with referrals and questions. Emergency physicians are interrupted—by nurses, students, technicians, pharmacists and other physicians—every 3–4 minutes on average (this has actually been studied). There are shifts when I cannot find time to make it to the bathroom.

Nurse staffing is often the rate-limiting step in the process. Nurses—they range from fresh-faced graduates in tight pink scrubs to ex-military medics covered with tattoos—are the front line of care at the county hospital. They see patients first and are responsible for screening the dozens that present to triage at any one time, and deciding which ones need to be seen immediately and which can wait. They bear the brunt of patients' frustration; they are the ones who undress them and find hidden wounds and weapons, medications and money, needles and crack pipes. Nurses have a maximum patient ratio of 1:4, mandated by California law and rigorously protected by the union. They also have mandatory protected break time and meals. Because physicians' orders—on medications, for example—cannot be executed without a nurse, patients often wait for hours to be roomed or get pain relief. The union is generally a force for good, though some feel that it has compromised physician–nursing relations—and even I, who was our union delegate for some years, feel that it has fostered some abuse of the county system.

A few doctors rail at the patients who come to the Emergency Department for routine care, but most who have chosen to work in the county system pride themselves on being jacks-of-all-trades, holding steady in the middle of the maelstrom, being a part of the safety net. So when patients cannot get primary care, we tell them to follow up in the ED on our next scheduled shift. I have started patients on medication for newly diagnosed diabetes and transitioned them to insulin before they could manage to see a primary-care doctor. I have prescribed first, second and third-line medications for blood pressure. I have seen three generations of women, plus an uncle, in one family. There are a cadre of regulars we know by name; we discuss their recent visits and send around emails when they die. So we do deliver primary care; some of us enjoy it, and the patients certainly need it. But in the end, we are simply not very good at it. An Emergency Department is a lousy place to manage chronic disease.

The failure of preventive, primary care creates emergencies that should never have happened. The County Hospital is where diseases become the worst version of themselves: what should have been a case of simple diabetes, requiring oral medication and diet change, presents as diabetic ketoacidosis, a life-threatening condition of acid in the blood. We see severe infection that can only be treated with amputation, but was once simple cellulitis requiring antibiotics; numerous strokes, which could have been prevented through blood-pressure control. While the Emergency Department tries to give patients what they need, it cannot offer them a phone number they can call for refills, a clinic to return to or the chance to see the same doctor year after year.

Frequently, the ED fails to take the whole patient into account. Given the volume and acuity of the patients we see, some stable patients just have too many problems to address in the course of a visit. We talk about the 'chief complaint' in medicine—the main reason for the visit. It might be abdominal pain, a sprained ankle, lost insurance or chest pain. When patients start on a list of several complaints, we sometimes ask them to identify the main thing that brought them in that day. A colleague recently signed out a patient to me as 'a 65-year-old man with vision loss in one eye for two weeks, seen here four days ago for indigestion, now waiting for a CT scan to rule out stroke'. I asked why we had not evaluated his vision loss when we had seen him four days ago, and was told that the patient had not mentioned it then. When we asked him why, the patient said he had been told he could only have one problem. He chose the indigestion because it hurt, while the vision loss was painless.

All Emergency Departments are legally required to examine patients and provide initial treatment, regardless of insurance status; but the definition of 'initial treatment' is broad. Frequently, we see patients with acute fractures diagnosed at a private hospital. They arrive with temporary splints in place and x-rays in hand, saying, 'I didn't have insurance, so they told me to follow-up here.' When we want to transfer patients to a nearby hospital for cardiac catheterization to treat a severe heart attack, we are asked to fax over the 'face sheet', a summary printout of the patient's basic demographic information: name, date of birth, address, phone number and insurance status. While it is technically illegal for hospitals who have room to refuse to accept a patient who needs a 'higher level of care', such as the cardiac catheterization that our hospital does not offer, we are frequently told there are no available beds. We are told this much more often for our uninsured patients than for those with Medicare, or those who have secured disability payments from the government.

Care delivery in America lags far behind our pharmaceutical and diagnostic science. Most applications for new drug approvals are in categories where good drugs are already available; more than new medicine for diabetes, we need good research on how to get the medicines we have to diabetic people. Our health system has generated an enormous cohort of patients who are diagnosed but untreated, or under-treated. These are not medical mysteries, but social ones. The barriers to appropriate healthcare are myriad, and not all are a function of the system. I have seen a homeless woman, probably schizophrenic, seeking her first care for a breast mass that must have been there for years before it took over half her chest. And a man brought in by the ambulance he had finally called when his legs became too swollen from heart failure and blood clots to get through his bathroom door. He hadn't been outside in a decade. Or the young man who had been diagnosed with mild renal failure two years earlier and re-presented with a complication so severe that the kidney specialist I called told me he had only seen it once before, thirty years ago in rural India. The young man seemed reasonable—he was responsible enough to hold two jobs and support one family in the US and two in Mexico. He spoke no English and had not really understood that he was supposed to come back. Until he had become too weak to work, he had just carried on. These are patients disenfranchised by much more than the healthcare system in our country—by a collision of poverty, poor social services and lousy public transportation, substance abuse, language barriers and more.

II

I have recently shifted my practice to the ED of the University of California, San Francisco Medical Center, 12 miles away, for a one-year speciality fellowship. This is a tertiary referral hospital, famous for treating patients with obscure diagnoses, syndromes that only affect five patients in the world; some are named for scientists who work upstairs in the same medical centre. The Hospital is a transplant centre and many of the patients are on drugs that suppress their immune systems; the very medications that keep them from rejecting their transplanted organs leave them vulnerable to severe, rapidly progressing infections. Many of the patients have heart or lung abnormalities. I recently saw a child with so little circulating oxygen that his lips were blue-black. Before I could put a breathing tube down his throat, his father told me that he always looks like that due to his unrepaired heart defect. They had come for his abdominal pain. While we sometimes complained about the simple cases in Oakland, here we complain that there are no simple patients. Chief complaints such as 'finger laceration' are inevitably followed by 'heart transplant 2 days ago', 'rash' by 'history of Gorlin's Syndrome', 'cough' by 'awaiting lung transplant next week'.

I have never been cursed at by a patient in the Emergency Department here, rarely asked for a sandwich, and only occasionally see a urine test that is positive for cocaine. Patients can almost always get their medi-cines, and frequently have follow-up appointments already scheduled. They can usually list their medications and often describe their entire medical history by memory. I have more than once been told that the chair of a subspecialty department would be coming down himself because the patient is a University Faculty member or some other VIP—on one surreal shift, two of my first three patients were doctors themselves. I almost never refill prescriptions for more than a two-day supply, because that is the purview of primary care. On an average shift I see at least three patients who are 90 or older, most of whom drive themselves to the hospital. Almost no one seems to live to 90 in the county system.

The healthcare proposals generated under the Obama administration take as given the profound inequalities in the distribution of medical care in the United States. Both House and Senate plans fall within a range of middle-ground options that legislate for even more money to be paid into the private system in return for only minimal concessions. They neither create the benefits of risk-sharing for the public system (which currently covers the oldest and sickest), nor make the insurance industry take on the total risk-pool of young and old, sick and well, which alone would make universal coverage feasible. With insurance mandatory and non-coverage penalized, millions more would be required to pay into the private system, while tens of millions out of the 46 million currently uninsured would remain without coverage in both the House and the

Senate plan. The Congressional debate has avoided medical and social realities to focus on rhetorical dilemmas. Reproductive medicine, which should be a matter of scientific standards of care, has been thrown into the package as a negotiating *quid pro quo*.

Healthcare in America is the civil-rights issue of our time. Extended insurance coverage will not tackle the huge social barriers that stand between patients and optimal medical treatment. Adequate primary care would mitigate the devastating effects of these social factors. In the current County system, a patient who misses a bus and therefore an appointment may wait months to get another, and may not even be able to reschedule by phone. In a functional primary-care system, patients who miss appointments—or a patient newly diagnosed with renal failure—would be called back, not lost to follow-up.

It is hard to talk about a middle ground for something that is a fundamental right. Some believe there is no harm in taking what we can get and going from there; but this is probably not true. The insurance industry makes great gains in the current plan that will be hard to reverse. More, the proposals validate much of the profoundly unjust current system, which has grown up ad hoc but which, up till now, has never been explicitly sanctioned as a workable plan by the Federal government. To tolerate a disastrous bricolage is one thing; to extol its virtues quite another.

I have been well aware of the fallout our imbalanced system has for county patients; but until recently I don't think I recognized the damage it was doing to the small minority it serves well. On one of my early shifts at the University of California hospital the triage nurse passed me a handwritten note from a patient in the waiting room. It read:

> Please help me. My jaw has been broken and I am in a lot of pain. I've been here over an hour and am still bleeding. My hands and feet are numb and I'm starting to shake. I need some care. I have insurance.

The young electrical engineer who wrote the note was in his mid-thirties, used neither drugs nor alcohol, and had never been in a fight in his life. He had been prescribed cough medicine with codeine for a viral illness and had passed out in his bathroom, breaking his jaw and several teeth on the sink as he fell. His injuries were no more and no less devastating than those resulting from violence in Oakland. What was striking was that a highly educated young man could feel that his pain, bleeding and shaking might not get him care in one of the best hospitals in the country, but that his insurance would; could assume that the brief delay before he was seen was due not to the acute stroke and heart-attack patients who had come in just before him, but to the suspicion that he did not have insurance. If even the privileged feel their access to care is so vulnerable, it becomes hard to argue that the system is working for anyone.

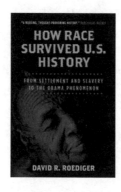

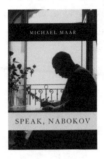

PERRY ANDERSON

TWO REVOLUTIONS

Rough Notes

I F THE TWENTIETH century was dominated, more than by any other single event, by the trajectory of the Russian Revolution, the twenty-first will be shaped by the outcome of the Chinese Revolution. The Soviet state, born of the First World War, victor in the Second, defeated in the cold replica of a Third, dissolved after seven decades with scarcely a shot, as swiftly as it had once arisen. What has remained is a Russia lesser in size than the Enlightenment once knew, with under half the population of the USSR, restored to a capitalism now more dependent on the export of raw materials than in the last days of Tsarism. While future reversals are not to be excluded, for the moment what has survived of the October rising, in any positive sense, looks small. Its most lasting achievement, huge enough, was negative: the defeat of Nazism, which no other European regime could have encompassed. That, at any rate, would be a common judgement today.

The outcome of the Chinese Revolution offers an arresting contrast. As it enters its seventh decade, the People's Republic is an engine of the world economy, the largest exporter at once to the EU, Japan and the United States; the largest holder of foreign-exchange reserves on earth; for a quarter of a century posting the fastest growth rates in per capita income, for the largest population, ever recorded. Its big cities are without rival for commercial and architectural ambition, its goods sold everywhere. Its builders, prospectors and diplomats criss-cross the globe in search of further opportunities and influence. Courted by former foes and friends alike, for the first time in its history the Middle Kingdom has become a true world power, whose presence reaches into every continent. With the fall of the USSR, no formula to describe the turn of events it signified became so canonized as 'the collapse of communism'. Twenty years later that looks a touch Eurocentric. Viewed in one light, communism has not just survived, but become the success story of the age. In the character and scale of that achievement, of course, there is more than one—bitter—irony. But of the difference between the fate of the revolutions in China and Russia, there can be little doubt.

Where does the explanation of this contrast lie? Despite the world-historical gravamen of the question, it has not been much discussed. At issue, of course, is not just a comparison of two similar but distinct upheavals, otherwise unrelated in their different settings, as in the once familiar pairing of 1789 and 1917. The Chinese Revolution grew directly out of the Russian Revolution, and remained connected with it, as inspiration or admonition, down to their common moment of truth at the end of the eighties. The two experiences were not independent of each other, but formed a consciously ordinal sequence.[1] That tie enters into any consideration of their differing outcomes. To explain these, in turn, involves reflection at a number of levels. Four of these will be distinguished here. Firstly, how far did the subjective political agencies of the two revolutions—that is, the respective parties in each country, and the strategies they pursued—differ? Secondly, what were the objective starting-points—socio-economic and other conditions—from which each ruling party set out on its course of reform? Thirdly, what were the effective consequences of the policies they adopted? Fourthly, which legacies in the *longue durée* of the history of the two societies can be regarded as underlying determinants of the ultimate outcome of revolutions and reforms alike? Since the PRC has outlived the USSR, and its future poses perhaps the central conundrum of world politics, the organizing focus of what follows will be China, as seen in the Russian mirror—not the only relevant one, as will become clear, but an ineludable condition of the rest.

I. MATRICES

The October Revolution, famously, was a swift urban insurrection that seized power in Russia's major cities in a matter of days. The speed

---

[1] Isaac Deutscher's remarkable essay 'Maoism—its Origins and Outlook' (1964) remains the starting-point for any consideration of the relationship between the revolutions: *Ironies of History*, Oxford 1966, pp. 88–120.

of its overthrow of the Provisional Government was matched by the crystallization of the Party that accomplished it. The Bolsheviks, numbering no more than 24,000 in January 1917, on the eve of the abdication of Nicholas II, had mushroomed to somewhere over 200,000 when they toppled Kerensky's regime nine months later. Their social base lay in the young Russian working class, which comprised less than 3 per cent of the population. They had no presence in the countryside, where over 80 per cent of the population lived, having never thought to organize among the peasantry—any more than had the Social Revolutionaries, though the SRs enjoyed an overwhelming rural following in 1917. Such rapid victory, from a still narrow ledge of support, was rendered possible by the shattering of the Tsarist state by German hammer-blows in the First World War—military failure detonating mutinies that dissolved its repressive apparatus, the February Revolution leaving only the shakiest lean-to of a successor authority.

But if power was taken easily in this vacuum, it proved hard to hold. Vast tracts of territory fell to German occupation. Once Germany was itself defeated in 1918, ten different expeditionary forces—American, British, Canadian, Serb, Finnish, Romanian, Turkish, Greek, French, Japanese—were dispatched to help White armies crush the new regime in a bitter Civil War that lasted till 1920. At the end of it, completing the destruction wrought in the World War, Russia was in ruins: famine in the villages, factories abandoned in the towns, the working class pulverized by the fighting and de-industrialization of the country. Lenin's Party, its social base disintegrated or absorbed into the structures of the new state, was left an isolated apparatus of power suspended over a devastated landscape: its rule now associated with the miseries of domestic war rather than the gifts of peace and land delivered after October.

The Union of Soviet Socialist Republics that, by a supreme effort, it brought into being covered the larger part of the former Russian empire. But, the first modern state in history to reject any territorial definition, the emergent USSR laid no claim to patriotic pride or national construction. Its appeal was international: to the solidarity of the labour movement across the world. Having taken power in a huge backward country, whose economy was overwhelmingly agrarian and population largely illiterate, the Bolsheviks counted on revolutions in the more developed, industrial lands of Europe to rescue them from the predicament of a radical commitment to socialism in a society without the preconditions of any coherent capitalism. A gamble the beleaguered rulers soon lost, it meant nothing to the mass of the ruled from the start. The Soviet Party would have to hold out on its own, attempting to move as far as it could towards another form of society, without much support at home or any assistance from abroad.

2

The Chinese Revolution, although it was inspired by the Russian, inverted virtually all its terms. The CCP, created in 1921, still had less than a thousand members four years later, when it started to become for the first time a significant force, born of the explosion of working-class militancy in coastal cities with the May 30th movement of 1925, and aided by the vital role of Soviet advisers and supplies in the fledgling GMD regime led by Sun Yat-sen in Canton. Between that founding moment and the Communist conquest of power across China lay struggles that extended through a quarter of a century. Its milestones are well known—the Northern Expedition of 1926, joining Nationalists and Communists against the leading warlord regimes; the massacre of Communists by Chiang Kai-shek in Shanghai in 1927; the ensuing White Terror; the establishment of the Jiangxi Soviet in 1931, and the five annihilation campaigns waged against it by the GMD; the Long March of the Red Army to Yan'an in 1934–35, and the creation of Border Regions ruled by the CCP in the north-west; the United Front again with the GMD against Japanese invasion in 1937–45; and the final civil war of 1946–49, in which the PLA swept the country.

More than just the wholly different temporality of this experience separated it from the overturn in Russia. The way in which power was won was altogether distinct. If the state is defined, in Weber's famous formula, by the exercise of a monopoly of legitimate violence over a given territory, a revolution always involves a breaking of that monopoly, and the emergence of what Lenin and Trotsky called a dual power. Logically, there are three ways in which this can arise, corresponding to the three terms of Weber's formula. A revolution can break the monopoly of the state's power by destroying the legitimacy of its rule, so that coercion cannot be exercised to repress the movement against it. The Iranian Revolution, in which there was no fighting, the royal army remaining paralysed as the monarchy fell, would be an example. Alternatively, a revolution can pit an insurgent violence against the coercive apparatus of the state, overwhelming it in a quick knock-out blow, without having secured any general legitimacy. This was the Russian pattern, possible only against a weak opponent.

Finally, a revolution can break the state's monopoly of power, not by depriving it from the outset of legitimacy, nor rapidly undoing its capacity for violence, but by subtracting enough territory from it to erect a counter-state, able in time to erode its possession of force and consent alike. This was the Chinese pattern. It was not exclusive to China, forming the general path of guerrilla forces—also Yugoslav or Cuban—to power. What was exceptional in the Chinese case was not the creation of successive 'rebel states' within the state, but their combined longevity. It is the conditions of this duration that require explanation.

At the turn of the century the Romanov monarchy, whatever its own weaknesses, was incomparably stronger than the Qing: a native institution that could draw not only on pockets of advanced industry and abundant natural resources, but on a huge army and deep reserves of patriotic loyalty, born of victory over Napoleon. In the Far East, it was foremost among the European powers in encroaching on the Chinese empire. Only massive defeat on the battlefield, first by Japan and then by Germany, triggered the revolutions of 1905 and 1917 against it. The Qing monarchy, by contrast, was already by the mid-19th century widely hated as an alien dynasty, and soon too as a corrupt dependency of the West. After the Taiping Rebellion, it never regained central control of force throughout the country. So enfeebled had the imperial state become that it fell in 1911 without even a concerted movement against it. No successor regime lived up to Weber's standard. The Republic dissolved, first into a chequerboard of rival warlord fiefs; then into the hybrid regime based in Nanjing, the GMD commanding the centre of the country around the Yangzi delta, assorted regional militarists the rest: never more than half of China's eighteen traditional provinces under Chiang Kai-shek's control, often less.

It was in this maze of competing power-centres that the CCP could anchor itself in gaps between jurisdictions, and build a movable counter-power. But although it never confronted a unified state machine, as the Bolsheviks had done, its adversary was paradoxically more formidable, and the risks of defeat higher. Restricted to its strategic strongholds though it was, the GMD was not an absolutist regime at the end of its life span, nor a spectral interim government. Nationalism and Communism were coeval as antagonists, formed in the same organizational mould: equally modern rivals, in their own fashion, for mastery of the country. The GMD, however, controlled vastly larger armies, equipped with heavy armour and trained in successive missions—Von Seeckt, Von Falkenhausen—by the cream of the Wehrmacht; it commanded the tax revenues of the richest regions of China. For all the heroism of the Long March, it would no doubt have wiped out the CCP by the end of the 30s, had Japan not launched a full-scale attack on the Nanjing regime in 1937.

In this emergency Chiang, cheated of his prey but still obsessed with communism as the greater danger, proved incapable of confronting the foreign enemy to any effect. A long-time collaborator with the Japanese military—with whom he planned the Shanghai massacre of 1927, flying to Tokyo shortly afterwards to seal a pact with its General Staff—who had acquiesced in its seizure of Manchuria, he retreated into the interior, hoping after Pearl Harbour to wait out the war for American victory and then turn on the CCP with his main forces intact. Japan's final campaign in China, the Ichigo Offensive of 1944, put paid to any easy realization of this prospect, shattering the GMD's best divisions beyond repair. No less damaging was the discredit Chiang's dictatorship incurred in refusing to commit all to the defence of the nation.

Beyond GMD reach or Japanese penetration, from its base in the remote Border Region of Yan'an the CCP waged increasingly effective guerrilla war against the invader across North China. The growth in its power came from its ability to combine reform in the villages—rent reduction, debt cancellation, limited land redistribution—with resistance to the foreigner. The union of the two gave it a depth of social racination the Russian Party never acquired, in an expanding mass base among the peasantry, the class that composed the vast majority of the population. In the eight years from 1937 to 1945, the Chinese Party grew from 40,000 to 1,200,000, and its armies from 90,000 to 900,000. Once Japan had surrendered, its implantation spread very rapidly across the North China plain: by the time civil war broke out in 1947, its ranks had more than doubled again, to some 2,700,000. Meanwhile, in the GMD-controlled zones of the Centre and South, unbridled corruption and inflation destroyed urban support for Chiang's regime, whose demoralized

ANDERSON: *Russia–China* 65

armies, however well-armed and equipped by the United States, proved no match for the PLA. In increasing numbers, his commanders surrendered or switched sides as it marched south: Beijing, Shanghai, Nanjing, Guangzhou—one after another, the great cities of China fell with scarcely a shot being fired.

In Russia, the civil war came after the Revolution, and as if in retribution for it, plunging the country into a far worse condition than it had been in before the Bolsheviks came to power. In China, the Revolution followed the civil war, and its immediate effects came as a redemption from it. For over a century, China had not known a central state capable of withstanding foreign aggression, or assuring order throughout the country. Communism brought both: national independence and internal peace. With the defeat of the Guomindang, US officers, British gunboats, Japanese hold-overs were sent packing. The victory of the PLA, far from leaving economy and society ravaged, delivered recovery and stability. Inflation was mastered; corruption banished; supplies resumed. In the countryside, landlordism was abolished. In the cities, no sweeping expropriation was needed, since over two-thirds of industry was already state-owned under the GMD, and comprador capital had fled to Hong Kong or Taiwan. The middle class was so alienated by the last years of Nationalist rule that much of it greeted the arrival of Communism with relief rather than resistance; as production revived, workers returned to normal employment and received wages again. The People's Republic, embodying patriotic ideals and social discipline, entered life enjoying a degree of popular assent that the Soviet Union never knew.

3

These differing matrices left their imprint on the course of each regime, in which the proportions of force and consent were always distinct. Under Stalin, Soviet communism acquired active popular support twice after the civil war: among the new generation of workers, from rural backgrounds, mobilized in the all-out industrialization drives of the first Five Year Plans, in a *Sturm und Drang* atmosphere of collective enthusiasm, real if never universal; and during the Second World War, when the regime could draw on a much broader Russian patriotism in a life-and-death struggle of the whole population against Nazi conquest. Neither altered the distrust of the rulers for the masses under them. The Soviet system utilized episodes of popular adhesion, when they arose. But it rested on repression. In the era of Stalin's dictatorship, the secret police became a more central and powerful institution than the Party itself. Violence, compulsively unleashed against real or imaginary enemies, not least within the regime's own ranks, was omnipresent.

Against a background of continual tension, its two great paroxysms were the collectivization of the late twenties, and the purges of the thirties. In the first, the regime launched an all-out war on the peasantry, in which mass deportations and famine cost perhaps 6 million lives, reducing it to a sullen, broken force from which Russian agriculture has never recovered. In the second, not only the entire Old Guard of Bolsheviks who had made the October Revolution, but virtually the whole next levy of cadres in leading positions of Party and state, and a huge number of further victims, were wiped out—at least 700,000 in all. Labour camps, to which those not executed outright in these savageries were dispatched, came to hold another 2 million in these years, amounting to a significant sector of the economy.[2] After victory in the Second World War, in which the USSR suffered an immense toll of destruction, terror abated. But for all the consecration he had won on the battlefield, fear remained the mainspring of Stalin's power to the end.

4

The Chinese Party inherited the Soviet model as it took shape under Stalin, developing much the same monolithic discipline, authoritarian structure, and habits of command. Organizationally and ideologically, the state it created in the early 50s resembled the USSR quite closely. More than this: in due course, Communist rule inflicted two parallel convulsions on China. Because of its roots in the countryside, where the peasantry by and large retained confidence in its leadership, the CCP was able to carry out a swift and complete collectivization within a few years of its original redistribution of land, without incurring the disaster that had occurred in Russia. But in 1958, determined to accelerate the tempo of development, it launched the Great Leap Forward, creating people's communes that were supposed both to produce backyard industries and

---

[2] For estimates of these tolls, see R. W. Davies, 'Forced Labour under Stalin: The Archive Revelations', NLR 1/224, Nov–Dec 1995, pp. 62–80; J. Arch Getty and Oleg Naumov, *The Road to Terror*, New Haven, CT 1999, pp. 587–94.

to deliver much higher quotas of grain. With labour diverted to home-made steelworks, and harvests failing in bad weather, the result was the worst famine of the century, in which at least 15 and perhaps 30 million died. Eight years later, the Cultural Revolution scythed through the Party itself, decimating its ranks in a series of purges that, as in Russia, then spread beyond it. To all appearances, as if in the grip of an unalterable common dynamic, the PRC had replicated the two worst cataclysms of the USSR.

But uncanny though the similarities might seem, the differing matrix of the Chinese Revolution had persisted. If the scale of the dead in the countryside was, relative to the population of each society, probably comparable, its mechanisms were distinct, as were its consequences. Soviet collectivization was conceived as an operation to destroy 'rich' peasants—typically those with some livestock—as a stratum, and executed with military levels of violence. Over 2 million kulaks were deported to wastelands, under the guns of the OGPU. The famine of 1932–33 that followed, though in part caused by bad weather, was basically an effect of the wreckage of rural society this second civil war left behind. Wildly voluntarist though it was, the Great Leap Forward, by contrast, was never intended as an attack on the peasantry, or any part of it. There were no deportations or troops of the Interior Ministry rounding up recalcitrants. Bureaucratic blindness, due to (naturally, self-inflicted) lack of truthful reports from below on grain actually harvested, rather than police ferocity, was the immediate cause of the disaster. By the same token, no comparable alienation of the peasantry ensued. The countryside was not durably demoralized by the Great Leap Forward, village life in even the worst afflicted regions recovering with surprising speed.

Contrasts of motivation and outcome were still more marked in the Cultural Revolution. In the second half of the 30s, Stalin sowed terror from top to bottom of the Soviet Party and state, targeting most of the very officials who had given him supreme power in the CPSU, shot out of hand during the Yezhovshchina, as spies, traitors or counter-revolutionaries. Though the full reasons for this dementia remain uncertain, it is clear that Stalin, whose legitimacy as personal dictator had never been altogether secure—he had played no significant role in the October Revolution, and Lenin had expressly warned the Party against him—was gripped by a morbid suspicion of all those around him, and operated on the belief that the only way to deal with potential doubters or opponents was to kill them.

In launching the Cultural Revolution, Mao too aimed at his immediate colleagues, in part because he had been obliged to acknowledge the failure of the Great Leap Forward and accept the reversal of agrarian policy they had imposed when it could no longer be denied. But his broader motive was to prevent any reproduction in China of the congealed bureaucratic caste that, as he saw it, was leading the USSR after Stalin towards a class society indistinguishable from capitalism. To block this development, he did not turn to the security organs, which in China never acquired the importance they had in Russia, but to student youth. Unleashing, against those he feared would take the Soviet path, mass turbulence from below, rather than decapitating them from above, Mao plunged the country into a decade of controlled chaos.

The cruelties that followed were legion. Uncoordinated violence—persecutions and dissensions; humiliations, beatings, shootings; factional warfare—spread from city to city; in the counties, organized executions. The number of victims, still to be properly computed, was well over a million.[3] Yet deaths, proportionately much fewer than in the Soviet maelstrom, were meted out not by central instruction but at vindictive local initiative, as authorities were overthrown and scores settled across the country. No Yezhov or Beria was in charge. But unlike the Great Terror, the Cultural Revolution was not just a gigantic repression. It was a sweeping attempt to shake up bureaucratic structures by mobilizing a younger generation in revolt against them, and was lived as a mental liberation—if only because of the temporary collapse of so much institutional authority—by many who would later become disillusioned with its outcome, or even passionate opponents of communism. Its self-proclaimed goal was an egalitarian transformation of outlooks that would no longer accept the 'three great differences': between town and country, between agriculture and industry, and—above all—between manual and intellectual labour.

Such ideals were utopian in any society at the time, let alone one still as backward as China. But they were not simply window-dressing. The suspension of universities and high schools to dispatch 17 million youngsters

---

[3] See Andrew Walder and Yang Su, 'The Cultural Revolution in the Countryside: Scope, Timing and Human Impact', *China Quarterly*, March 2003, pp. 82–107.

from the cities to undertake agricultural labour in the countryside, along-side peasants, was a more distinctive and longer-lasting process than the persecutions of the period. Carried out without violence, often with enthusiasm, it answered to other objectives. These in turn left their mark on the way the Cultural Revolution enacted successive purges of the Party itself. There was no wholesale slaughter. Humiliation, demotion and rustication was the typical fate of most of those targeted, rather than liquidation. The rituals of thought reform, 'curing the disease, rather than killing the patient' in the Yan'an phrase, remained in theory, and in—brutal enough—practice, the customary method for dealing with suspects of the capitalist road. When the Cultural Revolution came to an end, only about 1 per cent of the CCP had been permanently evicted from it, and—with the exception of Liu Shaoqi—virtually the entire top leadership of the Party on whom Mao had turned in 1966–69 had survived. Unlike Stalin, he had led the Chinese Revolution to victory, and there was no massacre of the Old Guard who had fought together with him.

Cultural and political variables intertwined in the differing *dénouement*. Mao had become a latter-day emperor, wielding an absolute personal power. But the imperial tradition in China had always placed more emphasis on indoctrination than coercion as an instrument of rule, however ruthless its exercise of violence when need or whim arose: the idea of the Cultural Revolution—altering minds to alter things, as if intellectual conceptions determined social relations—owed more to Confucian than to any Marxist notions of historical change. Yet this was still a regime born of a social revolution in which power—contrary to a dictum of Mao at the time—had grown not only out of the barrel of a gun, but also out of the moral confidence of millions in the party holding it. If the Cultural Revolution came close to destroying that political inheritance, it was nevertheless strangely shaped and, in the end, constrained by it, too.

II. MUTATIONS

Separated by thirty years at their origin, the two revolutions ended in projects of reform close enough in time to overlap. The background to each of these was the failure of a preceding attempt at reconstruction. In the USSR, once Stalin died, reaction against his tyranny was swift. Under Khrushchev, the machinery of terror was dismantled; censorship lightened; collective farms granted more autonomy; investment in consumption increased; and peaceful coexistence with capitalism pro-claimed. De-Stalinization proceeded for some five years, from the 20th to 21st Party Congresses of the CPSU, with considerable momentum. Thereafter, Khrushchev's erratic zig-zags in foreign and domestic policy—gambling and retreating in the Caribbean, pointlessly restructuring the Party, improvising schemes for agricultural revival—antagonized his colleagues and led to his summary removal. He had not envisaged any basic change in the economic system inherited from Stalin, of highly centralized planning and priority to heavy industry, which had assured Soviet triumph in 1945, and on which his own career had been based. Legitimizing all that Gosplan had achieved, the prestige of victory over the most industrialized power in Europe crippled the flexibility of the socio-economic system responsible for transforming the USSR into a Great Power just when it was most needed, at the entrance to a new era.[4]

When Khrushchev was ousted, growth was still respectable and the USSR's military power expanding. The price of his failure was the 'period of stagnation', as its long aftermath from the mid-60s to the mid-80s would come to be called. Freed from his restless initiatives, and now secure from arbitrary arrest, the Soviet bureaucracy settled into a com-placent inertia, contenting itself with a mounting stockpile of weapons and ignoring steadily declining returns from its routines of industrial investment. The USSR achieved nuclear parity with the USA, and was accorded the rank of a super-power. But twenty years of Brezhnevism left the Party a petrified forest of office-holders, presiding over a soci-ety in which life expectancy was falling, economic growth had virtually ground to a halt, and cynicism was universal. Such was the stage on which Gorbachev stepped in 1985.

The disarray in China when Deng Xiaoping came to power was more dramatic. Society was still traumatized by the upheaval of the Cultural Revolution. Higher education had effectively ceased for a decade. Vandalism had destroyed monuments, dogmatism snuffed out intellec-tual life. Vast numbers of youth remained immured in rural exile. Urban discontent was seething, the country's capital recently the scene of a massive popular riot in which the Public Security Bureau building on the edge of Tiananmen Square was sacked and set on fire by infuriated

---

[4] Negatively, collectivization and the purges had a not dissimilar effect on the politi-cal system: catastrophes whose success sealed off renewals, where the failures of the Great Leap Forward and the Cultural Revolution would allow them.

crowds: turmoil unthinkable in Moscow. Mao had wanted to avoid the kind of communism to which Khrushchev's policies, as he saw them, had led. In that goal, he had succeeded. No slow involution of a conservative bureaucracy, paralysing economy and society in a degenerative mould, as had gripped the USSR under Brezhnev, could now occur. His negative aim had been achieved. But his positive alternative had failed no less completely. By the time he died, his policies had ended in another kind of historical impasse.

2

Of the two states as they crossed the threshold of reform, the USSR enjoyed to all appearances much the better conditions, material and cultural, for success. Its GDP was four to five times higher than that of China. Its industrial base was far larger, employing over twice the relative labour force. It was richer in nearly every natural resource—fossil fuels, valuable minerals, abundant land. It was much more urbanized. Its population was better fed, with an average intake of calories half as much again as in China. Its infrastructure was considerably more developed. Last but not least, it was incomparably better educated: not only fully literate, but enrolling twenty times the relative number of students in higher education, and possessing a large pool of well-trained scientists.

Yet the 'period of stagnation' had progressively neutralized, and in critical respects degraded, these endowments. For twenty years, no political change ruffled the dead surface of Soviet life. Central planning taken to a caricatural extreme—specifying the prices of some 60,000 commodities—stifled innovation and accumulated every kind of irrationality. Labour productivity stagnated; capital–output ratios worsened; obsolete plant remained unscrapped; the new information technology was missed. But as the performance of the economy declined, the pressure of the arms race increased. Locked into strategic rivalry with the United States, an enormously wealthier and more advanced society, the Soviet leadership diverted a crippling portion of GDP to military expenditure, with little or no spin-offs to the rest of the economy, without ultimately being able to keep up with American weaponry. Its protectorates in Eastern Europe and Afghanistan, requiring subsidies and expeditionary forces, represented a further burden. For the USSR not just a diplomatic stand-off, the Cold War froze the springs of growth too.

But when the hour of reform came, long overdue, the greatest deficit in this deadlocked system was not economic, but political. The ruling Party was now four generations away from the Revolution. The insurrectionary spirit of Bolshevism was long gone. The rough dynamism of Stalinist *sturmovshchina*, in industry and war, was a thing of the past. Memory even of Khrushchev's boisterous show of combining something of the two, brief enough, had faded. The torpid bulk of the CPSU—the Soviet *nomenklatura* proper—consisted for the most part of mediocre administrative functionaries, incapable of imagination or initiative. But that it was not completely catatonic is suggested by the emergence of Gorbachev at its head. Once installed as General Secretary, he first moved rapidly to clear out the top layer of hold-overs from the Brezhnev period, consolidating his power in the Party with a hand-picked majority in the Politburo. He then proclaimed his watchwords: *glasnost* and *perestroika*—the need for greater openness of public life, and a makeover of the country's institutions.

The first of these, which saw a broad relaxation of censorship, was greeted with a great wave of enthusiasm in society, as long-suppressed energies were released in every kind of iconoclastic argument, exposé and debate. The second left its listeners more perplexed. What did *perestroika*—a term once fleetingly used by Lenin—actually mean, in practice? It soon became clear that Gorbachev, courageous in his intentions, was vague in his ideas: although morally distant from the Brezhnevized CPSU in which he had ascended, he had few intellectual resources independent of it, and only the haziest notion of the reforms he had in mind. Most of his appointees in the cupola of the Party had still less idea, and many were soon resisting him. So to circumvent their opposition, he increasingly turned to an alternative constituency for legitimacy and direction.

The Russian intelligentsia had long been alienated from the regime. The brilliant avant-garde culture of those who were not in exile after the Revolution was buried by Stalin. Hopes raised by the thaw after his death were quickly dashed, even before Khrushchev fell, by the crudity and philistinism of the successor regime. By the mid-80s, communism in any shape or form was anathema to nearly all currents in this historically influential stratum of Russian society. Slavophiles and Westernizers alike, its two traditional poles, were united in rejection of the Soviet order. The former, however, were—for all the fame of Solzhenitsyn—residual;

the latter were hegemonic. Liberals, convinced of the superiority of the West, and aspiring to become part of it, they were soon setting the pace in Gorbachev's entourage, supplying more decided ideas and objectives than he had developed himself. For them, real reform could mean only two, inter-related things: the introduction of democracy, with free competitive elections; and the establishment of a market economy, based on private ownership of the means of production.

As the General Secretary of the CPSU, Gorbachev was not in a position to espouse the second of these goals, even if he had wanted to, which he did not. But the first he embraced, provided the rules were such that he could count on winning endorsement of his own power from a popular consultation, helping to free him from dependence on a Party which he had come increasingly to mistrust, as it mistrusted him. Political reform, the creation for the first time in Russian history of a representative democracy, became the priority. Economic reform, which had originally been the principal meaning of *perestroika*, was deferred. This was the indicated order of battle for the liberal intelligentsia, which needed to break the communist monopoly of power before being able to attack the foundations of the planned economy. For Gorbachev, however, it had another attraction. Dismantling censorship and allowing free elections was relatively simple to do—essentially just a matter of lifting restrictions. Reorganizing the economy would be far more difficult—a huge task, by comparison. He opted for the less arduous route.

If Western-style democracy was to be introduced at home, what was the point of confrontation with it abroad? Winding down the Cold War could garner not only the applause of an intelligentsia that, now well entrenched in the media, had become the dominant opinion-maker in society, but real economic benefits, by reducing the burden of military spending. Not only that: the international prestige of a ruler consorting on the friendliest of terms with his Western counterparts, above all the President of the United States of America, and bringing peace and good-will to the nations of the world, could not but burnish his domestic image. From 1987 onwards, Gorbachev devoted himself more and more to foreign trips and confabulations, becoming the toast of Western opinion, and visibly intoxicated by the figure he was cutting on the world stage. Less and less time was spent on the ungrateful job of controlling the domestic economy.

There, after initial half-baked schemes for promoting cooperatives had come to nothing, one incoherent expedient for introducing greater enterprise autonomy after another was toyed with, to little or no effect, as a massive social crisis hit the USSR, stemming directly from the priority given to political over economic reanimation of the country. Growth was virtually zero when Gorbachev came to power, and oil prices—on which the government's foreign-exchange earnings critically depended—were already starting to fall, putting pressure on the budget that became steadily more acute as oil revenues continued to drop. These would have been difficulties in any circumstances. What converted them into a catastrophic free-fall was Gorbachev's sidelining of the CPSU in his quest for popular consecration. The planned economy depended on the ability of the Party to enforce the deliveries from enterprises that were required by the centre. Once it was removed from effective power, without any coherent replacement, managers simply ceased to supply the state with their output at its prescribed prices, selling it instead for whatever they could get to whomever they could. The result was a collapse of the central allocation mechanism that had held the system together, and a mounting disruption of economic exchange, particularly severe in inter-republican trade.

As the economy descended into chaos, the state became increasingly unable to collect taxes from enterprises or republics, and resorted to printing money instead, to cover food subsidies and social expenditures. Spiralling inflation was compounded by a widening balance of payments deficit, as the government tried to ward off unpopularity with consumer imports, and galloping foreign debt, which all but doubled in five years. By 1989 the Soviet state was not far from bankruptcy. More fatefully still, it was on the brink of disintegration, and for the same reason. Once Gorbachev pulled the linchpin of the Party out of the system, positioning himself as personal ruler apart from and above it, nothing held the republics together any longer.[5] Without the binding structure of the CPSU, the USSR lacked any all-Union ligaments. Gorbachev, immersed to the end in his role as stayer of the Cold War and liberator of Eastern

---

[5] For the dismantling of the all-union party, see Stephen Kotkin, *Armageddon Averted: The Soviet Collapse 1970–2000*, Oxford 2001, pp. 76–81; for the monetary chaos, spread of barter exchange and escalating theft of public assets as *perestroika* spiralled downwards, David Woodruff, *Money Unmade: Barter and the Fate of Russian Capitalism*, Ithaca 1999, pp. 56–78, and Andrew Barnes, *Owning Russia: The Struggle over Factories, Farms and Power*, Ithaca 2006, pp. 43–67.

Europe, proved blinder to the national question within his own country than even to its economic plight. When what was left of the old order finally revolted against him in 1991, and brought him down along with itself, the USSR dissolved overnight.

3

When, seven years before the CPSU, the CCP embarked on its reform course, China was a far poorer and more backward country than Russia.[6] Around 1980, the per capita GDP of the PRC was fourteen times lower than that of the USSR. Over 70 per cent of its labour force was engaged in agriculture, as against 14 per cent in the Soviet Union. Nearly every third Chinese could still not read or write. Its universities were a fraction of those even in India. It can safely be said that no observer, either inside or outside the country, could have predicted the reversal in the fortunes of the two societies three decades later. Yet from the start, there was a series of Soviet handicaps that China did not suffer from: a set of negative advantages that gave it initial conditions—economic, social, political—which, in less obvious respects, favoured it.

The first of these was the lesser weight of obsolescent plant in the economy, not because fixed capital was more advanced than in the USSR, but simply by virtue of a lower degree of industrialization. That what would become the Chinese rust-belt was still not inconsiderable, no-one who has seen Wang Bing's trilogy *West of the Tracks*—perhaps the greatest documentary of all time, on the ultimate fate of the smoke-stack district of Shenyang and its workers—could forget. But, relatively speaking, it was smaller than in the USSR. There were fewer factories to scrap. More significantly still, Chinese planning had always been much looser than its Soviet template. Mao had early on recognized the impossibility of imposing the ubiquitous directives of Gosplan on a far less articulated Chinese economy, with much deeper regional traditions and poorer infrastructures. From the beginning, provincial and township

---

[6] The relevant comparisons are set out in Peter Nolan's essential work, *China's Rise, Russia's Fall: Politics, Economics and Planning in the Transition from Stalinism*, Basingstoke 1995, pp. 110–59, which also contains one of the sharpest and still best critical accounts of *perestroika*: pp. 230–301. For regretful reflections on its failure to 'spark a capitalist revolution', compare Minxin Pei, *From Reform to Revolution: The Demise of Communism in China and the Soviet Union*, Cambridge, MA 1994, pp. 118–42.

authorities had enjoyed greater autonomy than in the Soviet system at any point in its history. Deliberately, the Cultural Revolution had further weakened the powers of the centre, leaving local governments more room for initiative. So output targets for industry were quite modest and pressure to fulfill them was not overwhelming. The result was a much more decentralized system, in which the number of allocated commodities whose prices were fixed in Beijing was at its maximum no more than 600, a hundredth of the Soviet plethora.[7] Less constraining, this was an institutional framework that allowed for greater flexibility and undisruptive change.

Socially, too, China had one huge, critical advantage over the USSR. The peasantry was not a listless, sullen rump of the class it had once been, as in Russia. It was neither tired nor disaffected, but full of potential energy, waiting to be released, as events would show. Historically, it had never possessed collective institutions comparable to the *mir*. Rural society, long atomized in the North and shaken loose by the Taiping upheaval in the South, could recover after the Great Leap Forward with centuries of market impulses behind it. The absence of deep agrarian alienation was not, moreover, simply a difference between the two countrysides. Making up the overwhelming majority of the population, the Chinese peasantry was the central pediment of the nation. Its nearest equivalent in the USSR, even if not so proportionately large a part of society, would have been the industrial working class. But it too, though not so demoralized as the *kolkhozniki*, was by the 80s thoroughly disabused as a social force, deeply cynical about the regime, inured to make-work and low productivity, in compensation for the vast gap between its nominal role as the leading class in the state and its actual position in the hierarchy of privilege. In China, where after the Great Leap Forward the rural population was barred entry into the cities, and had always lacked social benefits that urban workers received, formal inequalities between town and country were greater than in the Soviet Union. But the ruling ideology had never told peasants they were the vanguard class building socialism in the first place. There was less moral gulf between theory and reality, and less lived time between original hope and subsequent experience. For all that had been inflicted, as well as bestowed on it, the countryside remained a reserve of the Party in power.

---

[7] Barry Naughton, *Growing out of the Plan: Chinese Economic Reform, 1978–1993*, New York 1995, pp. 41–2.

Internationally, the situation of the PRC gave it further leeway. It was not burdened with any costly satellite zone, requiring soldiers and sub-ventions to hold down. It was not in a position, and did not attempt, to compete with the super-powers in the missile race. Beyond freedom from these fetters, however, was the radically different relationship of China to the United States. After a decade of extreme tension with the USSR, to the point of border hostilities, Mao had swung into an entente with the US during the Cultural Revolution itself. The Nixon visit and its aftermath, spectacular though these were, remained a diplomatic opening, without significant broader dimensions, as long as he lived. But it meant that when the turn towards domestic reform came, its external setting was propitious. A cautious amity rather than calculated antagonism had created conditions in which the headquarters of world capital, and its assorted regional affiliates, were already primed to extend financial support to any sign of a move towards the market in China. To absence of any deep peasant alienation at home corresponded lack of any direct imperialist threat abroad, for the first time in the modern history of the country.

Internally, moreover, the PRC was in no danger of disintegrating, as the USSR would do. It was not composed of fifteen different constituent republics. Ethnically more homogeneous than most nation-states, it confronted rebellious nationalities—Tibetan and Uighur—within its borders, as the Soviet Union had not done for half a century. But their weight within the population as a whole was minimal compared with the sum of the peoples who broke up the USSR a decade later. Higher on the agenda of the CCP than continuing problems of keeping control of these regions was the still unfulfilled task of recovering Taiwan, where the GMD had built an island redoubt under American protection, still claiming to represent the true Republic of China, and now flourishing economically. The Party's primary concern was not with risks of dissolution, but problems of repossession.

4

Yet, at the gateway to their reforms, perhaps the most decisive of all the differences between Russia and China lay in the character of their political leadership. In command of the PRC was not an isolated, inex-perienced functionary, surrounded by aides and publicists infused with a naive *Schwärmerei* for all that was Western, but battle-hardened veterans of the original Revolution, leaders who had been Mao's colleagues, and had suffered under him, but had lost none of their strategic skills or self-confidence. Deng Xiaoping, indeed, had been so indispensable to the regime that Mao had recalled him to office while still alive. After Mao's death, his authority was such that he soon emerged as the unquestioned arbiter of the Party, without having to seek this eminence personally, or even occupy the highest posts in it. But he was not alone. With him returned Chen Yun, Bo Yibo, Peng Zhen, Yang Shangkun and others, forming a compact, outspoken group of equals—the 'Eight Immortals'—who, often disagreeing vigorously with each other, steered the course towards reform with him. Collectively, they were in a strong position, enjoying not only the prestige of their roles in the Civil War and building of the nation, but the popularity of having brought the Cultural Revolution to an end, which was met with a surge of relief in the cities.

In confronting the situation of the country as Mao had left it, this leadership, with Deng at its head, remained the revolutionaries they had always been. Their temper was Leninist: radical, disciplined, imaginative—capable at once of tactical patience and prudent experimentation, and of the boldest initiatives and most dramatic switches of direction. It was this spirit that had inspired the Long March and won the Civil War. They now brought it to bear on the impasse into which the Cultural Revolution had taken China. In doing so, they were acutely aware of the transformation of its environment, in a way that the functionaries of the CPSU, presiding over a relatively more advanced society, were not of theirs. Western Europe was certainly richer and more developed than Russia, but it had always been so, and the difference between the growth rates of the two—the 70s and early 80s saw a long downturn in the EC itself—was not so vast as to shock Soviet rulers, even as late as the early Gorbachev, into rethinking the basic assumptions on which the success of the state had been built.

In East Asia, on the other hand, Japan had broken all historical records in its high-speed growth, from the 50s onwards—far outdistancing not just Europe, but the United States too. This spectacular recovery of an economy reduced to ashes at the end of the War—the creation of super-competitive export industries and a fully modernized consumer society—threw the relative poverty and autarchy of China, for all its substantial development under Mao, into pointed relief. Nor was Japan, towering above its neighbours though it now did, alone in its success. By the late 70s, South Korea had industrialized at a break-neck pace under Park Chung Hee and, most galling of all, the GMD regime in Taiwan was not far behind. The pressure of this setting on the PRC was inescapable. Deng gave vivid expression to it a decade later, at the height of the political crisis of 1989. After remarking that so long as China was isolated, 'there was no way the economy could develop, no way living standards could rise, and no way the country could get stronger', he went on: 'The world is galloping forward these days, a mile a minute, especially in science and technology. We can hardly keep up'.[8]

The task of making good the lag between communism in China and capitalism in East Asia was a formidable agenda for any programme of reforms. But the Immortals were not daunted. They tackled it with a vigour born not just from the momentum, still active, of the Revolution they had made, but from a millennial self-confidence, battered for a century, but ultimately unbroken, of the oldest continuous civilization in the world. Mao's dynamism, for better or worse, had been one expression of the recovery of that confidence. The Reform Era propelled by Deng would be another. In this historical self-assurance lay a fundamental difference between Russia and China.

5

Ideologically, Tsarism had from the start possessed a weak messianic streak, transmitted to Russian elites and in due course to the country's intelligentsia—notions of Russia as the Third Rome, the saviour of the Slavs, the redeemer of humanity from Western materialism. In the century leading up to the Revolution, versions of this strain could be found in the Aksakovs, Dostoevsky, Rozanov, Blok. But it was a compensation mechanism. Russia remained, as all Russians knew, a backward margin of Europe, redoubtable only by reason of its vastness. Westernization, devoid of religious or ethnic foibles, had been the driving vision of its greatest rulers, Peter and Catherine, and in one variant or another— liberal or radical—came to dominate its elites and intelligentsia alike by the early 20th century. Still, hankerings for a special Russian mission persisted, yielding a recurrent schizophrenia, visible to this day.

---

[8] *The Tiananmen Papers*, New York 2001, p. 327.

Leninism resolved this split mentality by waging war on Russian back-wardness, not in desperate imitation of the West, but in revolt against it, moved by its own deepest critique of itself.

Under Stalin, the Second World War and its aftermath brought a return to nationalism of a more traditional Great Russian stamp, with its train of defence mechanisms, though this always coexisted with Marxist themes. After Stalin, such chauvinism receded, without any real alternative succeeding it. The embers of internationalism, still extant under Khrushchev, were soon snuffed out, leaving only the ideological vacuum of Brezhnevism. By the time of *perestroika*, not only virtually the whole intelligentsia but elements within the ruling elite itself, despondent at the stagnation of the country, had reverted to what could be considered, historically speaking, the ideological default position of thorough-going Westernization—if, this time, in a spirit more of abasement than ambition.

China's geo-cultural traditions were altogether distinct. The Middle Kingdom had dominated its known world ever since the unification of the first Emperor, in the time of the Punic Wars in the West; sometimes conquered, but never rivalled by any comparable state in the region, where it was always far the largest, richest and most advanced power, to which others could only pay tribute, rather than hope for equal relations. Under the Qing, the empire had extended further than ever, stretching deep into Central Asia. The ideology of successive dynasties had varied—Manchu cults were more heteroclite than most—but the imperial claim to absolute preeminence over all lesser rulers, nearer or farther, did not. China was the centre of civilization, and its natural summit.

In the 19th century, Western intrusion shattered these age-old pretensions. Once it became clear that the monarchy was crumbling, under domestic and foreign blows, the alarm of the literati—normally the linchpin of imperial administration—became steadily more acute; and with the first failures of the new Republic, their reaction took a uniquely radical turn. Different currents criss-crossed in the May Fourth culture that crystallized around the student protests of 1919 against Japanese demands on China, and the Treaty of Versailles that upheld them. But its central thrust was a complete demolition of scriptural Confucianism, which had been the ruling doctrine of China's socio-political order and the moral framework of educated life since Han times. Within a few years, virtually nothing was left of it: an achievement no opponents of any comparable creed, world religions—Christian, Muslim, Hindu, Buddhist—occupying a similar position in the ideological firmament of their civilizations, have ever matched.[9] The assault on the Chinese past, intermittently passionate enough already in Liang Qichao, became uncompromising and comprehensive in Chen Duxiu, the intellectual polestar of *New Youth*.[10]

The vehemence of this rejection of native traditions, utterly unlike any current of feeling in Japan, did not reflect—this too was unlike Japan—any profound temptation by the West. In China, the predatory record of the Western powers was too blatant to permit a *zapadnichestvo*. The mutual slaughter of the First World War in Europe clinched the lessons of imperialist greed in Asia, their marriage at Versailles precipitating May Fourth itself. The hallmark of this intelligentsia, after the collapse of the examination system, was abhorrence of the traditional past and revulsion at the capitalist present, as these mingled in warlord China. Its greatest mind, Lu Xun, gave unforgettable expression to both. Without denying that something of value lurked in each system—in the spirit of a sardonic Montaigne, he urged his compatriots to take what good they could find of either, in a freebooting 'haptism'—he remained an irreconcilable enemy of both. But the very extremity of his positions sprang from the strength of the culture he criticized.

Mao, who admired Lu Xun, took his advice on a grand scale, transforming his negations into the positive synthesis of a Sinified Marxism, at once more systematically receptive of intellectual subversion from the West, and more profoundly attached to political traditions of the imperial past—composing 'On Contradiction' in the caves of Yan'an; neglecting affairs of state, at the height of his power, to re-read the chronicles of Sima Guang. Lu Xun knew little of dialectical materialism, and did not relish annals of autocracy. But today's liberals, detesting both men, are not wrong to see a connexion between the 'totalism' of the critic and the 'totalitarianism' of the ruler. In their own way, each

---

[9] For a coruscating analysis, see Mark Elvin, 'The Collapse of Scriptural Confucianism', in *Another History: Essays on China from a European Perspective*, Honolulu 1996, pp. 352–89.

[10] 'Where are the Babylonians today? What good is their culture to them now?', he asked: Jack Gray, *Rebellions and Revolutions: China from the 1800s to 2000*, Oxford 2002, p. 195.

embodied a Chinese response to the crises of their country of a creative vigour without counterpart in Russia after the mid-20s, drawn from
the deepest resources of a culture that was both much older and more
threatened by foreign domination. In productive or perverted form, from
May Fourth to the Cultural Revolution, related energies were at work.
From 1919 to 1949—confidence in negation; then in revolt. From 1958
to 1976—over-confidence in construction; then in destruction. Finally,
after 1978—confidence in reform and reconstruction.

<h1 style="text-align:center">6</h1>

The degree of inner security with which the senate of revolutionary elders
tackled the problems confronting them found early expression in the way
it dealt with the Party's past and future. De-Stalinization in Russia was
the sensational but surreptitious act of a single leader, Khrushchev, who
stunned the 20th Congress of his party with a speech denouncing the
crimes of Stalin about which he had consulted no-one. Emotional and
anecdotal, without more explanation of how the repressions he selectively
reported had been possible than the empty bureaucratic euphemism,
'cult of personality', this rambling address was never officially published;
nor was it followed by any more substantial documentation or analysis
from the leadership of that time or later, until the days of *perestroika*.

Deng and his colleagues proceeded very differently. Some 4,000 Party
officials and historians were involved in a retrospect of the Cultural
Revolution, out of whose discussions a drafting group of 20–40 distilled
a 35,000 word balance-sheet under Deng's supervision, formally adopted
as a resolution by the Central Committee of the CCP in June 1981. While
certainly no complete accounting of the Cultural Revolution—for which
it recorded Mao's responsibility, 'comprehensive in magnitude and pro-
tracted in duration', but confined its toll of repressions to the Party rather
than the population—it offered a reasoned explanation of it, beyond the
misdeeds of one man: the peculiar traditions of a party whose road to
power had inured it to harsh class struggle, as if this were a permanent task; the distorting effect of conflict with the USSR, fanning fears
of revisionism within; and last but not least, 'the evil ideological and
political influence of centuries of feudal autocracy'. Unlike Khrushchev's
commination, the Resolution accepted co-responsibility of the Central

Committee for the modern autocrat's rule, and made no attempt to diminish his contribution to the Chinese Revolution as a whole.

Looking forward, the Elders' approach was equally distinct. In the USSR, Khrushchev had given no thought to any passing of his powers. Those who ousted him, Brezhnev at their head, clung to their posts into senility. In the palsied gerontocracy that the CPSU became, new generations were less a promise than a threat, and only deaths could bring any renewal of the leadership. Three General Secretaries had to die within three years, all in their seventies, before a younger politician could finally take over. In the CCP, on the other hand, the Elders suffered from no such insecurity. They lost little time in finding a relay. Within two years of recovering power, they had delegated its daily exercise to the cohort below them, making Hu Yaobang head of the Party and Zhao Ziyang of the government.

7

The Reform Era began—if not quite in point of time, in substantial effect—with a transformation of relations on the land. First, procurement prices for grain were increased. Then, in a rolling process spreading across the country, after experimental success in two provinces, Anhui and Sichuan, the People's Communes were wound up and usufruct of their land carefully divided among the individual peasant families composing them, giving them control of their holdings to produce what they wanted, once deliveries to the state were met. The resulting 'household responsibility system' amounted to a second agrarian reform, as egalitarian as the first, but far more favourable to peasant production. Responding to the new incentives, productivity shot up: labour inputs fell and harvests rose, agricultural output jumping by a third. With work-times released from tillage, rural industry—textiles, bricks and the like—spread rapidly. The result was to lift peasant incomes from 30 to 44 per cent of national income in the space of a few years, 1978 to 1984.

In the industrial sector, no sudden wrench was thrown into the central allocation system, Russian-style. Rather, state enterprises were gradually permitted to charge market prices for output above the quotas required of them by the plan and sold at fixed prices—giving managers incentives, not unlike farmers, to produce profitably outside the official delivery system, without it being dismantled. Once such dual-track pricing was well tested, the size of the plan was in effect frozen, allowing further industrial growth to develop outside it. In practice the state now leased enterprises to managers on a contractual basis, much as peasants held their land on leases of thirty years from the state, which retained ultimate ownership of it.

For fifteen years or more, under these arrangements, the most dynamic sector of the economy proved to be the distinctive hybrid form of Chinese 'township and village enterprises'—firms intermediate between state, collective and private property, benefiting from low taxes and easy credit from local governments, often stake-holders in them—which mushroomed in the simpler branches of industry with astonishing speed and competitive success. Rural industrial output increased at an annual rate of over 20 per cent, as employment in TVES more than quadrupled from 28 to 135 million, and their share of GDP along with it, from 6 to 26 per cent, between the onset of the reforms and the mid-90s.[11] Highly profitable, the phenomenon of the TVES was ignored by Russian reformers of every stripe as *perestroika* got under way. Of all the contrasts between the changes in the two economies, their performance offers the most dramatic single antithesis to the careening Soviet plunge towards de-industrialization.

The spectacular growth of the TVES was based, of course, on unlimited supplies of cheap labour, absent in the USSR. With them, the PRC for the first time drew full benefit from its principal factor endowment, for which its earlier Soviet-inspired model of industrialization—focused on capital-intensive investment in heavy industry—had been a misfit, however necessary at the time. Reversing this pattern with labour-intensive investment in light industry, the TVES gained an enormous comparative advantage: by the end of the 80s, their ratio of labour to fixed capital was nine times that of state-owned enterprises. But the latter were also direct beneficiaries of the growth of the TVES, whose profits swelled peasant savings, which were then channelled by state banks into further investments in the big nationalized enterprises, re-equipping and modernizing them.

---

[11] Naughton, *The Chinese Economy: Transitions and Growth*, Cambridge, MA 2007, pp. 83, 274–6.

Very high levels of rural savings were in turn another feature of Chinese development rooted in the paradoxical legacy of the Revolution itself. For what determined them was a combination of the traditional limitation of full welfare coverage to the towns, the dismantling of the communes that had provided social services, lesser but real, in the countryside, and the effects of the one-child policy to restrain demographic growth. Without security against misfortune from the state, or sure prospect of family support from the next generation, peasant households had little option, even as their consumption increased, but to save a considerable portion of their income. The state benefited twice over. Unlike its Soviet counterpart, it was spared welfare expenditures on the larger part of its population, and had easy access to the funding required to finance its modernization programme.

Capital was also available from another source. As early as 1979–80, Special Economic Zones were opened along the southern coast to attract investment from the Chinese diaspora, targeting Hong Kong, Taiwanese and South-East Asian wealth. After a slow start, the Open Door shown to such foreign entrepreneurs became a success. Drawn by the privileges, absence of import duties and the cheaper labour of the mainland, diaspora firms arrived in force, bringing with them technologies beyond the reach of the TVEs, essentially in export processing. China was thus able to piggy-back on the accumulated experience and assets of diaspora capitalism for its entry into the world market as a low-cost manufacturing centre for assembly work; over time, principally in electronic and white goods. Here too lay a regional advantage that the Soviet economy, whatever else was possible for it, could not hope to match.

Last but not least, the Chinese reforms benefited crucially from the decentralization of state controls over the economy that was one of the most fruitful legacies of Maoism. This meant not only was there a much smaller planning empire to reconfigure, with far less muscle-bound paraphernalia of quotas and directives, but that the country already possessed in its provinces a web of autonomous centres of economic activity. Once these were further released from intervention by Beijing, their governments sprang into high gear, with every kind of incentive to increase investment and accelerate growth within their jurisdictions. In due course, this generated many an irrationality of its own: duplication of industries, gigantomania of public works, mushrooming of informal protectionism; not to speak of fiscal weakening of the centre, as local authorities competed with each other for best results. But, with all its tares, inter-provincial competition in China, as once rivalry between cities in Italy, was and remains a source of economic vitality. Russia is nominally a federation today; but its vast, featureless plains have never fostered strong regional identities, and its government remains as centralized as ever. The contrast with China is fundamental. Not in constitutional law, but in commercial reality, the People's Republic of today is as much a case of dynamic federalism as the United States.

III. BREAKING POINTS

A decade into the Reform Era, by the end of the 80s the Chinese economy had been substantially transformed. The scale and speed of such changes, naturally, had not left society or culture unaffected. In the countryside, income growth levelled off after 1984, but the peasantry had enjoyed such a major improvement in its conditions of life that in relative terms it remained a contented class. The intelligentsia, historically the other key to social order, had also gained greatly from the reform course. But its attitude to the regime was more ambiguous. Universities had been reopened, research institutes expanded, new employment opportunities created. Rusticated youth had been reintegrated into urban life, and victims of past repressions released. Freedom of expression was far greater than under Mao, access to foreign thought and literature by and large unhindered, giving rise to a veritable 'high-culture fever'. In a heady atmosphere of increasing emancipation, the future of the nation was debated, with an overwhelming consensus in favour of further reforms.

This was not a point of contention with the government itself, whose official aim was also to deepen the reform process. For many intellectuals the two were working in the same direction, with an exchange of consultation and advice between them, particularly around Zhao Ziyang and his aides. But there was also a certain tension, which grew as the decade progressed. The Party possessed the authority of its economic success. It had also enjoyed the legitimacy of its rescue of society from the Cultural Revolution. But this was a deliverance that did not outline any alternative political order. Here the Elders, themselves scarred by the experience of the upheaval, were without a message, beyond warnings of the need to avert any relapse into chaos. At the very outset of the

Reform Era, in 1978, voices calling for democracy were swiftly silenced, as a threat to stability. At the time, these were still relatively isolated.

But as the economic reforms developed, with more and more emphasis on the introduction of market relations, coherent theorization did not accompany them—there was no official explanation of the significance of the TVEs, for example. The result was a kind of ideological limbo, in which liberal ideas quite naturally spread. For if market principles of economic freedom were the order of the day, why should not juridical principles of political freedom—some nominally enshrined in the PRC constitution itself—follow them, as accredited doctrines in the West held they must? Historically, for all the distinction of Hu Shi, its one outstanding representative in the May Fourth generation, liberalism had been a very weak current in the Chinese intelligentsia. But in the 80s, without producing any comparable thinker, and with no very clear outlines, it became in the wake of the Cultural Revolution something like a dominant outlook among intellectuals. For the most part, this remained quite moderate, though over time more radical notes, closer to Russian norms, could be heard. By 1988, the popular television series *River Elegy* was offering a coded hymn to the West, contrasted with China's own grim traditions, of which any *zapadnik* could have been proud; though even this included a flattering portrait of Zhao Ziyang, evoking a great future ahead for the nation, and as history was widely criticized by scholars.

By this time, the mood among students differed. Among a generation no longer touched directly by the Cultural Revolution, spirits were higher, and ideas less fixed. Few were unaffected by the original ideals of the Liberation; some were influenced by liberal, others by more orthodox, teachers; most, attuned to culture and news from abroad—songs from Taiwan, music from America; strikes in Poland, elections in Russia; all, borne by the élan of a society in movement, excited by the opening of its horizons and frustrated by its continuing inertias. Conscious of its historic role in awakening the nation, in 1919 and again in 1935, this was the layer of the population readiest for collective action. In 1985 it showed its traditional nationalist mettle in protests against Japan. Then in the winter of 1986–87, it mounted demonstrations in Hefei and Beijing, calling for democratization. When Hu Yaobang, at the head of the Party, refused to suppress these, the Elders dismissed him. The movement was contained, but the sentiments behind it had not disappeared.

The following year, economic reform itself—hitherto the breakwater against demands for political reform—ran into its first serious crisis, as the cost of basic necessities started to rise, and urban wages stagnated. When Zhao and Deng hinted that full-scale liberalization of prices might be imminent, panic hoarding ensued, and in the summer inflation spiralled to an annualized rate of 50 per cent. Nor, in popular perception, was this the only baleful effect of the system of dual-track pricing. Corruption, unknown under Mao, was spreading, as officials took advantage of their position to exploit the difference between administered and market prices for the same products, and was detested. The combination of unexpected material hardship and anger at social injustice was an explosive mixture, creating a tense atmosphere in the cities.

In Beijing, students were already preparing demonstrations to coincide with the seventieth anniversary of May Fourth in 1989, when in April the death of Hu Yaobang—disgraced for his protection of them—suddenly provided a more immediate rallying-point for the expression of their feelings about the political clamp-down. Marching into Tiananmen Square to honour Hu, they caught the government off-balance. Zhao had been a party to the downfall of Hu, whom he replaced as Chairman of the CCP. But faced with this unrest he now temporized, and the Standing Committee split, leaving the authorities without direction. Showing extraordinary levels of self-organization, the student movement proved able to mobilize every campus in the city and keep up continual pressure on the government. By early May, the marches had become an occupation of the Square, demanding democratic change, backed by enormous demonstrations of the ordinary citizens of Beijing, on edge at the worsening of their economic situation and in open sympathy with the basic political aims of the students. Similar protests swept across the country, wherever there were universities to ignite them. Millions took to the streets, in a social movement without precedent in the history of the People's Republic.

The depth and scale of the upheaval of 1989 in China was far larger than anything in Eastern Europe in that year, let alone in Russia, then or later. The insurgent energy and idealism of the country's students, and the active solidarity with them of the urban population, were without comparison elsewhere: testimony in their way to the political vitality of a society still close to its revolutionary origins. But in China one kind of energy met another. When the crisis came, the post-revolutionary leadership charged with the daily running of the state and Party hesitated, and divided. But the Elders, veterans of decades of armed struggle to win power, were not going to lose it by indecision. They remained the combatants they had always been, unafraid to strike at a threat to the Party's rule, as they saw it, when the necessary force was assembled. In June, the PLA was ordered to clear the Square, and in a night of violence the movement was crushed.

2

Repression came at a high price. The CCP lost more legitimacy on June Fourth than in the Cultural Revolution, which not only had once enjoyed real support, but left a respected leadership in reserve to take charge once it was over. In 1989, no part of the nation supported the crackdown, and there was no opposition in the Party that survived—Zhao, dismissed for failing to vote for martial law, passed quietly away sixteen years later, still under house arrest. On the other hand, the regime still had the card of economic growth. Earlier ideological credentials spent, everything now had to be banked on this. A dose of austerity, to master inflation, lasted into 1991. What next?

Here Deng separated himself from his colleagues, and his own past. In May 1989, he had said: 'Some people, of course, understand "reform" to mean movement towards liberalism or capitalism. Capitalism is the heart of reform for them, but not for us. What *we* mean by reform is different and still under debate'.[12] In January 1992, Deng travelled to the South and declared in Shenzhen, the largest of the Special Economic Zones, that the principal danger facing China was not from the Right but Left opposition to further liberalization of the economy, of which the local stock-market was an exemplary innovation. While still maintaining that China needed socialism rather than capitalism, he now dismissed 'talk of capital C and capital S' as futile, explaining that since inequalities were functional for growth, individual accumulation of wealth was not reprehensible, but laudable: 'to get rich is glorious'. Hopes of collective liberty buried, compensation was to be found in private prosperity. All that mattered was growth, without anachronistic specifications: as the

---

[12] *The Tiananmen Papers*, p. 325.

official slogan, trumpeted to doubters, would put it: 'Development is the irrefutable argument'.

Development duly came, at a spectacular rate. Chinese growth in the 90s overtook even that of the 80s, as liberalization of the economy deepened. By the end of the decade, the industrial landscape had been transformed, with a massive shake-out of state-owned enterprises. As late as 1996, the state sector still accounted for the bulk of urban employment. But from 1997 onwards, provincial officials were allowed to dispose of most of them as they wished, closing down, transforming or privatizing them. In the process, some 7 million workers a year lost their jobs, until by 2004 total private employment was nearly double that in the public sector. Over the same period, the TVEs were privatized on an even more sweeping scale—leaving only about 10 per cent of them in any form of collective ownership. So too was 80 per cent of urban housing stock. But 'keeping the big and letting go the small', the state did not relinquish command of what it regarded as the strategic heights of the economy: energy, metallurgy, arms and telecoms. Accounting for a third of all industrial sales, and posting high rates of profit, its giant firms in these key sectors comprised some three-quarters of all SOE assets.[13]

Structurally, if controlled divestment was one of the two fundamental changes of the second reform period, after 1989, the other was maximization of foreign trade. The speed and degree of opening had few precedents. By the new century, average industrial tariffs were less than 10 per cent, about a third of Indian levels; agricultural not more than 15 per cent. Boosted by foreign investment, in which non-diaspora capital—American, Japanese, European—now played a significant, though minority role, exports of manufactures soared, increasingly in higher-tech lines, if still mainly assembly work in these. Within a generation, in effect, China had become the new workshop of the world, the value of its foreign trade in goods amounting to two-thirds of its GDP—an unheard-of figure for a large country, two to three times higher than that of the United States or Japan. But as in industry at home, so in commerce abroad, the state has to date reserved a critical lever for itself, retaining control of the exchange rate, capital account and banking system.

The material success of this model of development has made the PRC the contemporary wonder of the world. With a rate of investment of over

[13] Naughton, *The Chinese Economy*, pp. 186, 106, 286, 303–4.

40 per cent, in fifteen years GDP grew four times over, between 1989 and 2004. In the cities, the income of urban households rose at a rate of 7.7 per cent a year; in the countryside, at nearly 5 per cent.[14] From the beginning of the Reform Era to 2006, the average living standards of the Chinese increased eight times over, expressed in dollars. In a single decade, the urban population jumped by 200 million.[15] City-dwellers now comprise two-fifths of the nation, and sustain the largest car market in the world. Towering above even Japanese reserves, holdings of foreign exchange top $1.9 trillion, more than the GNP of Canada. China has arrived, with a vengeance.

IV. THE NOVUM

But is arrival the right term? Would not return be more appropriate? For centuries, after all, China was the wealthiest and most advanced civilization on earth: surely there must be some connexion between the prowess of this past and the formidable achievements of the present? Such questions take us to a terrain at once grander and more obscure than the relatively clear-cut field of comparison between two modern revolutions. Here three rival schools of thought can be stylized, without to date there being any systematic confrontation between them. The first, currently most in vogue among historians, attributes high-speed growth in the PRC essentially to millennial legacies of the imperial past—commercial dynamism based on intensive agriculture; deepening division of labour; flourishing urban networks and expansion of domestic trade; record demographic growth; an 'industrious revolution'. In this view the Chinese economy, long the largest and most sophisticated in the world, exhibiting a classically Smithian path of growth, was fully as developed as that of Western Europe—if not more so—down to the Opium War. Knocked off course for over a century by foreign penetration and internal disorder, it is now reverting to its natural position in the world.

---

[14] The overall figures mask a sharp break in both the model of growth and distribution of gains from it after 1989, favouring the cities at the expense of the countryside, and state and foreign enterprise at the expense of private firms. For an analysis of the change, see Yasheng Huang, *Capitalism with Chinese Characteristics: Entrepreneurship and the State*, New York 2008, who further argues that total factor productivity has been falling across it: pp. 288–90.

[15] Fred Bergsten, Bates Gill, Nicholas Lardy, Derek Mitchell, *China: the Balance Sheet*, New York 2006, pp. 5, 31.

For a second school, more prevalent among economists, the imperial past offers few clues to the modern present, if only because—as Smith emphasized—absence of foreign trade deprived the traditional economy of competitive stimulus, and inadequate security of property rights inhibited entrepreneurship, cramping Chinese development within limits closer to a Malthusian pattern. On this reading, contemporary high-speed growth is the product of the belated integration of China into a world capitalist economy from whose formation it was historically absent. With the opening of its markets to foreign investment, and gradual strengthening of property rights, factors of production were at last liberated for a new dynamism. The combination of abundant supplies of cheap labour with abundant overseas capital and technology has built an export machine with no precedent in the Chinese past.

For a third school, to be found (not exclusively) among sociologists, the key to China's economic ascent lies, on the contrary, in the Chinese Revolution. In this version, it is the achievements of the Mao period that laid the deep foundation for the feats of the Reform Era. Central to this legacy were the creation of a strong sovereign state for the first time in the modern history of the country, putting an end to semi-colonial bondage; the formation of an educated and disciplined labour-force, with high rates of literacy and life-expectancy for a still otherwise backward society; and the establishment of powerful mechanisms of economic control—planning, public sector, external account—within a relatively decentralized institutional framework, that allowed for provincial autonomies. Only on these transformative conditions has the performance of the Open Door period been possible.[16]

Plainly, none of these interpretations are absolutes. Mixtures can as often be found as pure cases. Generally lacking, however, are attempts to assess the relative weight of the alternative variables on offer. Analytically, the requisite causal hierarchy will not crystallize overnight. Here it is

---

[16] For foundations of the first view, see Kenneth Pomeranz, *The Great Divergence: Europe, China and the Making of the Modern World Economy*, Princeton 2000, and Sugihara Kaoru, 'The East Asian Path of Economic Development: a Long-Term Perspective', in Giovanni Arrighi, Hamashita Takeshi and Mark Selden, eds, *The Resurgence of East Asia: 500, 150 and 50 Year Perspectives*, London 2003, pp. 78–117; for illustration of the second, Jim Rowher, 'When China Wakes', *Economist* Special Report, 28 November 1992; for examples of the third, Chris Bramall, *Sources of Chinese Economic Growth, 1978–1996*, Oxford 2000, and especially Lin Chun, *The Transformation of Chinese Socialism*, Durham, NC 2006.

enough to indicate one relevant control for the contending hypotheses, which can be put as follows. How, and in what ways, has high-speed growth in the PRC differed from, or been similar to, that in Japan, South Korea or Taiwan? If the Chinese experience closely resembles these, the case for either pre-modern or late-capitalist explanations gains traction; if it diverges significantly from them, the revolutionary explanation will *prima facie* look more plausible. What does the evidence suggest?

A glance at the statistics yields a paradox. Impressively swift though it has been, PRC growth has not been that much faster than that of its East Asian neighbours at comparable stages of their development, though it has been sustained a decade longer. Nor has its economic basis been significantly different: in each case, the model of development has been overwhelmingly export-led. In these two respects, the family resemblance is strong. In five others, however, the contrast is marked. Since the 90s, export-dependence has been much higher in the PRC than in Japan, the ROK or Taiwan; the share of consumption in GDP much lower; reliance on foreign capital has been vastly greater; the gap between urban and rural incomes—and investment—much wider.[17] Finally, and no less fundamentally, the size and role of the state sector in the economy has been, and remains, structurally far greater. These features of Chinese growth, which set it apart within East Asia, are interrelated, and have a single explanation. In Japan, Korea and Taiwan, the post-war states were creatures of American occupation or protection, on a front-line of the Cold War. Strategically, they remain to this day wards of Washington— planted with US bases or ringed by US warships—without real diplomatic or military autonomy. Lacking political sovereignty, yet needing domestic legitimacy, their rulers—LDP, Park Chung Hee, GMD—compensated with policies of economic self-development, keeping foreign capital at bay with one hand, promoting domestic corporations with the other. So too, fearing peasant radicalization, with the spectre of the Chinese Revolution before them, they implemented agrarian reforms—here the US was with them—and were careful never to let the countryside fall too far behind the cities, as growth accelerated.

The opposite configuration held in the PRC. There, the post-revolutionary state was externally completely sovereign—capable, indeed, of fighting America to a halt in Korea—and domestically very strong, from the start.

---

[17] See the striking analysis, with accompanying graphs, of Hung Ho-fung, 'America's Head Servant?', NLR 60, Nov–Dec 2009.

Just for that reason, once the Reform Era arrived, the PRC could afford a massive influx of foreign capital, without fear of discredit or subversion by it. As a fully independent state, in tight command of its territory, it could be confident of its ability to control flows of alien capital by political power, much as Lenin had once hoped to do in the days of NEP; and, with a continuing grip on the strategic—financial and industrial—heights of the economy, of its ability to dominate or manipulate domestic capital. By the same token, it could also repress rural consumption, driving destitute peasants into the cities as migrant labour, in a way impossible for governments in Tokyo, Seoul or Taibei, whose farmers had to be looked after if the local regimes were to survive. If the CCP could do so without loss of control over urbanization—the planetary slums proliferating in South or South-East Asia—it was the *hukou* system separating cities and countryside, installed during the Great Leap Forward, that enabled it. Under Mao too, peasants had been victims of primitive accumulation, to the benefit of the towns. But once public health and education in the villages were dismantled after him, and under Jiang investment was switched away from the countryside, discrepancies between rural and urban incomes grew by bounds. The historical premise of both high levels of FDI and low levels of rural provision in the PRC has been the same—a regime born of revolution in a country with a population over seven times that of Japan, the ROK and Taiwan combined, capable of dealing toughly with peasants and foreigners alike. For both, the price has yet to be paid. But the direct or indirect bill for each is visibly increasing—still disconnected, but spreading unrest in the villages; still manageable, but mounting addiction to US Treasuries.

2

The Party that has presided over this transformation of the country has been transformed by it. The Immortals have passed away. But the advantages of being the second mover, rather than the first, have not. Learning from the fate of Brezhnevism, the CCP has institutionalized renovation of its leading ranks, with limits for tenure of office, and regular transfer of power from one generation to the next. Without any revolutionary background, those now in charge and to come have more formal education, and draw—much as imperial rulers once used the literati—on wider technical and intellectual resources, from many a think-tank and informal consultation with expert or interested opinion, than ever before. Economic growth and diplomatic success have restored political reputation: the Party of today enjoys greater popular legitimacy than at any time since the fifties. The mandate it has gained is at once powerful and brittle. Powerful: prosperity at home and dignity abroad are appeals few resist. Brittle: economic development without social justice, national assertion and international entanglement, are hard to square with the ideals of the Revolution which the Party claims as its own. Consumer nationalism is a shallow ideological construct, on which it cannot completely rely. Depoliticized as the principal discourse of the CCP has become, purging it of socialism altogether would be counter-productive. The inherited claim to another legitimacy, still inscribed in its name, remains a necessary reserve. For the revolutionary sentiments of injustice, and demands for equality, have not disappeared from the minds of citizens. Nor have the risks of ignoring them.

Explanation is one thing, classification another, evaluation a third. Taxonomically, the PRC of the 21st century is a world-historical *novum:* the combination of what is now, by any conventional measure, a predominantly capitalist economy with what is still, by any conventional measure, unquestionably a communist state—each the most dynamic of its type to date.[18] Politically, the effects of the contradiction between them are branded everywhere into the society where they fuse or intertwine. Never have so many moved out of absolute poverty so fast. Never have modern industries and ultra-modern infrastructures been created on so vast a scale, in so short a space of time, nor a flourishing middle class arisen at such speed along with them. Never has the rank-order of powers been altered so dramatically, to such unforced popular pride. Nor, in the same years, has inequality ever spiralled to such dizzying heights so swiftly, from such low starting-points. Nor corruption spread so widely, where once probity was taken for granted. Nor workers, till yesterday theoretical masters of the state, treated at will so ruthlessly— jobs destroyed, wages unpaid, injuries mocked, protests stifled.[19] Nor have peasants, the backbone of the revolution, been robbed in such

---

[18] For the clearest recent analysis of the structure of the economy, see Joel Andreas, 'Changing Colours in China', NLR 54, Nov–Dec 2008, pp. 123–52; and of the continuities in the Party, David Shambaugh, *China's Communist Party: Atrophy and Adaptation*, Berkeley–Los Angeles 2008, who stresses its learning abilities in the wake of the collapse of the CPSU.
[19] The fate of the Chinese working class, old and new, is the subject of a sociological masterpiece: Ching Kwan Lee, *Against the Law: Labor Protests in China's Rustbelt and Sunbelt*, Berkeley–Los Angeles 2007.

numbers of land and livelihood by developers and officials, in clearances as out of the Scottish Highlands. More users of the internet than in any country on earth, no terror, much freedom of private life; with more streamlined and effective machinery of surveillance than ever before. For minorities, affirmative action and cultural-political repression, hand in hand; for the rich, every luxury and privilege exploitation can buy; for the weak and uprooted, crumbs or less; for dissenters, gag or dungeon. Amid formal—even, not wholly unreal—ideological conformity, colossal social energy and human vitality. Emancipation and regression have often been conjoined in the past; but never quite so vertiginously as in the China that Mao helped to create and sought to prevent.

Judgement of so awesome a historical process, still in its early stages, is bound to be fallible. Difficult enough for those living through it, to keep the whole experience steadily in view and reach some dialectical balance-sheet of it may be all but impossible for those outside. In the West, Sinomania and Sinophobia have regularly alternated since the Enlightenment, the pendulum now swinging from the second back towards the first, amid a new wave of *chinoiserie*, popular and intellectual, not necessarily more enlightened than the original. In China their counterparts are recurrent moods of Westernism and Great Han chauvinism. A spirit of unintoxicated comparison, rarely achieved, is the only safeguard against such temptations. That goes for the future too. The scenarios, optimistic or pessimistic, heard from time to time among its citizens, are often drawn from Taiwan and Singapore: eventual democratization as living standards and political expectations rise, or authoritarian paternalism *in perpetuo*, with an electoral façade. Neither is particularly persuasive. Taiwanese democracy was less the product of a gradual change of heart by the GMD than of its need for a new kind of international legitimation, once America withdrew recognition from the island. The one-party regime in Singapore rests on a welfare system that can be so provident only because it is built for a city-state, not one of imperial proportions. Beijing neither requires the first, nor is likely to reproduce the second. Towards what horizon the mega-junk of the PRC is moving resists calculation, at least of any current astrolabe.

Talking with Sartre

Conversations and Debates

Edited and Translated by John Gerassi

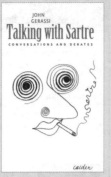

This breathtaking record of Sartre's spirited conversations with his godson is an essential companion to the works of one of the 20th-century's most important thinkers. These conversations add an intimate dimension to Sartre's more abstract ideas and also provide a clear lens through which to view the major conflagrations of the last century.

336pp. Cloth £30.00, Paper £15.00

Who Was Jacques Derrida?

An Intellectual Biography

David Mikics

This first intellectual biography of Derrida is a full-scale appraisal of his career, his influence and his philosophical roots. It is also the first attempt to define his crucial importance as the ambassador of 'theory', a phenomenon that has had a profound influence on academic life in the humanities.

296pp. £25.00

Czeslaw Milosz and Joseph Brodsky

Fellowship of Poets

Irena Grudzinska Gross

This intimate portrayal of the friendship between two Nobel prize-winning icons of twentieth-century poetry, Czeslaw Milosz and Joseph Brodsky, incorporates the author's personal reminiscences of both poets.

384pp. £30.00

yale university press

tel: 020 7079 4900 • www.yalebooks.co.uk

GlassHouse books from Routledge

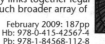

TARIQ ALI

PRESIDENT OF CANT

A YEAR SINCE THE White House changed hands, how has the American empire altered? Under the Bush Administration it was widely believed, in both mainstream opinion and much of the amnesiac section of the left, that the United States had fallen under an aberrant regime, the product of a virtual coup d'état by a coterie of right-wing fanatics—alternatively, ultra-reactionary corporations—who had hijacked American democracy for policies of unprecedented aggression in the Middle East. In reaction, the election to the Presidency of a mixed-race Democrat, vowing to heal America's wounds at home and restore its reputation abroad, was greeted with a wave of ideological euphoria not seen since the days of Kennedy. Once again, America could show its true face—purposeful but peaceful, firm but generous; humane, respectful, multi-cultural—to the world. Naturally, with the makings of a Lincoln or a Roosevelt for our time in him, the country's new young ruler would have to make compromises, as any statesman must. But at least the shameful interlude of Republican swagger and criminality was over. Bush and Cheney had broken the continuity of a multilateral American leadership that had served the country well throughout the Cold War and after. Obama would now restore it.

Rarely has self-interested mythology—or well-meaning gullibility—been more quickly exposed. There was no fundamental break in foreign policy, as opposed to diplomatic mood music, between the Bush 1, Clinton and Bush 2 Administrations; there has been none between the Bush and Obama regimes. The strategic goals and imperatives of the US imperium remain the same, as do its principal theatres and means of operation. Since the collapse of the USSR, the Carter Doctrine—the construction of another democratic pillar of human rights—has defined the greater Middle East as the central battlefield for the imposition of American power around the world. It is enough to look at each of its sectors to see that Obama is the offspring of Bush, as Bush was of Clinton and Clinton of Bush the father, as so many appropriately biblical begettings.

Ignoring Gaza

Obama's line towards Israel would be manifest even before he took office. On December 27, 2008, the IDF launched an all-out air and ground assault on the population of Gaza. Bombing, burning, killing continued without interruption for twenty-two days, during which time the President-Elect uttered not a syllable of reproof. By pre-arrangement, Tel Aviv called off its blitz a few hours before his inauguration on January 20, 2009, not to spoil the party. By then Obama had picked the ultra-Zionist Doberman from Chicago, Rahm Emanuel, a former volunteer for the IDF, as his Chief of Staff. Once installed, Obama called, like every US President, for peace between the two suffering peoples of the Holy Land, and again, like every predecessor, for Palestinians to recognize Israel and for Israel to stop its settlements in the territories it seized in 1967. Within a week of the President's speech in Cairo pledging opposition to further settlements, the Netanyahu coalition was extending Jewish properties in East Jerusalem with impunity. By the autumn, Secretary of State Clinton was congratulating Netanyahu on the 'unprecedented concessions' his government had made. Asked by Mark Landler of the *New York Times*, at a press conference in Jerusalem, 'Madame Secretary, when you were here in March on the first visit, you issued a strong statement condemning the demolition of housing units in East Jerusalem. Yet, that demolition has continued unabated, and indeed, a few days ago, the mayor of the city of Jerusalem issued a new order for demolition. How would you characterize this policy today?', she did not deign to reply.[1]

A month earlier, the UN Fact Finding Mission set up to look at the invasion of Gaza reported that the IDF had not always acted by the book, though naturally rocket-attacks by Hamas had provoked it. Chaired by one of the most notorious time-servers of 'international justice', the South African judge Richard Goldstone, a prosecutor at the pre-orchestrated Hague Tribunal on Yugoslavia and self-professed Zionist, the Mission's complaints against Israel could hardly have been feebler, in startling contrast to the testimony they heard in Gaza and which was made available

---

[1] 'Remarks with Israeli Prime Minister Binyamin Netanyahu', Jerusalem, 31 October 2009, available on State Department website.

on their website.[2] But unaccustomed to Establishment criticism of any kind, Tel Aviv reacted with dudgeon, and so Washington instructed its client at the head of the PLO, Mahmoud Abbas, that he must oppose any consideration of it at the UN.[3] This was too much even for Abbas's followers and amid the ensuing uproar he had to retract, discrediting himself even further. The episode confirmed that AIPAC's grip on Washington remains as strong as ever—contrary to delusions on the US left that the Israel lobby of old, never really much of a force, was now being superseded by a more enlightened brand of American Zionism.

In the Palestinian theatre of the American system, the lack of any significant novelty does not imply lack of movement. Viewed in a longer perspective, US policy has for some time been to coax Israel towards the creation of one or more bantustans, in its own best interests.[4] The condition of that has, of course, been the elimination of any prospect of a genuine Palestinian leadership or real Palestinian state. The Oslo Accords were a first step in this process, destroying the credibility of the PLO by setting up a 'Palestinian Authority' that was little more than a Potemkin façade for the real authority in the occupied territories, the IDF. Incapable of achieving even token independence, the PLO leadership in the West Bank settled down to make money, leaving the bulk of the Palestinian people helpless: mired in poverty and regularly subjected to settler violence. In contrast, by creating a primitive but effective welfare system, capable of distributing food and medical care in poor neighbourhoods and looking after the weak, Hamas was able to win enough popular support to triumph in the Palestinian elections of 2006. Euro-America reacted with an immediate politico-economic boycott, hoisting Fatah back into power on the West Bank. In Gaza, where Hamas was strongest,

---

[2] In an interview with Israeli Army Radio conducted in Hebrew, Nicole Goldstone, the judge's daughter, said: 'My father took on this job because he thought he is doing the best thing for peace, for everyone, and also for Israel . . . It wasn't easy. My father did not expect to see and hear what he saw and heard.' She told the radio station that had it not been for her father the report would have been harsher. One could add that had it not been for the presence on the Mission of a feisty Pakistani woman lawyer, Hina Jilani, the report would have been even softer.

[3] The Israelis applied the ultimate sanction: if Abbas endorsed the Goldstone Report, the mobile phone deal between an Israeli company and senior PLO personnel was off.

[4] Though it should be pointed out that both Bishop Tutu and Ronnie Kasrils, former Deputy Defence Minister in the Mandela government, vehemently dispute the analogy. They insist that the condition of Palestinians in the occupied territories is far worse than was that of blacks in the bantustans.

Israel had for some time been inciting a coup by Mohammed Dahlan, Washington's favourite thug in the PLO security apparatus. Defence Minister Ben-Eliezer has openly testified before the Knesset Foreign Affairs and Defence Committee that in 2002, when the IDF pulled out of Gaza, he had offered the Strip to Dahlan, who was quite willing to launch a Palestinian civil war, long a twinkle in the eye of many an Israeli colonizer. Four years later Dahlan was primed by Washington to implement a military putsch in Gaza,[5] but was beaten to the punch by Hamas, which took over the Strip in mid 2007. After Euro-American political and economic punishment of its voters for defiance of the West came Israeli military retribution, with the assault of late 2008, winked at by Obama.

But the result is not the impasse so regularly deplored by well-wishers of a 'peaceful settlement'. Under repeated blows, and amid increasing isolation, the Palestinian resistance is being gradually weakened to a point where Hamas itself—unable to develop any coherent strategy, or break with the Oslo Accords of which it, too, has become a prisoner—is edging towards acceptance of the pittance on offer from Israel, garnished with a solatium from the West. No meaningful Palestinian Authority exists. Elected representatives from the West Bank or Gaza are treated like mendicant NGOs: rewarded if they remain on their knees and follow Western bidding, sanctioned if they step out of line. Rationally, Palestinians would do far better to dissolve the Authority and insist on equal citizenship rights within a single state, backed by an international campaign for boycott, divestment and sanction till the apartheid structures of Israel are dismantled. Practically, there is little or no chance of this in the immediate future. In all probability what lies ahead is the convergence—already being hailed in *Haaretz* as even more enlightened than Rabin[6]—of Obama and Netanyahu on a final solution of 'Palestinian' entities Israel can live with, and Palestine can die in.

Harvesting Baghdad

For the moment, however, there are more pressing preoccupations: war-zones farther east have the first call on imperial attention. Iraq may have dropped from the headlines, but not from the daily security briefings in the Oval Office. In 2002, on his way up the political ladder

---

[5] See David Rose, 'The Gaza Bombshell', *Vanity Fair*, April 2008.
[6] For example, Ari Shavit, 'Netanyahu is Positioning Himself to the Left of Rabin', *Haaretz*, 6 December 2009.

as a low-profile state senator in Illinois, Obama opposed the attack on Iraq; it was politically inexpensive to do so. By the time he was elected President, American forces had occupied the country for six years, and his first act was to maintain Bush's Defense Secretary, Robert Gates, long-time CIA functionary and veteran of the Iran–Contra affair, in the Pentagon. A cruder and more demonstrative signal of political continuity could hardly have been conceived. In the last two years of the Republican Administration, US troop-levels were increased by a fifth, to 150,000, in a 'surge' that was hailed across the party spectrum as having crushed the Iraqi resistance, readying the country for a stable pro-Western, hopefully even democratic, future. The new Democratic Administration has not deviated at all from this script. The 3-year Status of Forces Agreement signed by Bush and his collaborators in Baghdad had stipulated that all US troops would leave Iraq by December 2011, although a subsequent agreement could obviously extend their stay, and the US 'combat' forces would quit Iraqi cities, villages and localities by June 2009. Before his election, Obama promised a withdrawal of all US 'combat' troops from Iraq within sixteen months of his taking office, i.e. by May 2010—adorned with a safety clause that this pledge could be 'refined' in the light of events. It promptly was, with the February 2009 announcement that combat troops would now leave Iraq by September 2010, while the 'residual' 50,000 forces could also engage in combat operations to 'protect our ongoing civilian and military efforts'.[7]

The slaughter and devastation wreaked on Iraq by the United States and its allies, chiefly Britain, are now well known: the destruction of the country's cultural patrimony, the brutal dismembering of its social infrastructure, the theft of its natural resources, the sundering of its mixed neighbourhoods, and above all the death or displacement of countless of its citizens—over a million dead; three million refugees; five million orphans, according to government figures.[8] Wasting no words on any of this, the Commander-in-Chief and his generals have other concerns. Can Iraq now be regarded as a tolerably secure outpost of

[7] Obama speech at Camp Lejeune, North Carolina, 27 February 2009.
[8] *Cultural Cleansing in Iraq: Why Museums were Looted, Libraries Burned and Academics Murdered*, edited by Raymond Baker, Shereen Ismael and Tareq Ismael, London 2009, contains detailed figures and sources, amongst which the fact that from 2003–07, Washington only allowed 463 refugees, mainly professional Iraqis of Christian origin, into the United States. For an illuminating survey of the history of Iraqi oil and the privatized looting now under way, see Kamil Mahdi, 'Iraq's Oil Law: Parsing the Fine Print', *World Policy Journal*, Summer 2007.

the American system in the Middle East? They have reason to exult, and reason to doubt. Compared with the situation at the height of the insurgency in 2006, most of the country today is under the thumb of Baghdad, and American casualties are few and far between. A predominantly Shia army—some 250,000 strong—has been trained and armed to the teeth to deal with any resurgence of the resistance. Sectarian cleansing of the capital, on a scale of which the Haganah could be proud, has wiped out most Sunni neighbourhoods, for the first time giving the Maliki regime set up by Bush a firm grip on the hub of the country. To the north, the Kurdish protectorates remain staunch bastions of US power. To the south, Moqtada al-Sadr's militias have been sent packing. Best of all, the oil-wells are returning to those who know how to make good use of them, as auctions distribute 25-year leases to foreign corporations. Some excesses may mar the scene in Baghdad,[9] but the new Iraq has the blessing of the saintly Sistani's smile.

Yet there persists the uneasy thought that the Iraqi resistance, capable of inflicting such damage on the US military machine only yesterday, might just be biding its time after its heavy losses and the defection of an important segment, and could still visit havoc on the collaborators tomorrow, should the US pull out altogether.[10] To ensure against any such danger, Washington has put down markers in the modern equivalents—vastly larger and more hideous—of the Crusader fortresses of old. The Balad military base, within easy bomber reach of Baghdad, is a small-town American city-state. Containing an airport that is reportedly the busiest in the world after Heathrow, it can house over 30,000 US soldiers and auxiliaries—an immigrant labour force composed largely of South Asian

---

[9] Here is the *Economist*: 'Old habits from Saddam Hussein's era are becoming familiar again. Torture is routine in government detention centres . . . Iraqi police and security people are again pulling out fingernails and beating detainees, even those who have already made confessions. A limping former prison inmate tells how he realized, after a bout of torture in a government ministry that lasted for five days, that he had been relatively lucky. When he was reunited with fellow prisoners, he saw that many had lost limbs and organs. The domestic-security apparatus is at its busiest since Saddam was overthrown six years ago, especially in the capital. In July the Baghdad police reimposed a nightly curfew, making it easier for the police, taking orders from politicians, to arrest people disliked by the Shia-led government.' See 'Could a Police State Return?', 3 September 2009.
[10] General Petraeus recently announced that attacks on US forces in Iraq were down to 'only' 15 a day: *Financial Times*, 2 January 2010. Not Maliki but Muntadhar al-Zaidi, the Baghdad shoe-thrower, represents the sentiments of most Iraqis, regardless of ethnic or confessional origin.

workers who clean homes, cook food and staff Subway sandwich bars; drug-dealers are never in short supply, while mobile Eastern European prostitutes serve Balad's other needs. Fifteen bus routes complement the airport, but commuting remains a problem for some of the service staff.[11] Another thirteen military and air-force bases are scattered throughout the country, among them Camp Renegade near Kirkuk, to guard the oil-wells, Badraj on the Iranian border, for espionage in the Islamic Republic, and a British base dating back to the 1930s at Nasiriyah, upgraded to serve American appetites. In Baghdad itself, meanwhile, the US proconsul can now enjoy the largest and most expensive embassy in the world—it is the size of the Vatican City—in the fortified enclave of the Green Zone.

After seizing Iraq as colonial prey in 1920 and installing the Hashemite dynasty as its local instrument, Britain was faced with full-scale rebellion which it suppressed only with difficulty and all-out savagery. For the next twelve years, London ruled the country as an imperial dependency, before finally relinquishing its 'mandate'—granted by the League of Nations—in 1932. But the client regime it left behind lasted another quarter of a century, until eventually it was overthrown in the revolution of 1958. The American seizure of Iraq provoked a full-scale insurgency even more swiftly, and one that has lasted longer, against an occupation enjoying this time a mandate of the United Nations. The US empire too will leave behind a puppet regime to hold down the country into the foreseeable future. In that venture there could be few more fitting successors to Ramsay MacDonald—that earlier handsome, willowy figure who was never at a loss for uplifting words—than Barack Obama. But history has accelerated since those days, and there is at least a chance that Maliki and his torturers will meet the fate of Nuri al-Said more rapidly, in another national uprising to root out alien military bases, outsize embassies, oil companies and their local collaborators alike.

Menacing Tehran

For American elites, Iran has long posed a conundrum: an 'Islamic Republic' publicly breathing fire against the Great Satan while quietly

---

[11] 'It takes the masseuse, Mila from Kyrgyzstan, an hour to commute to work by bus on this sprawling American base. Her massage parlour is one of three on the base's 6,300 acres and sits next to a Subway sandwich shop in a trailer, surrounded by blast walls, sand and rock', writes Marc Santora: 'Big US Bases Are Part of Iraq, but a World Apart', *New York Times*, 8 September 2009.

extending assistance to it wherever most needed, be it collusion with counter-revolution in Nicaragua, invasion of Afghanistan or occupation of Iraq. The rulers of Israel are not the recipients of any of these benefits, and have taken a dimmer view of the rhetoric of the mullahs, directed with greater ferocity at them and at the Little Satan in London, than at their patrons in Washington. Above all, once the prospect of an Iranian nuclear programme undermining the Israeli monopoly of weapons of mass destruction in the Middle East started to loom on the horizon, Tel Aviv galvanized its assets in the United States into a campaign to ensure that Washington became committed to striking it down at all costs. Not that there was much resistance to overcome, given the degree to which Israeli objectives have long been internalized as little less than second nature by US policy-makers. Scorning overtures from the Khatami regime for an across-the-board regional deal in 2003, the Republican Administration sought instead to force Iran into compliance with the Israeli monopoly by matching Tehran's oratorical tirades and tightening economic sanctions on it.

Without saying so too explicitly, Obama came into office allowing it to be understood that this was not the way to go about things. Much better would be to initiate a forgive-and-forget dialogue with Tehran, banking on the traditional pragmatism of the regime, and the manifest pro-Americanism of middle-class and youth layers in the population at large, to achieve a friendly diplomatic settlement in the interest of all parties, denuding Iran of a nuclear capability in exchange for an economic and political embrace. But the timing was unlucky and the calculation was upset by political polarization in Iran itself. Factional struggles in the clerical establishment escalated over the presidential election in June 2009, when a bid by its most openly pro-Western wing to take power on a wave of (mostly) middle-class protest was suppressed by an incumbent counter-strike that combined electoral fraud and militia violence. For Obama, the opportunity for ideological posturing was too great to resist. In a peerless display of sanctimony, he lamented with moist-eyed grief the death of a demonstrator killed in Tehran on the same day his drones wiped out sixty villagers, most of them women and children, in Pakistan. With the Western media in full cry behind the President, the thwarted candidate in the Iranian contest—historically one of the worst butchers of the regime, responsible for mass executions in the 80s— was converted into another icon of the Free World. Schemes for a grand reconciliation between the two states had to be set aside.

After this misadventure, the Democratic Administration has reverted to the line of its predecessor, attempting to corral Russia and China—European acquiescence can be taken for granted—into an economic blockade of Iran, in the hope of so strangling the country that the Supreme Leader will either be overthrown or obliged to come to terms. Should such pressure fail, an air-strike by Israeli or American fighter-bombers on Iranian nuclear facilities remains the back-up threat. While still unlikely, such a blitz cannot be altogether ruled out, if only because once the West at large—in this case not only Obama, but Sarkozy, Brown and Merkel—has pronounced any Iranian nuclear capability intolerable, little rhetorical room for retreat is left if this should materialize.[12] In the past, fear of Iranian retaliation against shaky American positions in Iraq would probably have been enough to deter such an assault. But Tehran's influence in Baghdad is not what it was. Once confident that Iraq would shortly become a sister Islamic Republic, it can no longer be sure that relations between the two will be any better than between the various Sunni states in the region. For the moment, the Maliki regime knows which side butters its bread—Iran could never match the dollars and arms it gets from the US, while Sistani's pretensions to pre-eminence over assorted divines across the border are of long standing. Whether Moqtada al-Sadr's militias are now equally biddable remains unclear.

Still, to date the Pentagon remains opposed to any adventure that could risk stringing its forces out across a war-zone which would stretch from the Litani to the Oxus, if the Revolutionary Guards were to foment operations in Lebanon or western Afghanistan. Nor should Tehran's threat to retaliate with conventional missiles against Israeli cities be discounted. There are also Washington's other allies to be considered. Israel and its lobbyists may be the prime movers in ongoing agitation against Iran, but they are not alone. The Saudi monarchy, a *sui generis* confessional dictatorship, remains fearful that a Tehran–Baghdad combination might destabilize the Peninsula: Shia constitute a large majority in Bahrain and the oil-producing region of the Saudi state itself. But the Saudis are also aware that any direct attack on Tehran could pose an even bigger threat to their rule, provoking Shia uprisings that might engulf them. For Riyadh, an alternative route under review in Washington is preferable—inserting

---

[12] In Illinois in 2004, I watched Obama interviewed on network television in the run-up to the Senate election he subsequently won. Asked whether he would back Bush if he decided to bomb Iran, the future President did not hesitate for a moment. He put on a warlike look and said that he would.

Turkey into the regional equation as a Sunni–NATO detachment of the empire, buttressing the Saudi petrodollars offered to Syria to break with Iran. This would serve as a counter-thrust against any future Tehran–Baghdad axis and cut off Hezbollah from Damascus, softening it up for another assault by the IDF.

Fabricating Kabul

From Palestine through Iraq to Iran, Obama has acted as just another steward of the American empire, pursuing the same aims as his predecessors, with the same means but with a more emollient rhetoric. In Afghanistan, he has gone further, widening the front of imperial aggression with a major escalation of violence, both technological and territorial. When he took office, Afghanistan had already been occupied by US and satellite forces for over seven years. During his election campaign Obama—determined to outdo Bush in prosecuting a 'just war'—pledged more troops and fire-power to crush the Afghan resistance, and more ground intrusions and drone attacks in Pakistan to burn out support for it across the border. This is one promise he has kept. A further 30,000 troops are currently being rushed to the Hindu Kush. This will bring the US army of occupation close to 100,000, under a general picked by Obama for the success of his brutalities in Iraq, where his units formed a specialist elite in assassination and torture. Simultaneously, a massive intensification of aerial terror over Pakistan is under way. In what the New York Times delicately described as a 'statistic that the White House has not advertised', it has informed its readers that 'since Mr Obama came to office, the Central Intelligence Agency has mounted more Predator drone strikes into Pakistan than during Mr Bush's eight years in office'.[13]

There is no mystery about the reason for this escalation. After invading Afghanistan in 2001, the US and its European auxiliaries imposed a puppet government of their own making, confected at a conference in Bonn, headed by a CIA asset and seconded by an assortment of Tajik warlords, with NGOs in attendance like page boys in a medieval court. This bogus construct never had the slightest legitimacy in the country, lacking even a modicum of the narrow but dedicated base the Taliban had enjoyed.

---

[13] David Sanger, 'Obama Outlines a Vision of Might and Right', New York Times, 11 December 2009.

Once installed in Kabul, it concentrated its energies on self-enrichment. Aid was diverted, corruption generalized, narcotics—repressed by the Taliban—set free. Karzai and company amassed a huge amount of wealth: over 75 per cent of the funds from donor countries were handed directly to Karzai's cronies, the Northern Alliance or private contractors used by both. The construction of a new 5-star hotel and a shopping mall became priorities in one of the world's poorest countries, while torture and murder proceeded routinely a short distance away; Bagram has become a chamber of horrors to make Guantánamo look civilized. Opium production reached an all-time high, soaring to over 90 per cent above its levels in 2001, when it was still confined to areas controlled by the Northern Alliance, spreading southwards and westwards under the aegis of the Karzai clan. The mass of the Afghan poor have received little or nothing from the new foreign-imposed order except increased risk to life and limb, as the re-organized neo-Taliban hit back at the occupation and NATO bombs rain so indiscriminately on villages that even Karzai has repeatedly been forced to protest.[14]

By June 2009 the Afghan guerrillas controlled large swathes of the country and had infiltrated official police and military units. Adopting Iraqi tactics of IEDs on the roads and suicide bombs in the cities, it was inflicting ever heavier blows on the Western occupation and its collaborators. Within the imperial camp itself, disarray was mounting.[15] American diplomatic and military functionaries publicly contradicted each other, quarrelling over how far the pretence of democratic elections staged by Karzai should be upheld or rejected. In the event, after vehement denunciations of fraud by the highest functionary in Washington, and a pro forma second round

---

[14] Most recently on 27 December when a US black-ops unit killed 10 civilians on the same day as Ahmadinejad's militias killed 5 demonstrators in Tehran.

[15] See the letter from Matthew Hoh, a former Marine captain who served as a political officer in Iraq and subsequently Afghanistan, and resigned in September 2009. 'The Pashtun insurgency, which is composed of multiple, seemingly infinite, local groups, is fed by what is perceived by the Pashtun people as a continued and sustained assault, going back centuries, on Pashtun land, culture, traditions and religion by internal and external enemies . . . In both RC East and South, I have observed that the bulk of the insurgency fights not for the white banner of the Taliban, but rather against the presence of foreign soldiers and taxes imposed by an unrepresentative government in Kabul . . . If honest, our stated strategy of securing Afghanistan to prevent al-Qaeda resurgence or regrouping would require us to additionally invade and occupy western Pakistan, Somalia, Sudan, Yemen, etc.' See Ralph Nader, 'Hoh's Afghanistan Warning', *CounterPunch*, 4 November 2009.

of voting, Obama consummated the farce by congratulating Karzai on a victory more blatantly rigged even than Ahmadinejad's two months earlier, on which—in top Uriah Heep form—the US President had spared no stern words. Unlike the regime in Tehran, which retains an indigenous base in society, however diminished, what passes for government in Kabul is a Western implant that would disintegrate overnight without the NATO praetorians dispatched to protect it.

Leaning on Islamabad

Desperate to claim victory in a self-chosen 'just war', Obama has plunged into the classic *fuite en avant* of dispatching a still larger expeditionary force, and expanding the war to a neighbouring country where the enemy is suspected of finding succour. From the start of his administration, it was announced that Pakistan and Afghanistan would henceforward be treated as an integrated war-zone: 'Afpak'. A stream of emissaries poured into Islamabad to man up the Pakistani state to the repressive tasks it was being called upon to perform.[16] The 2,460 km border between Afghanistan and what is now Pakistan has been porous ever since the Durand Line was laid down by the British Empire in 1893. Sixteen million Pashtuns live in southern Afghanistan, 28 million in the North-West Frontier Province of Pakistan. The frontier is impossible to police, and movement across it difficult to detect since tribes that speak the same dialect and are often inter-married live on either side. That Afghan insurgents seek and receive sanctuary in the area is hardly a secret. For NATO or the Pakistani Army to stop this flow would require at least a quarter of a million troops, and campaigns of annihilation like those of Chiang Kai-shek in the 1930s. Under Musharraf—and threats from Pentagon blowhards to bomb the country back into the Stone Age if it did not comply—the Pakistani Army was turned from patron to foe of the Taliban in Afghanistan, but never a whole-hearted one, since it was only too well aware that it was being forced to yield influence in Kabul to India, which wasted no time in taking Karzai under its wing. Musharraf did his best to please America by allowing US Special Forces

---

[16] Inter-Risk, the Pakistani subsidiary of US defence contractor DynCorp, was recently raided by local police, who seized 'illegal and sophisticated weaponry'. The company's boss, a retired Captain Ali Jaffar Zaidi, informed reporters that US officials in Islamabad had ordered the import of prohibited weapons 'in Inter-Risk's name', promising that payment would be made by the US embassy. Anwar Abbasi, 'Why the US security company was raided', *The News*, 20 September 2009.

and drones into the country, and handing over al-Qaeda operatives where he could. But he never really satisfied Washington that he was being vigilant enough, while managing to earn the contempt of the majority of Pakistanis for truckling to the US.

By the time Obama came to power, two developments had altered this scene. Incessantly goaded by the Pentagon, between 2004 and 2006 Musharraf sent the Pakistani Army nine times into the Federally Administered Tribal Areas (FATA), the seven mountainous sectors outside the jurisdiction of the North-West Frontier Province, where central governmental authority had always been vestigial, to crack down on Taliban infiltration. The result was simply to provoke solidarity with the Afghan resistance and an increasing will to emulate it. This led in December 2007 to the formation of the Tehrik-i-Taliban Pakistan, a brutal home-grown guerrilla dedicated to carrying the war back against Islamabad itself. (Contrary to Western assumptions, this outfit is not a subsidiary of the Afghan neo-Taliban, as evidenced in Mullah Omar's outburst against it. Revealingly, Omar insisted that it was wrong to target the Pakistan Army when the real enemy was the US and NATO.)

In 2008, Musharraf himself was ousted, fleeing impeachment to Mecca. His replacement as President became the infamous widower of Benazir Bhutto, Asif Zardari, a discredited crook who offered himself as an ideal straw-man for the US. Washington's Ambassador Anne Patterson—fresh from duty in arming Uribe in Colombia—was soon gushing over his cooperative good will. Its fruits were not long in coming. In April 2009, Zardari ordered the Army to occupy the Swat district in the North-West Frontier Province, taken over by the TTP two months earlier. An all-out military assault drove the TTP back into the hills, and 2 million refugees out of their homes. Emboldened by this humanitarian success, Obama pressed Zardari into sending the Army into FATA proper in October, to flush out Taliban fighters—it no longer mattered much whether Afghan or Pakistani—from South Waziristan and Bajaur. Hundreds of thousands more tribespeople were displaced, US bombers roaring overhead as they scattered to the winds.[17] In November the Pakistan Army announced that 'the offensive was over'. The guerrilla had disappeared.

---

[17] For the estimated number of refugees in Swat and FATA, see Mark Schneider, 'FATA 101: When the Shooting Stops', *Foreign Policy*, 4 November 2009. Schneider is Senior Vice President of the impeccably Establishment International Crisis Group.

How far domestic ethnic cleansing of this sort can be taken, and what kind of results it is likely to produce, have yet to be seen. What is clear is that in forcing the Pakistani Army to turn its guns on its own tribes, with whom it used to be on fairly good terms, Obama is de-stabilizing yet another society in the interests of the American empire. Suicide bombs are now exploding on a weekly basis in Pakistan's big cities, in vain acts of revenge for repression on the frontier. Zardari and his entourage are tottering, as the immunity against corruption charges granted them by Musharraf has been struck down by the Supreme Court. There is even a chance that the worm-eaten PPP—a curse to the country since Benazir Bhutto's second term in office—might break up and disappear after him.[18] Washington will be reluctant to let such a helpful stooge go, but can no doubt rely on the Army's top brass to provide a functional substitute, as it always has in the past. The Pakistani Army has never produced patriotic junior officers capable of eliminating the high command, expelling foreign agencies and instituting reforms, of the kind that Latin America or the Arab world has sometimes seen. Its subservience to the United States is structural, without ever being total. Dependent on massive infusions of American cash and equipment, it cannot afford to defy Washington openly, even when obliged to act against its own interests; covertly, it always seeks to retain a margin of autonomy, so long as confrontation with India persists. It will harry its own citizens at US behest, but not to the point of setting the tribal areas irretrievably on fire, or helping to extirpate all resistance across the border.

Duplicating Saigon?

With this expansion, what are the prospects for Obama's 'just war'? Comparing the American with the Soviet occupation of Afghanistan, two major differences stand out. The regime created by the US is far weaker than that protected by the USSR. The latter had a genuine local basis, however much it abused it: never just an alien graft, the PDPA

---

[18] The US-brokered deal that allowed Zardari and his late wife to return to the country during the Musharraf period was pushed through via a hurriedly concocted 'National Reconciliation Ordnance' pardoning politicians charged with various crimes. Last November, the National Assembly in Pakistan refused to vote in favour of renewing the Ordnance. The re-instated Chief Justice did the rest. On 16 December 2009, a cold, crisp winter afternoon in Islamabad, the full bench of the Supreme Court of Pakistan—sixteen senior judges and the Chief Justice—declared the Ordnance null and void. Few doubt that the Zardari interregnum is almost over. This particular US drone can now be returned safely to base in Dubai or Manhattan.

generated an army and administration capable of surviving the departure of Soviet troops. The Najibullah government was eventually overthrown only thanks to massive outside assistance from the US, Saudi Arabia and Pakistan. But in that assistance lies the second decisive contrast. Unlike the fighters who entered Kabul in 1992, bankrolled and armed to the teeth by foreign powers, the Afghan resistance of today is all but completely isolated: anathema not only to Washington, but to Moscow, Beijing, Dushanbe, Tashkent, Tehran, able at most to count on a sporadic, furtive tolerance from Islamabad.

That is why comparisons with Vietnam, though they are telling in so many other respects—moral, political, ideological—in military terms are less so. At one level Obama's arrogant escalation of the war in Afghanistan could be said to combine the hubris of Kennedy in 1961 with that of Johnson in 1965, even of Nixon in 1972, whose bombing of Cambodia bears more than one resemblance to current operations in Pakistan. But there is no draft to disaffect American youth; no Soviet or Chinese aid to sustain the guerrilla; no anti-imperialist solidarity to weaken the system in its homelands. On the contrary, as Obama likes to explain, no less than 42 countries are lending a hand to help his embarrassing marionette in Kabul dance a good show.[19] No world-historical spectacle could be more welcome than the American proconsul fleeing once again by helicopter from the roof of the embassy, and the motley expeditionary forces and their assorted civilian lackeys kicked unceremoniously out of the country along with him. But a second Saigon is not in prospect. Monotonous talk of the end of American hegemony, the universal cliché of the period, is mostly a way of avoiding serious opposition to it.

If a textbook illustration were needed of the continuity of American foreign policy across administrations, and the futility of so many soft-headed attempts to treat the Bush–Cheney years as exceptional rather than essentially conventional, Obama's conduct has provided it. From one end of the Middle East to the other, the only significant material

---

[19] In Oslo Obama could duly congratulate the Nobel Peace Prize committee on the Norwegian troop contingent in Afghanistan, along with those from Albania, Armenia, Australia, Austria, Azerbaijan, Belgium, Bosnia and Herzegovina, Bulgaria, Canada, Croatia, the Czech Republic, Denmark, Estonia, Finland, France, Georgia, Germany, Greece, Hungary, Iceland, Ireland, Italy, Jordan, Latvia, Lithuania, Luxembourg, Macedonia, the Netherlands, New Zealand, Poland, Portugal, Romania, Singapore, Slovakia, Slovenia, Spain, Sweden, Turkey, Ukraine, the United Arab Emirates and the UK.

change he has brought is a further escalation of the War on Terror—
or 'Evil', as he prefers to call it—with Yemen now being sighted as the
next target.[20] Beyond, the story is much the same. Renditions—torture
by proxy—are upheld as a practice, while their perpetrators continue
to lounge at their ease in Florida or elsewhere, ignoring extradition
warrants under Obama's protection. Domestic wire-taps continue. A
coup in Central America is underwritten. New military bases are set
up in Colombia.

Emulating Wilson

Still, it would be a mistake to think that nothing has changed. No
Administration is exactly like any other, and each President leaves a
stamp on his own. Substantively, vanishingly little of American imperial
dominion has altered under Obama.[21] But propagandistically, there has
been a significant upgrade. It is no accident that a leading columnist—
and one of the more intelligent—could, only half ironically, list the five
most important events of 2009 as so many speeches by Obama.[22] In
Cairo, at West Point, at Oslo, the world has been treated to one uplifting homily after another, each address larded with every egregious
euphemism that White House speech-writers can muster to describe
America's glowing mission in the world, and modest avowal of awe and
sense of responsibility in carrying it forward.

---

[20] On 27 December 2009 Obama announced the doubling of us military expenditure on Yemen. The *Economist* noted that 'On his [Obama's] watch American drones
and special forces have been busier than ever, not only in Afghanistan and Pakistan
but also, it is reported, in Somalia and Yemen': 30 December 2009.
[21] Hence in part the disenchantment of many erstwhile Obama partisans, which
has surfaced with striking rapidity compared to the relatively long liberal love affair
with Bill Clinton. Nonetheless, their explanations have tended to blame structural
constraints rather than the incumbent himself: Garry Wills sees the well-meaning
president as caught in the cogs of the us imperial state apparatus ('The Entangled
Giant', *New York Review of Books*, 8 October 2009), while Frank Rich has angrily
attacked lobbyists for undermining Obama's 'promise to make Americans trust the
government again' ('The Rabbit Ragu Democrats', *New York Times*, 3 October 2009).
For Tom Hayden, the 'expedient' decision to boost force levels in Afghanistan is 'the
last in a string of disappointments', despite the fact that Obama had pledged to do
so in his campaign; but though Hayden is removing his bumper sticker, he will still
be 'supporting Obama down the road' ('Obama's Afghanistan Escalation', *Nation*,
1 December 2009).
[22] Gideon Rachman, 'The Grim Theme Linking the Year's Main Events', *Financial
Times*, 23 December 2009.

'We must say openly to each other the things we hold in our hearts' is the characteristic tone. 'Our country has borne a special burden in global affairs. We have spilled American blood in many countries on multiple continents. We have spent our revenue to help others rebuild from rubble and develop their own economies. We have joined with others to develop an architecture of institutions—from the United Nations to NATO to the World Bank—that provide for the common security and prosperity of human beings'. 'The struggle against violent extremism will not be finished quickly, and it extends well beyond Afghanistan and Pakistan . . . Our effort will involve disorderly regions, failed states, diffuse enemies'. 'Our cause is just, our resolve unwavering. We will go forward with the confidence that right makes might'. In the Middle East, there are 'tensions' (the term recurs nine times in his address to Mubarak's claque at al-Azhar), and a 'humanitarian crisis' in Gaza. But 'the Palestinians must renounce violence', and 'the Iraqi people are ultimately better off' for American actions. In Oslo: 'Make no mistake: evil does exist in the world'. 'To say that force may sometimes be necessary is not a call to cynicism—it is a recognition of history; the imperfections of man and the limits of reason.' In Cairo: 'Resistance through violence and killing is wrong'. In short: if the US or Israel wage war, it is a regrettable moral duty. If Palestinians, Iraqis or Afghans resist them, it is an immoral dead-end. As Obama likes to say, 'We are all God's children', and 'This is God's vision'.[23]

If sonorous banality and armour-plated hypocrisy are the hallmarks of this Presidential style, that does not make it less functional for the task of servicing and repairing the imperial institutions over which Obama

---

[23] 'Remarks by the President on a New Beginning', Cairo, 4 June 2009; 'Remarks by the President to the Nation on the Way Forward in Afghanistan and Pakistan', West Point, 1 December 2009; Nobel Peace Prize acceptance speech, Oslo, 11 December 2009; 'Remarks by the President to the Ghanaian Parliament', Accra, 11 June 2009. The tropes of 'imperfect man' and 'limited reason' are borrowed from the vapourings of Reinhold Niebuhr, pastor of Cold War consciences, for whom see Gopal Balakrishnan, 'Sermons on the Present Age', below. Niebuhr could, however, on occasion be less of a humbug than his pupil. Rather than pious guff about the 'two suffering peoples', he had the honesty to call a Zionist spade a spade: in 1942, observing that 'the Anglo-Saxon hegemony that is bound to exist in the event of an Axis defeat will be in a position to see to it that Palestine is set aside for the Jews', he argued that 'Zionist leaders are unrealistic in insisting that their demands entail no "injustice" to the Arab population'. The latter would have to be 'otherwise compensated'. ('Jews after the War—II', *Nation*, 28 February 1942.)

and Clinton now preside. Nothing grated more on international opinion than the lack of requisite unction with which Bush and Cheney all too often went about their business, exposing allies and audiences otherwise well-disposed towards American leadership to inconvenient truths they would have preferred not to hear. Historically, the model for the current variant of imperial Presidency has been Woodrow Wilson, no less pious a Christian, whose every second word was peace, democracy or self-determination, while his armies invaded Mexico, occupied Haiti and attacked Russia, and his treaties handed one colony after another to his partners in war. Obama is a hand-me-down version of the same, without even Fourteen Points to betray. But cant still goes a long way to satisfy those who yearn for it, as the award to Obama of what García Márquez once called the Nobel Prize for War has graphically shown. After lying enough to voters—promising peace and delivering war—Wilson was re-elected to a second term, though it did not end well for him. In more combative times, Johnson was forced to step down in ignominy for his warmongering, without being able to gull the electors again. Twelve years later, a debacle in Tehran helped sink Carter. If the recent setbacks for Democrats in West Virginia and New Jersey—where Democratic voters stayed at home—become a pattern, Obama could be a third one-term President, abandoned by his supporters and mocked by those he tries so hard to conciliate.

FRANCO MORETTI

THE GREY AREA

Ibsen and the Spirit of Capitalism

ONSIDER THE SOCIAL universe of Ibsen's twelve-play cycle: shipbuilders, industrialists, financiers, merchants, bankers, developers, administrators, judges, managers, lawyers, doctors, headmasters, professors, engineers, pastors, journalists, photographers, designers, accountants, clerks, printers. No other writer has focused so single-mindedly on the bourgeois world. Mann; but in Mann there is a constant dialectic of bourgeois and artist (Thomas and Hanno, Lübeck and Kröger, Zeitblom and Leverkühn), and in Ibsen not quite, his one great artist—the sculptor Rubek, in *When We Dead Awaken*, who will 'work until the day he dies', and loves to be 'lord and master over his material'—is just like all the others.[1]

Now, many historians have doubts about the concept of the bourgeoisie: whether a banker and a photographer, or a shipbuilder and a pastor, are really part of the same class. In Ibsen, they are; or at least, they share the same spaces and speak the same language. None of the English semantic camouflage of the 'middle' class, here; this is not a class in the middle, threatened from above and below, and innocent of the course of the world: this is the *ruling* class, and the world is what it is, because they have *made* it that way. This is why Ibsen's 'settling of accounts' with the 19th century—one of his favourite metaphors—is so breathtaking: finally, what has the bourgeoisie brought to the world?

I will return to this, of course. For now, let me say how strange it is to have such a broad bourgeois fresco—and almost no workers in it (except for house servants). *Pillars of Society*, which is the first play of the cycle, opens with a confrontation between a union leader and a manager about safety and profits; and although the theme is never the centre of the plot, it is visible throughout, and is decisive for its ending. But then, the conflict between capital and labour disappears from Ibsen's world, even though, in general, nothing disappears here: *Ghosts* is the perfect Ibsen title because so many of his characters *are* ghosts: the minor figure of one play returns as the protagonist in another, or the other way around; a wife leaves home in one play, and stays to the bitter end in the following one. It's like a twenty-year-long experiment he is running: changing a variable here and there, to see what happens to the system. But, no workers in the experiment—even though the years of the cycle, 1877–99, are those when trade unions, socialist parties and anarchism are changing the face of European politics.

No workers, because the conflict Ibsen wants to focus on is not that between the bourgeoisie and another class, but that internal to the bourgeoisie itself. Four works make this particularly clear: *Pillars of Society*; *The Wild Duck*; *The Master Builder*; *John Gabriel Borkman*. All four have the same prehistory, in which two business partners, and/or friends, have engaged in a struggle in the course of which one of them has been financially ruined, and psychically maimed. Intra-bourgeois competition as a mortal combat: and since life is at stake, the conflict easily becomes ruthless, or dishonest; but, and this is important, ruthless, unfair, equivocal, murky—but seldom actually illegal. In a few cases it is also that—the forgeries of *A Doll's House*, the water pollution in *An Enemy of the People*, Borkman's financial manoeuvres—but in general, what's characteristic of Ibsen's wrongdoings is that they inhabit an elusive grey area whose nature is never completely clear.

This grey area is Ibsen's great intuition about bourgeois life, so let me give you a few examples. In *Pillars of Society* there are rumours that a theft has occurred in Bernick's firm; he knows the rumours are false, but he also knows they will save him from bankruptcy, and so, though they ruin a friend's reputation, he lets them circulate; later, he uses political influence in a barely legal way, to protect investments that are themselves barely legal. In *Ghosts*, Pastor Manders persuades Mrs Alving not to insure her orphanage, so that public opinion won't think that 'neither you nor I have adequate faith in Divine Providence'; divine providence

---

[1] All quotations from Ibsen come from *The Complete Major Prose Plays*, translated and introduced by Rolf Fjelde, New York 1978. Many many thanks to Sarah Allison for her help with the Norwegian original.

being what it is, the orphanage of course burns down—accident, more probably arson—and all is lost. There is the 'trap' that Werle might (or not) have laid for his partner in the prehistory of *The Wild Duck*, and the unclear business between Solness and his partner in the prehistory of *The Master Builder*; where there is also a chimney that should be repaired, isn't, and the house burns down—but, the insurance experts say, for a wholly different reason . . .

This is what the grey area is like: reticence, disloyalty, slander, negligence, half truths. As far as I can tell, there is no general term for these actions, which at first was frustrating; for I have often found the analysis of keywords illuminating for understanding the dynamic of bourgeois values: useful, serious, industry, comfort, earnest. Take 'efficiency': a word that had existed for centuries, and had always meant, as the OED puts it, 'the fact of being an efficient cause': causality. But then, in the mid-nineteenth century, all of a sudden the meaning changes, and efficiency starts indicating 'the fitness or power to accomplish . . . the purpose intended; adequate power'. Adequate; fit to the purpose: not the capacity to cause something in general any more, but to do so *according to a plan*, and *without waste*: the new meaning is a miniature of capitalist rationalization. 'Language is the instrument by which the world and society are adjusted', writes Benveniste, and he's right; semantic change, triggered by historical change; words catching up with things.[2] That's the beauty of keywords: they're a bridge between material and intellectual history.

But with the grey area, we have the thing, and not the word. And we really *do* have the thing: one of the ways in which capital accumulates is by invading ever new spheres of life—or even *creating* them, as in the parallel world of finance—and in these new spaces laws are more uncertain, and behaviour can quickly become profoundly equivocal. Equivocal: not illegal, but not quite right either. Think of a year ago (or today, for that matter): was it legal for banks to have a preposterous risk-to-asset ratio? Yes. Was it 'right', in any conceivable sense of the word? Clearly not. Or think of Enron: in the months that led to its bankruptcy, Kenneth Lay sold stock at prices that grossly overstated its value, as he knew perfectly well: in the criminal case, the government did not charge him; in

---

[2] Emile Benveniste, 'Remarks on the Function of Language in Freudian Theory', in *Problems in General Linguistics*, Miami 1971, p. 71.

the civil case it did, because the standard of proof was lower.[3] The same act that *is* and is *not* prosecuted: this is almost baroque, in its play of light and shadow, but typical: the law itself acknowledging the existence of the grey area. One does something because there is no explicit norm against it; but it doesn't feel right, and the lurking fear of being held accountable remains, and instigates endless cover-up. Grey on grey: a dubious act, wrapped in equivocations. 'The substantive conduct may be somewhat ambiguous', a prosecutor put it a few years ago—ambiguous, because of the 'fog of financialization', 'opaque data', 'dark pools', 'shadow banking': fog, opaque, dark, shadows: all images of inextricable black and white. The initial act may be ambiguous, 'but the obstructive conduct may be clear.'[4] The first move may remain forever undecidable: what followed it—the 'lie', as Ibsen calls it—that, is unmistakable.

The initial act may be ambiguous: that's how things begin, in the grey area. An unplanned opportunity arises all by itself: a fire; a partner ousted from the picture; rumours; finding a rival's lost papers. Accidents. But accidents that repeat themselves so often that they become the structural, hidden foundation of modern life. The initial event had been punctual, unrepeatable; the lie endures for years, or decades; it becomes 'life'. That's probably why there is no keyword, here: just as some banks are too big to fail, the grey area is too pervasive to be acknowledged; it casts too bleak a shadow on the value which is the bourgeoisie's justification in the face of the world: honesty. Honesty is to the bourgeoisie what honour was to the aristocracy; etymologically, it even derives from honour (and there is a *trait d'union* between them in the female 'chastity'—honour and honesty at once—so central in early bourgeois drama). Honesty tells the bourgeoisie apart from all other classes: the word of the merchant, as good as gold; transparency ('I can show my books to anyone'); moral-ity (Mann's bankruptcy as 'shame, dishonour worse than death'). Even McCloskey's 600-page extravaganza on *Bourgeois Virtues*—which ascribes to the bourgeoisie courage, temperance, prudence, justice, faith, hope, love—even there, the apex are the pages on honesty. Honesty, the theory goes, is *the* bourgeois virtue because it is so perfectly adapted to a market economy: market transactions require trust, honesty provides it, and the

---

[3] See Kurt Eichenwald, 'Ex-Chief of Enron Pleads Not Guilty to 11 Felony Counts', *New York Times*, 9 July 2004.
[4] Jonathan Glater, 'On Wall Street Today, a Break from the Past', *New York Times*, 4 May 2004.

market rewards it. Honesty *works*. 'By doing evil we do badly'—we lose money—McCloskey concludes, 'and we do well by doing good.'[5]

By doing evil we do badly—this is true neither in Ibsen's theatre, nor outside of it. Here is a contemporary of his, a German banker, describing the 'undecipherable machinations' of finance capital:

> Banking circles were and are dominated by a striking, very flexible moral- ity. Certain kinds of manipulation, which no good *Bürger* would in good conscience accept . . . are approved by these persons as clever, as evi- dence of ingenuity. The contradiction between the two moralities is quite irreconcilable.[6]

Machinations, manipulation, no good conscience, flexible morality; the grey area. Within it, an 'irreconcilable contradiction between two morali- ties': words that echo almost verbatim Hegel's idea of tragedy—and Ibsen is a playwright. Is it this that draws him to the grey area? The dramatic potential of a conflict between honest *Bürger* and scheming financier?

II

The curtain rises, and the world is solid: rooms full of armchairs, bookcases, pianos, sofas, desks, stoves; people move calmly, carefully, speaking in low voices. Solid. Old bourgeois value: the anchor against the fickleness of Fortune—so unstable atop her wheel and her waves, blindfolded, garments blown by the winds . . . Look at the banks built around Ibsen's time: columns, urns, balconies, spheres, statues—gravity. Then the action unfolds, and there is no business that is safe from ruin; no word which is not hollow at the core. People are worried. Sick. Dying. It's the first general crisis of European capitalism: the long depression of 1873–96, which Ibsen's twelve plays follow almost year by year.

The crisis reveals the victims of the bourgeois century: *I vinti*: 'the defeated', as Verga entitled, one year after *Pillars*, his novelistic cycle. Krogstad, in *Doll's House*; old Ekdal and his son, in *The Wild Duck*;

---

[5] Deirdre McCloskey, *The Bourgeois Virtues: Ethics for an Age of Commerce*, Chicago 2006.
[6] Cited in Richard Tilly, 'Moral Standards and Business Behaviour in Nineteenth-Century Germany and Britain', in Jürgen Kocka and Allan Mitchell, eds, *Bourgeois Society in Nineteenth-Century Europe*, Oxford 1993, pp. 190–1.

Brovik and his son, in *Master Builder*; Foldal and his daughter, but also
Borkman and his son, in *John Gabriel Borkman*. Ekdal and son, Brovik
and son . . . In this naturalist quarter-century, failure flows from one generation to the next, like syphilis. And there is no redemption, for Ibsen's
defeated: the victims of capitalism, yes, but its *bourgeois* victims, made of
exactly the same clay as their oppressors. Once the struggle is over, the
loser is hired by the man who ruined him, and turned into a grotesque
Harlequin, part parasite, part worker, confidante, flatterer. 'Why did you
put us into this little box where everybody is wrong?' a student once
asked about *The Wild Duck*. She was right, it's unbreathable.

Irreconcilable contradiction between honest and fraudulent bourgeois?
That's not Ibsen's point. Someone *was* deceitful, in the prehistory of
many plays, but his antagonist was often more stupid than honest—and
anyway, he's neither honest nor an antagonist anymore. The only conflict between good *Bürger* and corrupt financier is *An Enemy of the People*:
Ibsen's worst play (and of course, the one the Victorians immediately
loved). But in general, 'cleaning up' the bourgeoisie from its murky side
is not Ibsen's project; it's Shaw's. Vivie Warren: who leaves her mother,
her boyfriend, her money, everything, and—'goes at her work with a
plunge', as the final stage direction has it. When Nora leaves everything
at the end of *Doll's House*, she walks into the night, not to a good white-
collar job waiting for her.

What draws Ibsen to the grey area? Not the clash between a good and a
bad bourgeoisie. Not an interest in the victims, for sure. The victors? Take
old Werle, in *The Wild Duck*. Werle occupies the same structural position
as Claudius in *Hamlet*, or Philip in *Don Carlos*: he is not the protagonist
of the play (that's his son Gregers—just like Hamlet, or Carlos), but he is
certainly the one with most power; he controls all the women on stage;
buys people's complicity, or even affection; and he does all this without
emphasis, in an almost subdued way. Possibly, because of his past. Many
years earlier, after 'an incompetent survey', his business partner Ekdal
'carried out illegal logging on state property'.[7] Ekdal was ruined; Werle

[7] As Sarah Allison pointed out to me, this 'incompetent survey' is a *very* grey area:
the word *uetterrettelig* is given as 'false, mistaken' in Brynildsen's *Norsk-Engelsk
Ordbog* (Kristiania 1917) and translated as 'misleading' by Michael Meyer in his
edition (London 1980); 'inaccurate' in Christopher Hampton's (London 1980);
'fraudulent' in Dounia B. Christiani's (New York 1980); 'disastrously false' in Brian
Johnston's (Lyme, NH 1996); and 'crooked' in Stephen Mulrine's (London 2006). The

survived, then prospered. As usual, the initial act remains ambiguous: was the logging truly the result of incompetence? Was it fraud? Did Ekdal act alone? Did Werle know—did he even 'lay a trap' for Ekdal, as Gregers suggests? The play doesn't say. 'But the fact remains', says Werle, 'that [Ekdal] was convicted and I was acquitted'. Yes, replies his son: 'I'm aware that no proof was found'. And Werle: 'Acquittal is acquittal.'

There is a piece by Barthes, 'Racine is Racine', on the arrogance of taut-ology: this trope 'that resists thought', like 'a dog owner pulling the leash'. Pulling the leash is certainly in Werle's style, but that's not the point, here. Acquittal is acquittal, that is to say: the outcome of a trial is a legal act—and legality is *not* justice: it's a formal notion, not an ethical one. Werle accepts this potential contradiction, and so does Ibsen: some kind of legal injustice is for him almost intrinsic to bourgeois success. Other writers react differently. Take the masterpiece of bour-geois Britain. One of the main characters of *Middlemarch* is a banker, Bulstrode, who begins his career by cheating a mother and child of their inheritance—without however being 'in danger of legal punishment' for that. A banker—in fact, a profoundly *Christian* banker—in the grey area: a triumph of bourgeois ambiguity, made even more so by Eliot's use of free indirect style, which makes it almost impossible to find a standpoint from which to criticize Bulstrode (a consequence of this style that was famously denounced at the trial of *Madame Bovary*):

> The profits made out of lost souls—where can the line be drawn at which they begin in human transactions? Was it not even God's way of saving His chosen? . . . Who would use money and position better than he meant to use them? Who could surpass him in self-abhorrence and exaltation of God's cause?[8]

A triumph of ambiguity—had Eliot stopped here. But she couldn't. A petty swindler, Raffles, knows the old story, and by a series of coincidences this 'incorporate past', in Eliot's wonderfully Ibsenesque formulation, locates both Bulstrode and the child.[9] While at Bulstrode's house to

---

etymology—a negative prefix 'u' + 'efter' (='after') + 'rette' (='right') + adjectival suf-fix 'lig'—indicates something, or someone, which cannot be relied upon to be right: misleading, unreliable, or untrustworthy seem the best equivalents for a word in which an objective untrustworthiness neither assumes nor excludes the subjective intent to provide false information.

[8] Eliot, *Middlemarch*, New York 1994, pp. 615, 616, 619.

[9] Eliot, *Middlemarch*, p. 523.

blackmail him, Raffles falls ill; Bulstrode calls the doctor, receives his orders, and follows them; later, though, he lets a house-keeper disregard them—he doesn't suggest it: he just lets it happen—and Raffles dies. 'It was impossible to prove that [Bulstrode] had done anything which hastened the departure of that man's soul', the narrator says.[10] 'Impossible to prove'; 'no proof was found'. But we don't need proof; we have *seen* Bulstrode acquiesce in manslaughter. Grey has become black; dishonesty has been forced to shed blood. 'Forced', because this is such an incredibly implausible sequence that it's hard to believe that someone with Eliot's profound intellectual respect for causality could have actually written it.

But she did; and when a great writer contradicts her own principles so openly, something important is usually at stake. Probably, this injustice protected by the cloak of legality—Bulstrode, guilty, wealthy, and unscathed by his early actions—this is for Eliot too bleak a view of how society works. Mind you, this is indeed how capitalism functions: uneven exchange, 'equalized' by contracts; expropriation and conquest, rewritten as 'improvement' and 'civilization'. Past might becomes present right. But Victorian culture—even at its best: 'one of the few English books written for grown-up people', as Woolf said of *Middlemarch*—cannot accept the idea of a world of *perfectly lawful injustice*. The contradiction is unbearable: lawfulness must become just, or injustice criminal: one way or the other, form and substance must be aligned, making capital ethically comprehensible. That's what Victorianism *is*: social relations cannot always be morally good—but they must be morally *legible*. No ambiguity.

Ibsen doesn't need this. In *Pillars of Society* there is a hint in that direction, when Bernick's 'incorporate past' boards a ship that he knows will sink, yet he lets it sail, just like Bulstrode with the housekeeper. But then he changes the ending, and never does anything like it again. He can look at bourgeois ambiguity without having to resolve it: 'signs against signs', as they say in *The Lady from the Sea*: moral signs saying one thing, and legal signs another.

Signs against signs. But, just as there is no real conflict between Ibsen's victims and their oppressors, so that 'against' does not indicate an opposition in the usual dramatic sense. It's more like a paradox: lawful injustice; unfair legality: the adjective grates against the noun, like chalk on a

---

[10] Eliot, *Middlemarch*, p. 717.

blackboard. Enormous discomfort, but no action. What draws Ibsen to the grey area? This: it reveals with absolute clarity the great *unresolved dissonance* of bourgeois life. Dissonance, not conflict. And unresolved: strident, unsettling—Hedda and her pistols—precisely because there are no alternatives. *The Wild Duck*, writes Adorno, the great theorist of dissonance, does not solve the contradiction, but articulates its insoluble nature.[11] This is where Ibsen's claustrophobia comes from: the box where everybody is wrong: the paralysis, to use the keyword of the early Joyce, who was one of his greatest admirers. It's the same prison of other sworn enemies of the post-1848 order: Baudelaire, Flaubert, Manet, Machado, Mahler. Everything they do is a critique of bourgeois life; all they see is bourgeois life. *Hypocrite lecteur,—mon semblable,—mon frère!*

III

So far, I have considered what Ibsen's characters 'do' in his plays. Now I'll turn to how they speak, and specifically to how they use metaphors. The first five titles of the cycle—*Pillars, Doll's House, Ghosts, An Enemy of the People, The Wild Duck*—are all metaphors; and (with one possible exception) they are all, in one way or another, delusions. Take *Pillars of Society*. Pillars: Bernick and his associates: exploiters that the metaphor turns into benefactors, in the semantic somersault which is typical of ideology. Then a second meaning emerges: the pillar is that (sham) 'moral credibility' which saved Bernick from bankruptcy in the past, and that he now needs again to shield his investments. And then, in the last lines of the play, two more transformations: 'Another thing I have learned', says Bernick, is that 'it's you women who are the pillars of society'. And Lona: 'No, my dear—the spirit of truth and the spirit of freedom—*those* are the pillars of society.'

One word; four totally different meanings. Here, the metaphor is flexible: it's there, like a sort of pre-existing semantic sediment, but characters can bend it to their different views of things. Elsewhere, it's a more threatening sign of a world that refuses to die:

> I almost believe we *are* ghosts, all of us, Pastor. It's not only what we inherit from our fathers and mothers that keeps on returning in us. It's all kinds of old dead doctrines and opinions and beliefs, that sort of thing. They aren't

---

11 Theodor W. Adorno, *Problems of Moral Philosophy* (1963), Stanford 2001, p. 161.

alive in us; but they hang on all the same, and we can't get rid of them. I just have to pick up a newspaper, and it's as if I could see the ghosts slipping between the lines. They must be haunting our whole country, ghosts everywhere . . .

They hang on and we can't get rid of them . . . One Ibsen character can:

> Our home has been nothing but a playpen. I've been your doll-wife here, just as at home I was Papa's doll-child. And in turn the children have been my dolls. I thought it was fun when you played with me, just as they thought it fun when I played with them. That's been our marriage, Torvald.

Nothing but a playpen. It's a revelation, for Nora. And what makes it truly unforgettable is that it's followed by a switch to a wholly different style. 'Doesn't it occur to you', she says, after changing from her tarantella costume into everyday clothes, 'that this is the first time we two . . . have ever talked seriously together?' Serious; another great bourgeois keyword: serious as in mirthless, of course; but also sober, concentrated, precise. Serious Nora takes the idols of ethical discourse ('duty'; 'trust'; 'happiness'; 'marriage'), and measures them against actual behaviour. She has spent years waiting for a metaphor to come true: 'the most wonderful thing in the world' (or 'the greatest miracle', as it's also translated); now the world, in the person of her husband, has forced her to become 'realistic'. 'We are closing our accounts, Torvald'. How do you mean that, he reacts; I don't understand you, What's that, What do you mean, What a thing to say . . . And of course it's not that he doesn't understand what she is saying: it's that for him language should never be so—serious. It should never be *prose*.

Prose: unavoidable, if one wants to do justice to the achievements of bourgeois culture. Prose as *the* bourgeois style; style as conduct, as a way of *living* in the world, not just of representing it. Prose as analysis, first of all: trying to see clearly: 'unmistakable definiteness and clear intelligibility', as Hegel's *Aesthetics* has it. Prose as the acknowledgment—half melancholy, half proud—that meaning will never be as intuitive and memorable as it is in verse: it will be delayed, scattered, partial; but also articulated, also strengthened by the effort. Prose as, not inspiration— this absurdly unjustified gift from the gods—but work: hard, tentative, never perfect. And, finally, prose as rational polemic, like Nora's: emotions, fortified by thought. It's Ibsen's idea of freedom: a style that understands the delusions of metaphors, and leaves them behind. A woman who understands a man, and leaves him behind.

Nora's dispelling of lies at the end of *Doll's House* is one of the great pages of bourgeois culture: on a par with Kant's words on the Enlightenment, or Mill's on liberty. How telling, that the moment should be so brief. From *The Wild Duck* on, metaphors multiply—the so-called 'symbolism' of the late Ibsen—and the prose of the early phase becomes unimaginable. And this time, the source of the metaphors is not the past, not a cultural old regime, but the bourgeoisie itself. Two very similar passages, from Bernick and Borkman—two versions of the financial entrepreneur, one at the beginning and one at the end of the cycle—will explain what I mean. This is Bernick, describing what a railway will bring:

> Think what a lift this will give the whole community! Just think of the vast tracts of forest that'll be opened up! The rich lodes of ore to mine! And the river, with one waterfall after another! The possibilities of industrial development are limitless!

Bernick is excited here: sentences are short, exclamative, with those 'think!' (think what a lift, think of the forest) that try to arouse his listeners' imagination, while the plurals (tracts, lodes, waterfalls, possibilities) multiply results in front of our eyes. It's a passionate passage—but fundamentally descriptive. And here is Borkman:

> Do you see those mountain ranges *there* . . . That's my deep, my endless, inexhaustible kingdom! The wind works on me like the breath of life. It comes to me like a greeting from captive spirits. I can sense them, the buried millions. I feel the veins of metal, reaching their curving, branching, beckoning arms out to me. I saw them before like living shadows—the night I stood in the bank vault with a lantern in my hand. You wanted your freedom then—and I tried to set you free. But I lacked the strength for it. Your treasures sank back in the depths. *(His hands outstretched)* But I'll whisper to you here in the silence of the night. I love you, lying there unconscious in the depths and darkness! I love you, you riches straining to be born—with all your shining aura of power and glory! I love you, love you, love you!

Bernick's was a world of forests, mines, and waterfalls; Borkman's, of spirits and shadows and love. Capitalism is de-materialized: the 'lodes of ore' become kingdom, breath, life, death, aura, birth, glory . . . Prose withdraws in front of tropes: a greeting from captive spirits, veins of metal beckoning, treasures sinking into the depths, riches straining to be born. Metaphors—this is probably the longest metaphorical string in the entire cycle—no longer interpret the world; they obliterate it and then remake it, like the night fire which clears the way for master-builder

Solness. Creative destruction, Schumpeter will call it: the grey area, become seductive. Typical of the entrepreneur, writes Sombart, is 'the poet's gift—the metaphorical gift—of calling up to the eyes of his audience ravishing pictures of realms of gold . . . he himself, with all the passionate intensity he is capable of, dreams the dream of the successful issue of his undertaking.'[12]

He dreams the dream . . . Dreams are not lies. But they aren't the truth, either. Speculation, writes one of its historians, 'retains something of its original philosophical meaning; namely, to reflect or theorize without a firm factual basis'.[13] Borkman speaks with the same 'prophetic style' that was typical of the director of the South Sea Company (one of the first bubbles of modern capitalism);[14] the grand—and blind—vision of the dying Faust; the faith 'that the golden age lies not behind, but ahead of mankind' that Gerschenkron saw as the 'strong medicine' needed for economic take-off:

> Can you see the smoke from the great steamers out on the fjord? No? I can . . . Hear that? Down by the river, the factories whirring! *My* factories! All the ones *I* would have built! Can you hear how they're going? It's the night shift. Night and day they are working.

Visionary; despotic; destructive; *self*-destructive: this is Ibsen's entrepreneur. Borkman renounces love for gold, like Alberich in *The Ring*; is jailed; imprisons himself at home for eight more years; and in the rapture of his vision, marches into the ice to certain death. That's why the entrepreneur is so important for the late Ibsen: he brings *hubris* back into the world—hence tragedy. He is the modern tyrant: *The Banker's Tragedy* would have been the title of *John Gabriel Borkman* in 1620. Solness's vertigo is the perfect clue: the body's desperate attempt to preserve itself from the deadly daring demanded of a founder of kingdoms. But, unfortunately, the spirit is too strong: he *will* climb to the top of the house he's just built, challenge God—'Hear me, Almighty . . . from now

---

[12] Werner Sombart, *The Quintessence of Capitalism*, London 1915, pp. 91–2. It's impossible to miss the erotic component of Sombart's thesis, which, after all, identifies 'the classic type of the entrepreneur' in Faust, Goethe's most destructive—*and* creative—seducer. In Ibsen, too, the entrepreneur's metaphoric vision has an erotic origin in Solness's hysterically chaste adultery with Hilda (whom he had already 'seduced' when she was twelve).
[13] Edward Chancellor, *The Devil Take the Hindmost: A History of Financial Speculation*, New York 1999, p. xii.
[14] Chancellor, *Devil Take the Hindmost*, p. 74.

on, I'll build only what is most beautiful in all this world'—wave to the crowd below . . . and fall.

And this uncanny act of self-immolation is the right prelude to my last question: so, what is Ibsen's verdict on the European bourgeoisie? What has this class brought to the world?

IV

The answer lies in a wider arc of history than the 1880s and 90s; an arc, at the centre of which lies the great industrial transformation of the 19th century. Before then, the bourgeois is not the ruling class: what he wants is to be left alone, as in the famous reply to Frederick the Great, or at most to be recognized and accepted. He is, if anything, too modest in his aspirations; too narrow: Robinson Crusoe's father, or Wilhelm Meister's. His great desire is 'comfort': this almost medicinal notion, halfway between usefulness and leisure: pleasure, as mere wellbeing. Caught in a never-ending struggle against the vagaries of *Fortuna*, this early bourgeois is orderly, careful, with the 'almost religious respect for facts' of the first Buddenbrooks. He is a man of details. He is the prose of capitalist history.

After the great industrialization, though more slowly than we used to think—chronologically, all of Ibsen falls within Arno Mayer's 'persistence of the old regime'—the bourgeoisie becomes the dominant class; and one with the immense means of industry at its disposal. The realistic bourgeois is ousted by the creative destroyer; analytical prose, by world-transforming metaphors. Drama captures better than the novel this new phase, where the temporal axis shifts from the sober recording of the past—the double-entry book-keeping practised in *Robinson* and celebrated in *Meister*—to the bold shaping of the future which is typical of dramatic dialogue. In *Faust*, in the *Ring*, in late Ibsen, characters 'speculate', looking far into the time to come. Details are dwarfed by the imagination; the real, by the possible. It's the *poetry* of capitalist development.

The poetry of the possible . . . The great bourgeois virtue is honesty, I said earlier; but honesty is retrospective: you're honest, if, in the past, you haven't done anything wrong. You can't be honest in the future tense—which is the tense of the entrepreneur. What is an 'honest' forecast of the price of oil, or of anything else for that matter, five years from now? Even if you *want* to be honest, you can't, because honesty needs firm facts, which 'speculating'—even in its most neutral etymological sense—lacks. In the Enron story, for instance, a big step towards the great swindle was the adoption of so-called mark-to-market accounting: entering as actually existing earnings that are still in the future (at times, years in the future). The day the Securities and Exchange Commission authorized this 'speculation' on the value of assets, Jeff Skilling brought champagne to the office: accounting as 'professional scepticism', as the classical definition had it—and it sounds so much like the poetics of realism—scepticism was over. Now, accounting was vision. 'It wasn't a job—it was a mission . . . We were doing God's work.'[15] This was Skilling, after the indictment; Borkman, who can no longer tell the difference between conjecture, desire, dream, hallucination, and fraud pure and simple.

What has the bourgeoisie brought to the world? This mad bifurcation between a much more rational and a much more *ir*-rational rule over society. Two ideal-types—one before and one after industrialization—made memorable by Weber and Schumpeter. Coming from a country where capitalism arrived late, and encountered few obstacles, Ibsen had the opportunity—and the genius—to compress a history of centuries into just twenty years, making it explosive and irrevocable. The realistic bourgeois inhabits the early plays: Lona; Nora; perhaps Regina in *Ghosts*. The realist as a woman: an odd choice, for the times (*Heart of Darkness*: 'it's queer how out of touch with truth women are'). A radical choice, too, in the spirit of Mill's *Subjection of Women*. But also profoundly pessimistic about the scope of bourgeois 'realism': imaginable within the intimate sphere—as the solvent of the nuclear family and all its lies—but not in society at large. Nora's prose at the end of *Doll's House* echoes the writings of Wollstonecraft, Fuller, Martineau:[16] but their public arguments are now locked inside a living room (in Bergman's staging, a bedroom). What a paradox, this play that shocks the European public sphere, but doesn't really believe in the public sphere. And then, once creative destruction emerges, there are no Noras left, to counter Borkman's and Solness's destructive metaphors; the opposite: Hilda, inciting '*my*

---

[15] Bethany McLean and Peter Elkind, *The Smartest Guys in the Room: The Amazing Rise and Scandalous Fall of Enron*, London 2003, p. xxv.
[16] The sources of Nora's speech have been identified by Joan Templeton; see Alisa Solomon, *Re-Dressing the Canon: Essays on Theatre and Gender*, London and New York, p. 50.

master-builder' to his suicidal hallucination. The more indispensable realism is, the more unthinkable it becomes.

Remember the German banker, with his 'irreconcilable contradiction' between the good *Bürger* and the unscrupulous financier. Ibsen of course knew the difference between them; and he was a playwright, looking for an objective collision on which to base his work. Why not use this intra-bourgeois contradiction? It would have made so much sense to do so; so much sense for Ibsen to be Shaw, instead of being Ibsen. But he did what he did because the difference between those two bourgeois is perhaps 'irreconcilable', but is not really a contradiction: the good *Bürger* will never have the *strength* to withstand the creative destruction of capital; the hypnotic entrepreneur will never yield to the sober Puritan. Recognizing the impotence of bourgeois realism in the face of capitalist megalomania: here lies Ibsen's unforgettable political lesson.

Telos Press Publishing

www.telospress.com

HAMLET OR HECUBA:
THE INTRUSION OF THE TIME INTO THE PLAY
by Carl Schmitt

Translated by David Pan and Jennifer R. Rust

Though Carl Schmitt is best known for his legal and political theory, his 1956 *Hamlet or Hecuba* provides an innovative and insightful analysis of Shakespeare's tragedy in terms of the historical situation of its creation. Schmitt argues that the significance of Shakespeare's work hinges on its ability to integrate history in the form of the taboo of the queen and the deformation of the figure of the avenger. He uses this interpretation to develop a theory of myth and politics that serves as a cultural foundation for his concept of political representation. More than literary criticism or historical analysis, Schmitt's book lays out a comprehensive theory of the relationship between aesthetics and politics that responds to alternative ideas developed by Walter Benjamin and Theodor W. Adorno. Jennifer R. Rust and Julia Reinhard Lupton's introduction places Schmitt's work in the context of contemporary Renaissance studies, and David Pan's afterword analyzes the links to Schmitt's political theory. Presented in its entirety in an authorized translation, *Hamlet or Hecuba* is essential reading for scholars of Shakespeare and Schmitt alike.

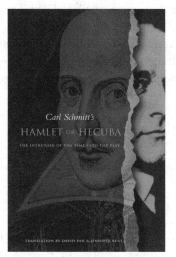

$19.95 | Paperback | 120 pages
ISBN: 978-0-914386-42-1

"Beyond ancient tragedy and the Atreides, through the themes of vengeance, of the brother and of election, this essay also questions the political destiny of the 'European spirit.'"

—Jacques Derrida,
The Politics of Friendship

Telos Press Publishing
431 East 12th Street · New York, NY · 10009
Tel: 212 · 228 · 6479 | Fax: 212 · 228 · 6379
Order online at www.telospress.com

ERIC HOBSBAWM

Interview

WORLD DISTEMPERS

Age of Extremes *ends in 1991 with a panorama of global landslide—the collapse of Golden Age hopes for world social improvement. What do you see as
the major developments in world history since then?*

I SEE FIVE MAIN changes. First, the shift of the economic centre of
the world from the North Atlantic to South and East Asia. This was
beginning in Japan in the seventies and eighties, but the rise of
China from the nineties has made a real difference. Secondly, of
course, the worldwide crisis of capitalism, which we had been predicting,
but which nevertheless took a long time to occur. Third, the clamorous
failure of the US attempt at a solo world hegemony after 2001—and it has
very visibly failed. Fourth, the emergence of the new bloc of developing
countries as a political entity—the BRICS—had not taken place when I
wrote *Age of Extremes*. And fifth, the erosion and systematic weakening
of the authority of states: of national states within their territories, and in
large parts of the world, of any kind of effective state authority. It might
have been predictable, but it has accelerated to an extent that I would
not have expected.

What else has surprised you since then?

I never cease to be surprised at the sheer lunacy of the neocon project,
which not merely pretended that America was the future, but even
thought it had formulated a strategy and tactics for achieving this end.
As far as I can see, in rational terms, they didn't have a coherent strategy.
Second—much smaller, but significant—the revival of piracy, which we
had largely forgotten about; that is new. And the third, which is even
more local: the collapse of the CPI(M) in West Bengal, which I really

wouldn't have expected. Prakash Karat, the CPI(M) general secretary, recently told me that in West Bengal, they felt themselves beleaguered and besieged. They look forward to doing very badly against this new Congress in the local elections. This after governing as a national party, as it were, for thirty years. The industrialization policy, taking land away from the peasants, had a very bad effect, and was clearly a mistake. I can see that, like all such surviving left-wing governments, they had to accommodate economic development, including private development, and so it seemed natural for them to develop a strong industrial base. But it does seem slightly surprising that it should have led to such a dramatic turn-around.

Can you envisage any political recomposition of what was once the working class?

Not in traditional form. Marx was undoubtedly right in predicting the formation of major class parties at a certain stage of industrialization. But these parties, if they were successful, were operating not purely as working-class parties: if they wanted to extend beyond a narrow class, they did so as people's parties, structured around an organization invented by and for the purposes of the working class. Even so, there were limits to class consciousness. In Britain, the Labour Party never got beyond 50 per cent of the vote. The same is true in Italy, where the PCI was much more of a people's party. In France, the left was based on a relatively weak working class, but one which happened to be politically reinforced by the great revolutionary tradition, of which it managed to make itself the essential successor—and that gave it and the left far more leverage.

The decline of the manual working class in industry does seem terminal. There are, or will be, plenty of people left doing manual work, and defence of their conditions remains a major task for all left governments. But it can no longer be the principal foundation of their hopes: they no longer have, even in theory, political potential, because they lack the potential for organization of the old working class. There have been three other major negative developments. One is, of course, xenophobia—which, for most of the working class is, as Bebel once put it, 'the socialism of fools': safeguard my job against people who are competing with me. The weaker the labour movement is, the more xenophobia appeals. Second, a lot of manual labour and work in what the British Civil Service used to call 'minor and manipulative grades' is not permanent, it's temporary:

students or migrants, working in catering, for instance. And therefore it's not easy to see it as potentially organizable. The only readily organizable form of that kind of labour is that employed by public authorities, and this is because those authorities are politically vulnerable.

The third and most important development, in my view, is the growing divide produced by a new class criterion—namely, passing examinations in schools and universities as an entry ticket into jobs. This is, if you like, meritocracy; but it is measured, institutionalized and mediated by educational systems. What this has done is to divert class consciousness from opposition to employers to opposition to toffs of one kind or another—intellectuals, liberal elites, people who are putting it over on us. America is a standard example of this, but it's not absent in the UK, if you look at the British press. The fact that, increasingly, getting a PhD or at least being a postgraduate also gives you a better chance of getting millions complicates the situation a bit.

Can there be new agencies? It can no longer be in terms of a single class, but then in my view it never could be. There is a progressive politics of coalitions, even such relatively permanent coalitions as that between, say, the educated, *Guardian*-reading middle class and the intellectuals— the highly educated, who on the whole tend to be more on the left than the others—and the mass of the poor and the ignorant. Both groups are essential to such a movement, but they are perhaps harder to unify than before. In a sense, it is possible for the poor to identify with multi-millionaires, as in the United States, saying, 'If only I was lucky, I could become a pop star'. But you can't say, 'If only I was lucky, I'd become a Nobel Prize winner'. This is a real problem in coordinating the politics of people who objectively might be on the same side.

How would you compare the contemporary crisis to the Great Depression?

Nineteen twenty-nine didn't start with the banks—they didn't collapse until two years later. Rather, the stock exchange set off a production slump, with far higher unemployment and a greater actual decline in production than there have ever been since. The current depression had more preparation than that of 1929, which came almost out of the blue. It should have been apparent from quite early on that neoliberal fundamentalism produced an enormous instability in the operations of capitalism. Until 2008 it seemed to affect only the marginal areas—Latin America in the nineties and earlier 2000s; Southeast Asia; Russia. In the major countries, all it meant was occasional stock-exchange collapses, which were then recuperated quite quickly. It seemed to me that the real sign of something bad happening should have been the collapse of Long-Term Capital Management in 1998, which proved how wrong the whole growth model was; but it wasn't seen as such. Paradoxically, it did get a number of businessmen and journalists to rediscover Karl Marx, as somebody who wrote something of interest about a modern, globalized economy; it had absolutely nothing to do with the former left.

The world economy in 1929 was less global than at present. This, of course, had some effect—for instance, it would have been a great deal easier for people who lost their jobs to go back to their villages than it is today. In 1929, in much of the world outside Europe and North America, the global parts of the economy were really patches that left what surrounded them largely unchanged. The existence of the USSR had no practical effect on the Depression, but it had an enormous ideo- logical effect—there was an alternative. Since the 1990s, we have seen the rise of China and the emerging economies, which actually has had a practical effect in the current depression, because they have helped to keep the world economy on a far more even keel that it would have been otherwise. In fact, even in the days when neoliberalism claimed that it was flourishing, the actual growth was very largely occurring in these newly developing economies—particularly in China. I'm sure that if China had not been there, the 2008 slump would have been much more serious. So, for those reasons, I think we are likely to emerge from it more quickly; though certain countries—notably Britain—will continue to be fairly depressed for quite some time.

What about the political consequences?

The 1929 Depression led overwhelmingly to a shift to the right, with the major exception of North America, including Mexico, and Scandinavia. In France, the Popular Front in 1936 had only 0.5 per cent more votes than they had had in 1932, so their victory marked a shift in the composi- tion of political alliances rather than anything more profound. In Spain, despite the quasi- or potentially revolutionary situation, the immediate effect was also a move to the right, and indeed also the long-term effect. In most of the other states, particularly in central and eastern Europe, politics moved very sharply to the right. The effect of the current crisis is not so clear-cut. One would suspect that the major political changes or shifts in policy would come not in the United States or in the West, but almost certainly in China. But one can only speculate about what they're likely to be.

Do you see China continuing to resist the downturn?

There's no particular reason to think that it will suddenly stop growing. The Chinese government has had a bad shock with the depression, because it brought an awful lot of industries to a stop, temporarily. But the country is still in the early stages of economic development, and there is enormous room for expansion. I don't want to speculate about the future, but one would imagine China in twenty or thirty years' time to be relatively more important than it is today, on the world scale—at least economically and politically; not necessarily in military terms. Of course, it has enormous problems—there are always people who ask if the country can hold together. But I think both the real and the ideological reasons for people wishing for China to be united continue to be very strong.

How would you assess the Obama administration, one year on?

People were so pleased at a man like that being elected, and in a situation of crisis, that they thought he was bound to be a great reformer, to do what Roosevelt did. But he didn't. He started badly. If you compare the first hundred days of Roosevelt with the first hundred days of Obama, what leaps out is Roosevelt's readiness to take on unofficial advisers, to try something new, compared to Obama's insistence on staying right in the centre. I think he's blown his chance. His real opportunity was in the first three months, when the other side was totally demoralized, and before it was able to remobilize in Congress—and he didn't do it. One might wish him well, but I think the prospects don't look terribly encouraging.

Looking at the hottest theatre of international conflict in the world at present, do you think a two-state solution, as currently envisaged, is a credible prospect in Palestine?

Personally, I doubt whether it's on at the moment. Whatever the solution is, nothing is going to happen until the Americans decide to change their mind totally, and put pressure on the Israelis. And it doesn't look as though this is happening.

Are there any parts of the world in which you think positive, progressive projects are still alive, or likely to revive?

Certainly in Latin America, politics and general public discourse are still conducted in the old Enlightenment—liberal, socialist, communist— terms. Those are the places where you find militarists who talk like socialists—who *are* socialists. You find a phenomenon like Lula, based on a working-class movement, and Morales. Where it's going to lead is another matter, but the old language can still be spoken, and the old modes of politics are still available. I'm not absolutely sure about Central America, although there are indications of a slight revival of the tradition of the Revolution in Mexico itself; not that this will go very far, since Mexico has been virtually integrated into the American economy. I think Latin America benefited from the absence of ethnic-linguistic national-ism, and of religious divisions; that made it a lot easier to maintain the old discourse. It always struck me that, until quite recently, there were no signs of ethnic politics. It has appeared among indigenous move-ments in Mexico and Peru, but not on the scale of anything that there was in Europe, Asia or Africa.

It's possible that in India, because of the institutional strength of the Nehru secular tradition, progressive projects could revive. But this doesn't seem to reach very far into the masses, except for some areas where the Communists have, or had, mass support, such as Bengal and Kerala, and possibly some groups like the Naxalites or the Maoists in Nepal. Beyond that, the heritage of the old labour, socialist and communist movements in Europe remains quite strong. The parties founded under Engels are still, almost everywhere in Europe, potential parties of government or the chief parties of opposition. I suspect that at some stage the heritage of communism, for example in the Balkans and even in parts of Russia, may come out in ways we can't predict. What will happen in China, I don't know. But there can be no question that they are thinking in differ-ent terms, and not in modified Maoist or Marxist terms.

You've always been critical of nationalism as a political force, warning the left against painting it red. But you've also come out strongly against violations of national sovereignty in the name of humanitarian interventions. What kinds

of internationalism, after the demise of those born of the labour movement, are
desirable and feasible today?

First of all, humanitarianism, the imperialism of human rights, doesn't
have anything much to do with internationalism. It's an indication either
of a revived imperialism, which finds a suitable excuse for violations of
state sovereignty—they may be perfectly sincere excuses—or else it is,
more dangerously, a reassertion of belief in the permanent superiority
of the area which dominated the globe from the sixteenth until the late
twentieth century. After all, the values which the West seeks to impose are
specifically regional values, not necessarily universal ones. If they were
universal values they would have to be reformulated in different terms. I
don't think we're dealing here with something that is in itself national or
international. Nationalism does enter into it, however, because the international order based on nation-states—the Westphalian system—has in
the past been, for good or ill, one of the best safeguards against outsiders
coming into countries. There's no question that once that is abolished,
the road is open for aggressive and expansionist warfare—indeed, that's
why the United States has denounced the Westphalian order.

Internationalism, which is the alternative to nationalism, is a tricky
business. It's either a politically empty slogan, as it was, for practical purposes, in the international labour movement—it didn't *mean* anything
specific—or it's a way of ensuring uniformity for powerful, centralized
organizations like the Roman Catholic Church, or the Comintern.
Internationalism meant that, as a Catholic, you believed in the same
dogmas and took part in the same practices, no matter who you were
and where you were; the same thing was theoretically the case with
Communist parties. To what extent this really happened, and at what
stage it ceased to happen—even in the Catholic Church—is another
matter. This is not really what we meant by 'internationalism'.

The nation-state was and remains the framework for all political decisions, domestic or foreign. Until quite recently, the activities of labour
movements—in fact, all political activities—were almost entirely conducted within the framework of a state. Even within the EU, politics is still
framed in national terms. In other words, there is no super-national power
to act—only separate states in coalition. It is possible that missionary fundamentalist Islam is an exception here, which spreads across states, but
this hasn't actually yet been demonstrated. Earlier attempts at pan-Arab

super-states, as between Egypt and Syria, broke down precisely due to the persistence of the existing state—formerly colonial—frontiers.

Do you therefore see inherent obstacles to any attempts to exceed the boundaries of the nation-state?

Economically and in most other respects—even to some extent culturally—the revolution of communications has created a genuinely international world, in which there are powers of decision that go transnational, activities that are transnational, and of course movements of ideas, communications and people that are far more easily transnational than they ever were before. Even linguistic cultures are supplemented now by international communications idioms. But in politics there has been no sign of this happening at all; and that's the basic contradiction at the moment. One of the reasons why it hasn't occurred is that, in the twentieth century, politics was democratized to a very great extent—the mass of the ordinary people were involved in it. For them, the state is essential to normal daily operations and to their life possibilities. Attempts to break up the state internally, by decentralization, have been undertaken, mostly in the past thirty or forty years, and some of them not unsuccessfully—certainly in Germany decentralization has been successful in some respects, and in Italy, regionalization has actually been beneficial. But the attempt to set up supra-national states hasn't worked. The EU is the obvious example. It was to some extent handicapped by its founders thinking precisely in terms of a super-state analogous to a national state, only bigger—whereas that wasn't, I think, a possibility, and certainly isn't now. The EU is a specific reaction within Europe. There were signs, at one time or another, of a super-national state in the Middle East and elsewhere, but the EU is the only one that seems to have got anywhere. I don't believe, for instance, that there's much chance of a greater federation arising in South America. I would bet against it, myself.

The unsolved problem, then, remains this contradiction: on the one hand, there are transnational entities and practices, which are in the process of hollowing out the state, perhaps to the point at which it collapses. But if this happens—which isn't an immediate prospect, not in developed states—who, then, will undertake the redistributive and other functions, which so far only the state has undertaken? At the moment, you have a sort of symbiosis and conflict. This is one of the basic problems of any kind of popular politics today.

Nationalism was clearly one of the great driving political forces in the nineteenth and throughout most of the twentieth century. What's your reading of the situation today?

There's no question that historically, nationalism was, to a great extent, part of the process of the formation of modern states, which required a different form of legitimation from the traditional theocratic or dynastic state. The original idea of nationalism was the creation of larger states, and it seems to me that this unifying and expanding function was very important. Typical was the French Revolution, where in 1790 people appeared saying, 'We're no longer Dauphinois, or Southerners, we are all Frenchmen'. At a later stage, from the 1870s on, you get movements of groups within these states pushing for their own independent states. This, of course, produced the Wilsonian moment of self-determination— although fortunately, in 1918–19, it was still corrected to a certain extent by something which has since completely disappeared, namely, the protection of minorities. It was recognized, if not by the nationalists themselves, that none of these new nation-states were in fact ethnically or linguistically homogeneous. But after the Second World War, the weaknesses of the existing arrangements were addressed, not just by the Reds but by everybody, with the deliberate, forcible creation of ethnic homogeneity. This brought an enormous amount of suffering and cruelty, and in the long run, it didn't work either. Nevertheless, up to that period the separatist type of nationalism operated reasonably well. It was reinforced after the Second World War by decolonization, which by its nature created more states; and it was bolstered still further at the end of the century by the collapse of the Soviet empire, which also created new mini-separate states, including many, as in the colonies, which actually hadn't wanted to secede, and which had independence imposed on them by the force of history.

I can't help feeling that the function of small, separatist states, which have multiplied tremendously since 1945, has changed. For one thing, they are recognized as existing. Before the Second World War, the mini-states, like Andorra and Luxembourg and all the rest, weren't even reckoned as part of the international system, except by stamp collectors. The idea that everything down to the Vatican City is now a state, and potentially a member of the United Nations, is new. It's also quite clear that, in terms of power, these states are not capable of playing the part of traditional states—they do not possess the capacity to make war against other states. They've become at best fiscal paradises, or useful sub-bases for transnational deciders. Iceland is a good example; Scotland is not far behind.

The historic function of creating a nation as a nation-state is no longer the basis of nationalism. It's no longer, as it were, a very convincing slogan. It may once have been effective as a means of creating communities and organizing them against other political or economic units. But today, the xenophobic element in nationalism is increasingly important. The more politics was democratized, the more potential there was for it. The causes of xenophobia are now much greater than they were before. This is cultural rather than political—look at the rise of English or Scottish nationalism in recent years—but not the less dangerous for that.

Did fascism not include such forms of xenophobia?

Fascism was still, to some extent, part of the drive to create large nations. There's no question that Italian fascism was a great step forward in turning Calabrians and Umbrians into Italians; and even in Germany it wasn't until 1934 that Germans could be defined as Germans, and not German *because* they were Swabian, or Frank, or Saxon. Certainly, German and central and east European fascisms were passionately against outsiders—largely, but not only, Jews. And of course, fascism provided less of a guarantee against xenophobic instincts. One of the enormous advantages of the old labour movements used to be that they *did* provide such a guarantee. This was very clear in South Africa: but for the commitment of traditional left-wing organizations to equality and non-discrimination, the temptation to exact revenge on the Afrikaners would have been much harder to resist.

You've emphasized the separatist and xenophobic dynamics of nationalism. Would you see this as something that now operates at the margins of world politics, rather than in the main theatre of events?

Yes, I think this is probably true—although there are areas in which it has done an enormous amount of harm, such as south-east Europe. Of course, it is still the case that nationalism—or patriotism, or identification with a specified people, not necessarily ethnically defined—is an enormous asset for giving legitimacy to governments. It is clearly the case in China. One of the problems in India is that they don't have anything quite like that. The United States obviously can't be based on ethnic unity, but it certainly has strong nationalist sentiments. In quite a lot of the well-functioning states, those sentiments remain. This is why mass immigration creates more problems today than it did in the past.

How do you foresee the social dynamics of contemporary immigration work-
ing out, now that as many newcomers arrive every year in the EU as in the
US? Would you foresee the gradual emergence of another melting pot, not dis-
similar to the American, in Europe?

But in the US, the melting pot stopped melting as of the 1960s. Moreover, at the end of the twentieth century, migration had become really quite different from that in earlier periods, largely because, by emigrating, one no longer breaks links with the past to the same extent as before. You can continue living in two, possibly even three, worlds at the same time, and identify with two or three different places. You can go on being a Guatemalan while you're in the United States. There are also situations as in the EU where, *de facto*, immigration does not create the possibility of assimilation. A Pole who comes to the UK isn't supposed to be anything except a Pole who comes to work.

This is clearly new, and quite different from the experience of, say, people of my generation—that of political émigrés, not that I was one of them—in which one's family was British, but culturally one never stopped being Austrian or German; yet nevertheless, one really believed that one ought to be English. Even when they went back afterwards to their own countries, it wasn't quite the same—the centre of gravity had shifted. There are always exceptions: the poet Erich Fried, who lived in Willesden for fifty years, in fact went on living in Germany. I do believe it is essential to maintain the basic rules of assimilation—that citizens of a particular country should behave in a certain way and have certain rights, and that these should define them, and that this should not be weakened by multicultural arguments. France had, in spite of everything, integrated about as many of its foreign immigrants as America, relatively speaking, and still the relationship between locals and former immigrants is almost certainly better there. This is because the values of the French Republic remain essentially egalitarian, and make no real concession in public. Whatever you do privately—it was also the case in America in the nineteenth century—publicly this is a country that speaks French. The real difficulty is going to be not so much with the immigrants as with locals. It's in places like Italy and Scandinavia, which previously had no xenophobic traditions, where this new immigration has created serious problems.

Today, the view is widespread that religion—whether in evangelical, Catholic, Sunni, Shia, neo-Hindu, Buddhist, or other forms—has returned as an immensely powerful force in one continent after another. Do you regard this as a fundamental phenomenon, or a more passing one, of surfaces rather than depths?

It's clear that religion—as the ritualization of life, the belief in spirits or non-material entities influencing life, and not least, as a common bond of communities—is so widespread throughout history that it would be a mistake to regard it as a superficial phenomenon, or one destined to disappear, at least among the poor and the weak, who probably have more need of its consolations, as well as of its potential explanations of why things are the way they are. There are systems of rule, such as the Chinese, which for practical purposes lack anything corresponding to what we would regard as religion. They demonstrate that it is possible, but I think one of the errors of the traditional socialist and communist movement was to go for violent extirpation of religion at times when it might well have been better not to do so. One of the major interesting changes after Mussolini fell in Italy came when Togliatti no longer discriminated against practising Catholics—and quite rightly. He wouldn't otherwise have had 14 per cent of housewives voting Communist in the 1940s. This changed the character of the Italian Communist Party from being a Leninist vanguard party to a mass class party or people's party.

On the other hand, it's true that religion has ceased to be the universal language of public discourse; and to this extent, secularization has been a global phenomenon, even though it has only undercut organized religion severely in some parts of the world. In Europe, it's still doing so; why this hasn't occurred in the United States isn't so clear, but there's no question that secularization has taken hold to a large degree among intellectuals and others who don't need religion. For people who continue to be religious, the fact that there are now two languages of discourse produces a sort of schizophrenia, which you can see quite often, say, in fundamentalist Jews in the West Bank—they believe in what is patently baloney, but work as experts in IT. The present Islamist movement is largely composed of young technologists and technicians of this kind. Religious practices no doubt will change very substantially. Whether that actually produces a further secularization isn't clear. For instance, I don't know how far the major change in the Catholic religion in the West— namely, the refusal of women to abide by the sexual rules—has actually made Catholic women believers to a lesser extent.

The decline of the Enlightenment ideologies, of course, has left far more political scope for religious politics and religious versions of national-ism. But I don't think there has been a major rise in all religions. Many are clearly on the way down. Roman Catholicism is fighting very hard, even in Latin America, against the rise of evangelical Protestant sects, and I'm sure it's only maintaining itself in Africa by concessions to local habits and customs which I doubt would have been made in the nine-teenth century. Evangelical Protestant sects are rising, but to what extent they are more than a small minority of the upwardly mobile—as noncon-formists used to be in England—is not clear. It's also not apparent that Jewish fundamentalism, which does such harm in Israel, is a mass phe-nomenon. The one exception to this trend is Islam, which has continued to expand without any effective missionary activity over the past few cen-turies. Within Islam, it's unclear whether tendencies such as the present militant movement for restoring the caliphate represent more than an activist minority. Islam, however, does seem to me to have great assets for continuing to expand—largely because it gives poor people the sense that they're as good as anybody else and that all Muslims are equal.

Couldn't the same be said of Christianity?

But a Christian doesn't believe that he's as good as any other Christian. I doubt whether Christian blacks believe that they're as good as Christian colonizers, whereas Muslim blacks do. The structure of Islam is more egalitarian and the militant element is rather stronger there. I remem-ber reading that slave-traders in Brazil stopped importing Muslim slaves because they kept rebelling. From where we stand, there are consider-able dangers in this appeal—to some extent Islam makes the poor less receptive to other appeals for equality. Progressives in the Muslim world knew from the start that there was no way of shifting the masses away from Islam; even in Turkey they had to come to some kind of *modus vivendi*—probably the only place where this was successfully done.

Elsewhere the rise of religion as an element in politics, in nationalist politics, has been extremely dangerous. In places like India, it has been a very strong middle-class phenomenon, and all the more alarming because linked with militant and quasi-fascist elites and organizations such as the RSS, and therefore more easily mobilized as an anti-Muslim movement. Fortunately, the upper-class secularization of Indian politics has so far blocked its advance. Not that India's elite is anti-religious; but the basic idea of Nehru was a secular state in which religion is obviously omnipresent—nobody in India could suppose otherwise, or would necessarily want it to be otherwise—but it is limited by the supremacy of the values of the secular civil society.

Science formed a central part of the culture of the left before the Second World War, but over the next two generations it virtually disappeared as a leading element in Marxist or socialist thinking. Do you think that the growing salience of environmental issues is likely to rejoin science and radical politics?

I'm sure radical movements will be interested in science. The environment and other concerns produce sound reasons for countering the flight from science, and from the rational approach to problems, which became fairly widespread from the 70s and 80s. But with regard to the scientists themselves, I don't believe it will happen. Unlike social scientists, there is nothing which edges natural scientists towards politics. Historically speaking, they have in most cases either been non-political or had the standard politics of their class. There are exceptions—say, among the young in early nineteenth-century France, and very notably in the 1930s and 1940s. But these are special cases, due to the recognition by scientists themselves that their work was becoming increasingly essential to society, but that society didn't realize it. The crucial work on this is Bernal's *The Social Function of Science*, which had an enormous effect on other scientists. Of course, Hitler's deliberate attack on everything that science stood for helped.

In the twentieth century, the physical sciences were the centre of development, whereas in the twenty-first century it's clearly the biological sciences which are. Because these are closer to human life, there may be a greater element of politicization. But there is certainly one counter-factor: increasingly, scientists have been integrated into the system of capitalism, both as individuals and within scientific organizations. Forty years ago it would have been unthinkable for somebody to speak of patenting a gene. Today one patents a gene in hopes of becoming a millionaire, and that has removed quite a large body of scientists from left politics. The one thing which may still politicize them is the struggle against dictatorial or authoritarian governments which interfere with their work. One of the most interesting phenomena in the Soviet Union was that Soviet scientists were forced to become politicized, because they were given the privilege of a certain degree of citizen rights and freedoms—so that people who otherwise had been nothing except loyal manufacturers of H-bombs became dissident leaders. It is not impossible for this to occur in other countries, though there aren't very many at the moment. Of course, the environment is an issue which may keep a number of scientists mobilized. If there is a massive development of campaigns around climate change, then clearly the experts will find themselves engaged, largely against know-nothings and reactionaries. So all is not lost.

Turning to historiographical questions: what originally drew you to the subject-matter of archaic forms of social movement in Primitive Rebels, *and how far did you plan for it in advance?*

It developed out of two things. Travelling around Italy in the 1950s, I kept discovering these aberrant phenomena—Party branches in the South electing Jehovah's Witnesses as Party secretaries, and so on; people who were thinking about modern problems, but not in the terms that we were used to. Second, particularly after 1956, it expressed a general dissatisfaction with the simplified version we had of the development of working-class popular movements. In *Primitive Rebels*, I was very far from critical of the standard reading—on the contrary, I pointed out that these other movements would not get anywhere unless they sooner or later adopted the modern vocabulary and institutions. But, nonetheless, it became clear to me that it wasn't enough simply to neglect these other phenomena, to say that we know how all these things operate. I produced a series of illustrations, case studies, of this kind, and said, 'these don't fit'. It led me to think that, even before the invention of modern political vocabulary, methods and institutions, there were ways in which people practised politics that encompassed basic ideas about social relations—not least between the powerful and the weak, rulers and ruled—which had a certain logic and fitted together. But I didn't really have a chance to follow this up any further, although later, reading Barrington Moore's *Injustice,* I found a clue as to how one might be able to get at it. It was the beginning of something that was never really carried on, and I rather regret it. I'm still hoping to try and do something about it.

In Interesting Times, *you expressed considerable reservations about what were then recent historical fashions. Do you think the historiographic scene remains relatively unchanged?*

I'm increasingly impressed by the scale of the intellectual shift in history and the social sciences from the 70s on. My generation of historians, who on the whole transformed the teaching of history as well as a good deal else, were essentially trying to establish a permanent liaison, a mutual fertilization, between history and the social sciences; an effort that dated back to the 1890s. Economics went down a different road. We took it for granted that we were talking about something real: objective realities; even though, ever since Marx and the sociology of knowledge, we knew that one didn't simply record the truth as it was. But what was really interesting were social transformations. The Depression was instrumental in this, because it reintroduced the part played by great crises in historical transformations—the fourteenth-century crisis, the transition to capitalism. It wasn't actually Marxists who introduced this—it was Wilhelm Abel, in Germany, who first reread the developments of the Middle Ages in light of the Great Depression of the 1930s. We were a problem-solving lot, concerned with the big questions. There were other things we downgraded: we were so against traditionalist, top people's history, or for that matter history of ideas, that we rejected all that. It was not a particularly Marxist position—this was a general approach adopted by Weberians in Germany; by people in France who had no Marxist background, who came from the *Annales* school; and, in their own way, by American social scientists.

At some stage in the 70s, there was a sharp change. *Past & Present* published an exchange between myself and Lawrence Stone in 1979–80 on the 'revival of narrative'—'what's happening to the great *why* questions?' Since then, the big, transformative questions have generally been forgotten by historians. At the same time, there was a huge expansion of the range of history—you could now write on anything you wanted: objects, sentiments, practices. Some of this was interesting, but there was also an enormous increase in what you might call fanzine history, which groups write in order to feel better about themselves. The intention was trivial; the results were not always trivial. Just the other day

I noticed a new labour history journal which has an article on blacks in Wales in the eighteenth century. Whatever the importance of this to blacks in Wales, it is not in itself a particularly central subject. The most dangerous instance of this, of course, is the rise of national mythology, a by-product of the multiplication of new states, which had to create their own national histories. A large element in all this is people saying, we're not interested in what happened, but in what makes us feel good. The classical example is that of the Native Americans who refused to believe that their ancestors had migrated from Asia, and said, 'We've always been here'.

A good deal of this shift was in some sense political. The historians who came out of 68 were no longer interested in the big questions—they thought they'd all been answered. They were much more interested in the voluntary or personal aspects. *History Workshop* was a late development of this kind. I don't think the new types of history have produced any dramatic changes. In France, for instance, history post-Braudel is not a patch on the generation of the 1950s and 1960s. There may be the occasional very good work, but it's not the same. And I'm inclined to think the same is true of Britain. There was an element of anti-rationalism and relativism in this reaction of the 1970s, which on the whole I found was hostile to history.

On the other hand, there have been some positive developments. The most positive one was cultural history, which unquestionably we had all neglected. We didn't pay enough attention to history as it actually presents itself to the actors. We had assumed that you could generalize about actors; but if you go back to saying that men make their history, how do they make it, in their practices, in their lives? Eric Wolf's book, *Europe and the People without History*, is an example of a good change in this regard. There has also been an enormous rise in global history. Among non-historians, there has been a great deal of interest in general history—namely, how the human race started. Thanks to DNA research, we now know a good deal about the settlement of humans across the globe. In other words, we have a genuine basis for a world history. Among historians, there has been a break with the Eurocentric or Occidentalocentric tradition. Another positive development, largely from the Americans and partly also the postcolonial historians, has been the reopening of the question of the specificity of European or Atlantic civilization, and of the rise of capitalism—Pomeranz's *The Great*

Divergence and so on. That seems to me very positive, even though there is no denying that modern capitalism arose in parts of Europe, and not in India or China.

If you were to pick still unexplored topics or fields presenting major challenges for future historians, what would they be?

The big problem is a very general one. By palaeontological standards the human species has transformed its existence at astonishing speed, but the rate of change has varied enormously. Sometimes it has moved very slowly, sometimes very fast, sometimes controlled, sometimes not. Clearly this implies a growing control over nature, but we should not claim to know whither this is leading us. Marxists have rightly focused on changes in the mode of production and their social relations as the generators of historical change. However, if we think in terms of how 'men make their own history', the great question is this: historically, communities and social systems have aimed at stabilization and reproduction, creating mechanisms to keep at bay disturbing leaps into the unknown. Resistance to the imposition of change from outside is still a major factor in world politics today. How is it, then, that humans and societies structured to resist dynamic development come to terms with a mode of production whose essence is endless and unpredictable dynamic development? Marxist historians might profitably investigate the operations of this basic contradiction between the mechanisms bringing about change and those geared to resist it.

Architecture | Art | Media | Politics

Grey Room

Editors: Karen Beckman, Branden W. Joseph, Reinhold Martin, Tom McDonough, and Felicity D. Scott

Grey Room joins scholarly and theoretical articles from the fields of architecture, art, media, and politics to forge a unique, cross-disciplinary discourse.

SPECIAL ISSUE #39: WALTER BENJAMIN'S MEDIA TACTICS: OPTICS, PERCEPTION, AND THE WORK OF ART

MIT Press Journals
238 Main Street, Suite 500
Cambridge, MA 02142
tel: 617-253-2889
toll-free US/Canada: 800-207-8354
fax: 617-577-1545
http://mitpressjournals.org/greyroom

NEW LEFT REVIEW
Index of Articles and Authors

1960–2010

Visit www.newleftreview.org for details

ROBIN BLACKBURN

STATE OF THE UNION

Marx and America's Unfinished Revolution

OWARDS THE CLOSE of the American Civil War Friedrich Engels wrote to Joseph Weydemeyer with the following prophecy: 'Once slavery, the greatest shackle on the political and social development of the United States, has been broken, the country is bound to receive an impetus from which it will acquire quite a different position in world history within the shortest possible time, and a use will then soon be found for the army and navy with which the war is providing it.'[1] Northern capitalism did indeed receive great impetus from the War, after which it embarked on headlong continental expansion. For three decades this proved to be such an absorbing task that little was done to project US power outside its own borders. William Seward, Secretary of State under Lincoln and then Johnson, wanted Caribbean acquisitions but the Radical Republicans were not interested. Troops were sent to repress the resistance of the Sioux and Apache, Alaska bought, and steps taken to modernize the navy; but for a generation the terrible losses of the Civil War bequeathed a great distrust of military adventures. The main issues in contention were, instead, three intimately interlinked processes that were of supreme interest to Marx and Engels: the advance of capitalism in North America, the unfolding of an epic class struggle and the progress made towards building a genuine workers' party. The outcome of this mighty contest was to determine the possibility, timing and character of any US bid for empire.

In the post-Civil War era the recently reunited United States was the most dynamic and soon largest capitalist state in the world. No country illustrated Marx's ideas with greater precision. Great railroads spanned the continent, vast factories sprouted up producing steel, agricultural machinery, sewing machines. The emancipation of nearly four million slaves, the demobilization of a million and a half soldiers, and the arrival of a stream of new immigrants swelled the size of the most diverse labouring class in the world. Marx predicted that capitalist conditions would gener- ate class conflict as workers were brought into contact with one another and discovered their common condition. While they might at first fol- low their employers, workers' attempts to acquire security and improved pay or conditions would repeatedly bring labour into conflict with them. This would teach the workers the need to organize and seek political representation. And since capitalism would create wealth at one pole and misery at another, and since it would be gripped by recurrent crises, the workers would be drawn to support increasingly radical measures.

'After the Civil War phase the United States are only now really entering the revolutionary phase', Marx wrote to Engels in April 1866.[2] The two men clearly expected more from the victory of the Union than the end- ing of slavery, momentous as that was. They also expected the producers to assert new political and social rights. If the freedmen moved simply from chattel slavery to wage slavery, if they were denied the right to vote, or organize, or receive education, then the term 'emancipation' would be a mockery. As it turned out, the era of Reconstruction did indeed bring a radical surge in both South and North, with the Republican Party seeking to keep abreast of events by adopting the ideas of radical abo- litionists, black as well as white, and with pressure being exerted by a shifting coalition of labour unions, social reformers, African-American conventions, feminists and, last but not least, the multiplying American sections of the International Workingmen's Association.

The post-Civil War radicalization in North America in some ways may be compared with the British experience of slave emancipation and political reform in the 1830s. In both countries abolitionism and the 'free labour' doctrine seemed at one moment to consecrate wage labour and its central role within capitalism, only to give rise to popular movements— Chartism in Britain, a wave of class struggles and popular radicalism in the US—which challenged the given form of the bourgeois order. While the banner of free labour expressed bourgeois hegemony at one moment, it furnished a means of mobilizing against it at another. In one

---

[1] Friedrich Engels to Joseph Weydemeyer, 24 November 1864.
[2] Marx and Engels, *The Civil War in the United States*, New York 1961, p. 277.

register the ideal of free labour encouraged the aspiration of workers to become independent small producers, with their own workshop or farm. Hence the Republican slogan 'free soil, free labour, free men' and its embodiment in the Homestead Act of 1862.[3] But in the United States of the 1860s and 1870s, as in the Britain of the 1840s, there were increasing numbers of wage workers who did not want to become farmers and who looked to a collective improvement in the rights of working people.[4] Of course some workers did take up the offer of land, but many realized that this could prove a trap. Already by the late 1860s the farmers' Grange movement was attacking exorbitant railroad freight rates and cut-throat competition from large producers.

The Gilded Age, with its robber-baron capitalists and titanic labour conflicts, served as a laboratory test for Marx's ideas, and it vindicated many of them. But, despite several attempts, no broad-based working-class party emerged in the United States, and the country proved a laggard in developing a welfare state. In these respects much greater progress was made in Europe, especially in Marx's native Germany, where the rise of a Social Democratic Party inspired by Marx's ideas persuaded the German Chancellor, Otto von Bismarck, to begin construction of a social security system. In what follows, I will look at the tremendous opportunities and challenges which Reconstruction, dubbed by Eric Foner 'America's unfinished revolution', bequeathed to Marx and the supporters of the International in the United States.[5]

Reconstruction

Marx had observed that labour in the white skin would not be truly free so long as labour in the black skin was in chains. This should be understood as a complex sociological proposition as much as a simple moral statement. The Thirteenth Amendment (1865) abolishing slavery in the

---

[3] The classic study of the free-labour doctrine is Eric Foner, *Free Soil, Free Labor, Free Men: The Ideology of the Republican Party Before the Civil War*, New York 1970.

[4] David Montgomery takes a sample of over seventy labour organizers of the later 1860s about whom information is available and finds that most of them were second-generation wage workers, with about half of them being British immigrants. Their efforts focused not on acquiring land but on regulating the conditions of labour and securing political and industrial representation for the working man. Montgomery, *Beyond Equality: Labor and the Radical Republicans, 1862–1872*, New York 1967, pp. 197–229.

[5] Foner, *Reconstruction: America's Unfinished Revolution, 1863–1877*, New York 1988.

United States ended a formal legal status that was already crumbling because of massive slave desertions, the Emancipation Proclamation and deep, disruptive inroads by the Union armies. The greater part of the Confederate forces melted away, and the planter class reeled from its spectacular defeat. But paradoxically local white power emerged in some ways stronger in the post-bellum era than before. Alarmed at the sight of free black people, former Confederate officers and men formed militia and patrols designed to defend white families from luridly imagined threats, to deny land or hunting to the freedmen and to ensure that they were still available for work. The new President in Washington shared and condoned this Southern white reaction, issuing thousands of pardons to Confederate officials. On 15 July 1865 Engels wrote to Marx attacking President Johnson: 'His hatred of Negroes comes out more and more violently . . . If things go on like this, in six months all the old villains of secession will be sitting in Congress at Washington. Without coloured suffrage nothing whatever can be done there.'[6]

The Republican Radicals in Congress narrowly failed to impeach Lincoln's successor but imposed much of their own vision of Reconstruction—including votes for the freedmen—on the former slave states, thanks to the presence of Union troops and to the emergence of Union Leagues drawing support from the freedmen and from Southern whites who resented the power of the planters. Nevertheless armed white vigilantes still lurked in the shadows and mounted attacks after dark.[7]

As the Northern public became aware of the new President's gross indulgence of traitors and of the planters' resort to violence in their attempt to rebuild a coercive labour regime, support for the Radicals grew. Northern outrage at the presidential pardons and at the vicious racial revanchism of the Ku Klux Klan and kindred groups led the Congressional Republican majority to support more radical measures and propose extending the vote to the freedmen of the South. The enfranchisement of black males was promoted by the Reconstruction Acts of 1867–68 and the Fourteenth (1868) and Fifteenth (1870) Amendments. In 1866–68 the Radical Republicans managed to overrule the President on key issues, and they retained some leverage in 1868 by endorsing General Ulysses S. Grant,

---

[6] Marx and Engels, *The Civil War in the United States*, pp. 276–7.
[7] Foner, *Reconstruction*; and William McKee Evans, *Open Wound: The Long View of Race in America*, Urbana, IL 2009, pp. 147–74. See also David Roediger, *How Race Survived US History*, London and New York 2008, pp. 99–135.

the Union commander, as the Republican candidate in the presidential election. The new President gave his backing to a Republican strategy of restoring some of the sanctions on former Confederate officials and obliging the reconstructed states to give freedmen the vote as the price of re-entry to the Union.

Reconstruction set out to make freedom and equality more tangible, and for a while succeeded in curbing white terror and promoting black representation and equality. In Louisiana attempts had been made to segregate public space and means of transport. The state's 1868 Constitutional Convention asserted the novel concept of 'public rights', which would give equal access to public space. The Constitution's Bill of Rights declared that all citizens of the state should enjoy 'the same civil, political and public rights and privileges, and be subject to the same pains and penalties'. The concept was clarified by a prohibition of racial discrimination on public transport, and in places of public resort or accommodation. Rebecca Scott contrasts this clear requirement with the 'oblique language' of the Fourteenth Amendment.[8]

Many abolitionists and Radical Republicans believed that the suppression of slavery was not enough and that the freedmen deserved at least free education, and preferably land and the vote as well. In this situation it was important that some Union Leagues were responsive to abolitionist appeals and that a convention of 144 black men from 18 states met in Syracuse, NY in October 1864. The Syracuse convention, and subsequent gatherings in Charleston and New Orleans, framed a broad programme for equal civic and political rights. Many of the participants in these events were already free before the War. They articulated the aspirations of black communities in Louisiana, the South Carolina islands and Tennessee—areas occupied by Union forces long before the final collapse. The African-American leaders argued that black soldiers had earned citizenship by helping to save the Union. They also paid their taxes and therefore deserved representation. At Syracuse, Charleston and elsewhere the call was not simply for rights in the abstract but for tangible expressions of a new status—the right to vote and serve on juries, and a Homestead Act for the South that would give land to the freedmen. A 'Declaration of Rights and Wrongs' adopted at both Syracuse and Charleston warned that measures favourable to the freedmen would

---

[8] Rebecca Scott, *Degrees of Freedom: Louisiana and Cuba after Slavery*, Cambridge, MA 2005, pp. 43–5.

be a hollow mockery if planters were still at liberty to intimidate and dragoon them.[9]

With Union soldiers on call, the freedmen voted in new officials and sent black Representatives and Senators to Washington. The Reconstruction administrations fostered a variety of social programmes. Lasting for between four and ten years, the Reconstruction regimes saw many black elected officials, both locally and in Washington. As Eric Foner explains, the Reconstruction governments were innovative: 'Public schools, hospitals, penitentiaries, and asylums for orphans and the insane were established for the first time or received increased funding. South Carolina funded medical care for poor citizens and Alabama funded free legal counsel for indigent defendants.'[10] With some charitable assistance, the Reconstruction administrations laid the basis for an educational system that comprised university colleges as well as high schools open to the freed-people and their descendants. But the empowerment of the freedmen was carried through in the teeth of fierce resistance from white 'rifle clubs', the Ku Klux Klan and similar organizations. The Northern public was disturbed by the white terror and murderous 'race riots', but it had little patience for the heavy costs of an extended occupation and was demoralized by reports of carpet-bagger corruption. As the size of the Union occupation forces was continuously whittled down, white vigilantism was emboldened. Some attempts were made in South Carolina to defend Reconstruction by relying on local mixed militia, but eventually in the key states the Republican governors relied on Federal troops.[11] The deadlocked presidential election of 1876 led to a deal whereby the Republican went to the White House but the Federal Army was withdrawn from the South. The last Reconstruction governments collapsed, to be replaced by white 'Redeemers'.

New voices

During the heyday of Radical Reconstruction, Northern white working men also made important strides forward. Whereas the freed-people were in a struggle for the control of space, both public and private, the Northern workers sought to control time. In this industrializing

---

[9] Steven Hahn, *A Nation under Our Feet: Black Political Struggles in the Rural South from Slavery to the Great Migration*, Cambridge, MA 2003, pp. 103–5.

[10] Foner, *Reconstruction*, p. 364.

[11] Hahn, *A Nation under Our Feet*, pp. 302–13.

era the average working day was over eleven hours. In 1868 Congress was persuaded to establish an eight-hour legal working day for Federal employees. Eight states had similar laws though implementation was weak. Radical Reconstruction also favoured the first attempts to regulate the railroads. The stirrings of a new social utopianism and a very practical trade-union movement were encouraged by the polarizations around Radical Republicanism. Wendell Phillips led prominent abolitionists and some—but by no means all—Radicals in supporting Eight-Hour Leagues. In demanding the eight-hour day the 'labour reformers' were accepting 'clock time' and a degree of labour discipline as part of a wider scheme of improvement. Starting from free-labour principles Ira Steward argued that shorter hours meant higher pay and that higher pay would combat unemployment. As he bluntly put it, 'new employments depend upon a more expensive style of living'.[12]

In 1866 a National Labor Union was formed to spread the eight-hour day demand. At its first national meeting the NLU declared: 'The National Labor Union knows no north, no south, no east, no west, neither colour nor sex, on the question of the rights of labour.'[13] Some blacks joined the movement. The *New Orleans Tribune*, published by black journalists, supported the eight-hour movement, and a State Labor Convention in South Carolina called for a nine-hour day. A Colored Workers' Convention in Washington in 1869 sought to build a bridge between organized labour and the freedmen. The mining districts of Tennessee were to be one of the few areas of the South where labour organizers made some headway, sometimes bringing together white and black workers.[14]

The North American Central Committee of the International Workingmen's Association was founded in May 1871. Marx and his followers had moved the IWA's headquarters to New York following the European panic occasioned by the Paris Commune. This is often seen as a ploy by Marx and his followers to prevent the IWA falling into anarchist hands. No doubt there is truth in this. Yet there was indeed, as Marx claimed, a promising opening in the United States in which the

[12] Quoted in David Roediger and Philip Foner, *Our Own Time: A History of American Labor and the Working Day*, London and New York 1989, p. 85.
[13] Quoted in Timothy Messer-Kruse, *The Yankee International: Marxism and the American Reform Tradition, 1846–1876*, Chapel Hill, NC 1998, p. 191.
[14] Karin Shapiro, *A New South Rebellion: The Battle Against Convict Labor in the Tennessee Coalfields, 1871–1896*, Chapel Hill, NC 1998.

International could begin to sink real roots in North America. By the early 1870s the IWA had fifty sections in a dozen urban areas, ranging from Boston and New York to San Francisco and Chicago. An African-American militia in New York was said to have affiliated to the International, but no such developments were possible in the South. A section of the International played a lead role in the first city-wide general strike, organized in St Louis in 1877.[15]

Some leading female abolitionists declined to support the Fourteenth Amendment on the ground that, while promoting the enfranchisement of black men, it left women without the vote.[16] This was an argument about priorities since nearly all abolitionists supported female suffrage. The great majority of abolitionists insisted that there were exceptional arguments for black male enfranchisement. The fact that African-Americans had risked their lives for the Union carried great weight with Northern voters, making it an immediately practical proposal.[17] Furthermore the black communities were more vulnerable to physical attack than white women, giving the former a greater claim to priority. Indeed, even with the vote, the difficulty of defending black communities in the South was to prove very great. However, these unhappy disputes did not prevent new attempts in the 1870s to explore the making of a progressive coalition, including female suffrage.

The appearance of the labour movements encouraged the view that a fresh start could be made in the 1870s, with the emergence of new issues and voices. Racism, sexism and conscious, or unconscious, bourgeois ideology continued to hold much of the population in thrall and to

[15] David Burbank, *Reign of the Rabble: The St Louis General Strike of 1877*, New York 1966.
[16] See Angela Davis, *Women, Race and Class*, New York 1981, pp. 30–86.
[17] Robert Dykstra shows that military service was a trump card in the debate over enfranchising black men in Iowa. See Dykstra, *Bright Radical Star: Black Freedom and White Supremacy on the Hawkeye Frontier*, Cambridge, MA 1993. Women had been lauded for their contribution to the war as nurses and home-makers but the passage from this to enfranchisement proved more difficult. See also the introductions to Elizabeth Cady Stanton and Susan B. Anthony, *Correspondence, Writings, Speeches*, edited by Ellen Dubois, New York 1981, pp. 92–112, 166–9. Dubois argues that both women were, in different ways, both trying to adapt the women's movement to the need for wider alliances. While Anthony drew on 'free labour' ideology to criticize women's dependence, Stanton sketched the programmatic basis for an alliance between the women's and labour movements.

weaken progressive movements. But much more remarkable than this predictable state of affairs was the emergence of challenges to racism, including institutional racism, to male privilege in the home and workplace as well as ballot box, and to the divine right of employers to dictate to their employees and to accumulate vast personal fortunes.

For a brief span—about half a dozen years—the US sections of the IWA became the sounding board and banner for a diverse series of radical initiatives after the International itself had been formally dissolved. The IWA and the NLU were seen as sister organizations. The German-American Marxists wielded what was then a very novel doctrine—the idea that if labour was only sufficiently well-organized it would become a mighty lever for social advance, opening the way for all sections of the oppressed. The privileges of white and male workers were not addressed and all attention was focused on the great concentration of privilege represented by capital. In theory female and black workers were welcome to join the workers' organizations and would enjoy equal rights within them, though the practice often lagged behind. Some of the IWA's US sections developed a primitive and sectarian Marxism that contrasts with the programme and practice of the German Social Democratic Party. Marx and Engels themselves were often uneasy at the narrow-mindedness of their American followers, but they were partly responsible for this, since they had not yet developed a conception of the different character and goals of trade unions, on the one hand, and political parties, on the other.

The fact that the International embraced, or mixed, both types of organization was no bad thing, but because there had been no theorization of their distinct and different purposes there was often confusion and tension. There was also a dilemma posed by the scope for social alliances. The workers needed to organize themselves as a distinct body, yet they also needed to reach out to potential allies—farmers, farm labourers, progressive members of the middle class, home workers—on a range of issues. The implicit labour metaphysic of some of the German-American Marxists failed to tackle these issues. However, in the short run the International actually thrived by avoiding a clear stance on such questions and simply allowing each section to organize in its own way and according to its own priorities. The German-American Marxists might have been narrow-minded, but they were committed to the ideals of racial and gender equality, albeit that they soft-pedalled these issues when seeking to recruit *bona fide* wage workers who did not share such principled commitments, arguing that it would be easier to educate them once they had joined the IWA.

Rights of all living things

The IWA became a rallying point for many of the disparate forces of emancipation seeking to take part in the reconstruction of the social order. It attracted the attention of Victoria Woodhull—in some ways the Arianna Huffington of the 1870s—who edited the widely selling and much-discussed *Woodhull & Claflin's Weekly*, and used it to publicize the initiatives of the IWA. In 1870 and 1871 the *Weekly* published several articles summarizing the *Communist Manifesto* and explaining the documents of the IWA. It exposed the schemes of the railway promoters and argued that the greed of the owners of the Staten Island ferry led them to skimp on safety, leading to a disaster in which a hundred passengers perished. An editorial explained: 'This is the age of rights when, for the first time in human history, the rights of all living things are, in some way, recognized as existing. We are far enough yet from according to all their rights, but we talk about them, we see them, and thought is busy to determine how best they should be secured.'[18]

A series of articles entitled 'Man's Rights, or How Would You Like It?' explored the idea of women taking leading positions in economic affairs while it was the turn of men to be 'housekeepers and kitchen girls'.[19] Other articles sought to reconcile a needed collectivism with the rights of the individual. The banks and the corporations should be taken into truly public ownership, and democratic institutions should ensure 'the personal participation of each in the preparation, administration and execution of the laws by which all are governed'. But the state should not seek to prescribe how people lived: 'Social freedom means the absolute immunity from impertinent intrusion in all affairs of exclusively personal concernment, such as scientific or religious belief, the sexual relationship, habits of dress, diet or the like.'[20] With her sister Tennie Claflin, Woodhull was the founder of Wall Street's first female brokerage, and used her rewards from this to finance the *Weekly*, 'the lady broker's

[18] 'The Rights of Children', *Woodhull & Claflin's Weekly*, 6 December 1870.
[19] 'Man's Rights, or How Would You Like It?', *Woodhull & Claflin's Weekly*, 8 September 1870.
[20] 'The International: Appeal of Section No. 12', *Woodhull & Claflin's Weekly*, 23 September 1871.

paper'. Eclectic, literate and radical, the *Weekly*'s lively interest in social-ism and new forms of collective self-government led it to publish a special edition of Marx's *Address on the Civil War in France*. Marx wrote a friendly note to Woodhull and suggested that his daughter Jenny could supply an article on her experiences in France following the suppression of the Paris Commune in 1871.[21]

In Europe respectable opinion was outraged by the supposed excesses of the Paris Commune. But in the United States the bloody suppression of the Commune provoked sympathy for its victims. Marx's *Civil War in France* was widely read by reformers and radicals. The IWA mustered a demonstration of 70,000 or more in New York in December 1871 to pay tribute to the Commune's tens of thousands of martyrs. The parade brought together the Skidmore Guards (a black militia), the female leadership of Section 12 (Woodhull and Claflin), an Irish band, a range of trade unions, supporters of Cuba's fight for independence march-ing under the Cuban flag, and a broad spectrum of socialist, feminist, Radical and Reform politics. In its aftermath Section 12, and its support-ers within a new reform body, the Equal Rights Convention, proposed running a ticket in the forthcoming presidential election, with Victoria Woodhull and Frederick Douglass as the candidates. For a brief moment an attempt was made to present a progressive alternative in the 1872 elections, but it passed.[22]

Many of Marx's US followers distrusted Woodhull. She was the President of the American Association of Spiritualists and her Wall Street broker-age had the support of Cornelius Vanderbilt, the richest man in America. The IWA Council declared that wage-earners should comprise at least 66 per cent of the membership in all sections. Section 12 was suspended for failing to reach this figure. The inability to distinguish between trade union and party was part of the problem here. So too was the concep-tion that workers' interests were somehow natural and sociologically

---

[21] Unfortunately this cordial tone was not maintained. Marx casually refers to Woodhull as 'a banker's woman, free lover and general humbug' in a later text; so far as sexual matters were concerned, Marx, the likely father of Frederick Demuth, was more deserving of the term 'humbug' than Woodhull. Messer-Kruse, *Yankee International*, p. 171.

[22] The classic survey of this moment is Montgomery, *Beyond Equality*, with the IWA discussed on pp. 414–21. See also Samuel Bernstein, *The First International in America*, New York 1962; and Herbert Gutman, *Work, Culture and Society in Industrializing America*, Oxford 1976, pp. 293–343.

given without benefit of ideology or politics. The sectarian exclusion of Section 12 weakened the International, though in the short run the dissension it aroused was eclipsed when Woodhull and her *Weekly* became embroiled in an unrelated obscenity suit which briefly led to her imprisonment and prevented her from developing her political profile. Her uncompromising attacks on sexual prudery led mainstream feminists and spiritualists, as well as socialists, to take their distance from her.[23]

Party vs union?

There was to be a legacy of distrust and factional strife between those of Marx's German-American followers who believed that party building was the priority and others who saw the trade unions as the first task. The huge mid-century German immigration had had a transformative impact on American culture, as Bruce Levine shows in *The Spirit of 1848*. At a time when immigration was rising to new heights, Germans comprised roughly half of all newcomers, many of them radicalized by the experiences of 1848. With their breweries, beer gardens, musical concerts and *Turnvereine* (exercise clubs), the German radicals had furnished a strong secular current of anti-slavery before the Civil War. The more radical among them supported women's rights and suffrage: Mathilde Anneke published a German-language women's paper, while Margarethe Schurz was influential in the introduction of public kindergartens.[24]

In the 1870s, both 'Yankee' and German Internationalists deplored racial violence and supported female enfranchisement, but the trade unionists

---

[23] Amanda Frisken, *Victoria Woodhull's Sexual Revolution*, Philadelphia 2004.
[24] The founding statement of the American Workers League (*Amerikanische Arbeiterbund*) drafted by Weydemeyer and others in 1853 had declared that 'all workers who live in the United States without distinction of occupation, language, colour or sex can become members.' Today such a formula sounds entirely conventional, but in the 1850s it was very fresh. Bruce Levine, *The Spirit of 1848: German Immigrants, Labor Conflict and the Coming of the Civil War*, Urbana, IL 1992, p. 125. There was a conservative, familistic formation within early German-American Marxism, sometimes regrettably endorsed by Marx; but the subsequent evolution of the Socialist Labor Party, the main German-American Marxist body, was towards more progressive positions on the 'woman question', as Mari Jo Buhle explains in *Women and American Socialism*, Urbana, IL 1981, pp. 1–48. The change was due both to an influx of women labour activists and to the influence of August Bebel's *Woman Under Socialism* (1879). Bebel, then chairman of the SPD, insisted that Social Democrats should fight for full equality for women, including the vote, and access to equal work at equal pay.

gave low priority to such issues, while many Socialists despised the narrowness and caution of the trade-union leaders. The prize was clear—steps that would lead to the establishment of a farmer–labour party on American soil. Robin Archer has recently shed new light on why this possibility was nipped in the bud. He sees this as happening because of a combination of ferocious repression, socialist sectarianism and the reluctance of workers' organizations to address political questions, since to do so would risk antagonizing the large number of religious workers with their ties to the existing two-party system.[25]

The party system was difficult to beat because it adjusted to the threat of third parties either by stealing their slogans or by ganging up against them—as the Republicans and Democrats did with their joint slate in Illinois in the 1880s. Successful labour leaders were wooed as candidates by the two established parties. But both parties took hand-outs from the robber barons, with state assemblies becoming the pawns of railway promoters and awarding them large tracts of public land in return for kickbacks. The state authorities also frequently used the state militia as strikebreakers. While striking workers sometimes enjoyed public support, the newspapers and middle-class opinion easily turned against them.

From the Great Railroad Strike of 1877 and the Illinois and Pennsylvania miners and steelmen of the 1880s to the Pullman and Homestead strikes of the 1890s, the United States was shaken by epic and desperate industrial struggles. These battles involved tens, sometimes hundreds, of thousands of workers and had no equal in Europe. The Great Strike of 1877 has been described as 'one of the bitterest explosions of class warfare in American history'.[26] It was provoked when the rail companies, responding to the economic crisis, sought to cut wages by 10 per cent. The rail workers had much public sympathy, and the large employers faced labour militancy in mines and steelworks as well as on the railroads. The strikes also tapped into widespread urban unrest. The strike gathered

---

[25] Robin Archer, *Why Is There No Labour Party in the United States?*, Oxford 2008. This carefully researched and argued study is the most provocative work on its theme since Mike Davis, *Prisoners of the American Dream*, London and New York 1985, and extends the latter's comparison of the US and Australia.

[26] Foner, *Reconstruction*, p. 383. For this momentous event see also Robert Bruce, *1877: Year of Violence*, New York 1959 and Philip Foner, *The Great Labor Uprising of 1877*, New York 1977.

momentum because the militia units were loath to threaten lives. One of the militia commanders, Major General Alfred Pearson, explained: 'Meeting an enemy on the field of battle you go there to kill. But here you had men and fathers, and brothers and relatives mingled in the crowd of rioters. The sympathy of the people, the sympathy of the troops, my own sympathy was with the strikers proper. We all felt that these men were not receiving enough wages.'[27]

Just as the withdrawal of Federal troops abandoned the field to semi-private white militias in the South, so the employers in the North were able to pay for thousands, sometimes tens of thousands, of National Guards, specially recruited 'deputy marshals' and Pinkerton men to break the strike which spread until it had national scope.[28] One hundred strikers lost their lives in the course of the struggle. The employers brought in black workers to take their place. Some labour organizers concluded from this that blacks must be welcomed and organized too, but it took time for formal recognition to be translated into practical action.[29]

By the 1880s there were as many as 30,000 Pinkerton men, making them a larger force than the Army of the Republic. The latter's strength had dropped to less than 27,000, with those soldiers not in the West reduced to strikebreaking roles. By 1877 the Democrats were calling for Army strength to be further reduced to no more than 20,000. The robber barons of the North and West, and the planters of the South, had found brutally effective ways to cow the direct producers. Both distrusted the Army and both hated the Federal taxing power. The steep reductions in the Federal military establishment reflected the conviction of many employers in all sections that the Army that stemmed from the Civil War and Reconstruction was not well adapted to enforcing labour discipline. Stephen Skowronek describes the closing decades of the nineteenth century as the epoch of the 'patchwork state' and emphasizes the role of labour struggles in shaping its peculiar formation.[30] While the

---

[27] Quoted in John P. Lloyd, 'The Strike Wave of 1877', in Aaron Brenner, Benjamin Day and Immanuel Ness, eds, *The Encyclopedia of Strikes in American History*, Armonk, NY 2009, p. 183. On subsequent struggles, see Theresa Ann Case, 'Labor Upheavals on the Nation's Railroads, 1877–1922', in this valuable reference work.

[28] Samuel Yellin, *American Labor Struggles, 1877–1934*, New York 1937.

[29] Gutman, *Work, Culture and Society*, pp. 131–208.

[30] Stephen Skowronek, *Building a New American State: The Expansion of National Administrative Capacities, 1877–1920*, Cambridge 1982, pp. 38–84.

ante-bellum regime defended plantations without regulating them, the post-bellum one performed a similar service for the new corporations.

Defeats and triumphs

The double defeat of Reconstruction had suppressed black rights in the South and curtailed labour rights in the North. Jim Crow in the South, and the widespread use of Pinkerton's men and other goons in the North, were both victories for privatized violence and for a minimal view of the state. They were a defeat for the republican ideal of a unified and responsible Federal authority. In the great battles of the 1880s and 1890s hundreds of strikers were killed, thousands imprisoned and tens of thousands blacklisted. These gruelling labour battles are a civilian echo of the Civil War. The railroad corporations sought to cultivate military-style discipline, furnishing their workforce with uniforms and insignia, with a famous general or two on the board.

While there was orchestrated violence in the North it was put into the shade by Jim Crow. From 1884 to 1899, between 107 and 241 blacks were murdered each year by lynch mobs, with total victims numbering over 3,000. Lynchings were concentrated in the South and the great majority targeted blacks, but they were not unknown elsewhere and sometimes targeted white labour organizers, Chinese and Mexicans. Along the Mexican border, dozens of Hispanics were lynched during these years. And there were also lynchings of whites in other parts of the Union, especially the 'wild' West.[31] The intensification of Jim Crow in the South was accompanied by the spread of onerous, if less extreme, practices of racial exclusion in other areas, affecting residence, employment and education.[32]

The freed-people of the South and the labour organizers of the North not only faced physical threats but also found their attempts to organize and negotiate assaulted in the name of the same conservative strain

---

[31] Joel Williamson, *The Crucible of Race: Black–White Relations in the American South since Emancipation*, Oxford 1984, pp. 117–8, 185–9; Ida B. Wells-Barnett, *On Lynchings* (1892), with an introduction by Patricia Hill Collins, Amherst, NY 2002, pp. 201–2.
[32] Desmond King and Stephen Tuck, 'De-Centring the South: America's Nationwide White Supremacist Order after Reconstruction', *Past and Present*, February 2007, pp. 213–53.

in free-labour ideology—that which construed any regulation or combination as a violation of 'freedom of contract'. The Republicans and Democrats deferred to this doctrine and the Supreme Court codified it. These rulings pulverized the workers and sharecroppers, leaving them to negotiate only as individuals.

American social democracy?

Without a political order capable of regulating the employers, the case for a social democratic party was more difficult to make, and to some a syndicalist perspective seemed more realistic. Another obstacle to proposals for a labour party was the fact that the Federal state was fiscally hamstrung, rendering impractical projects for a welfare state. The Union's vast Civil War outlays had been met, in part, by a progressive income tax. This tax had been proposed by Schuyler Colfax, a Radical Republican representative from Indiana, who later served as Grant's Vice President.[33] However, in the early 1870s the income tax was dropped—and then declared unconstitutional by the Supreme Court. The Fourteenth Amendment had promised 'all persons' the equal protection of the laws. While this proved a dead letter so far as the freedmen were concerned, the corporations—who enjoyed the legal status of persons—successfully invoked it against measures of corporate taxation and regulation.

These and other reactionary developments might themselves have increased the willingness of the trade unions to back a labour party. Indeed those trying to organize general or industrial unions aimed at the mass of workers realized that they needed the support of government. But Archer claims that many key craft leaders—especially Samuel Gompers—had greater industrial bargaining power and feared that their organizations might be put at risk if they teamed up with political adventurers.

Several key trade unions had been inspired by the agitation surrounding the IWA and Marx's writings on the importance of the self-organization of workers. A number of US unions were to describe themselves as 'International' organizations—the International Longshoremen or International Garment Workers Union and so forth—echoing the IWA. Sometimes the word 'International' was justified by reference to organizing in Canada, but its resonance also owed something to the

---

[33] W. Elliot Brownlee, *Federal Taxation in America*, Cambridge 1996, p. 26.

IWA. If Marx's followers—many of them German-Americans—can take a share of the credit for the impetus given to trade-union organization they must also accept some of the blame for the failure of the US workers' movement to develop a labour party, and for the related weakness and tardiness of the development of a US welfare state. Indeed some blame the influence of Marx for these failures.[34]

Yet Marx favoured both trade unions and social-democratic or socialist parties in the 1870s, as may readily be seen in the case of Germany. The German SPD was clearly linked to and supportive of organized labour, but its Erfurt programme committed it to revolutionary and demo-cratic objectives, and to immediate reforms. It campaigned for votes for women and the defence of the German forests. It later supported rights for homosexuals and an end to Germany's imperial exploits in Africa, and it debated the 'agrarian question'.[35] The breadth of the SPD's pro-gramme did not, of course, wholly stem from Marx but from several other currents, including that of the Lassalleans. Though Marx had tena-ciously fought against what he saw as Lassalle's misguided belief in the progressive character of the German state, he nevertheless went out of his way to cultivate his acquaintance, gently to warn him of his mistakes and above all to remain in touch with the tens of thousands of German socialists who were influenced by Lassalle.

The programmatic scope of the SPD is not the only evidence of the approach favoured by Marx and Engels. The platform of the French work-ers party was directly inspired by a conversation with Marx. Its very first clause declared that 'the emancipation of the class of producers involves all mankind, without distinction of sex or race.'[36] Other clauses com-mitted the party to universal suffrage and equal pay for equal work. No doubt economism still lurked, but in 1879 it was not such a bad starting point. The counterposing of trade union and political organization as

---

[34] Both Messer-Kruse, *Yankee International* and Archer, *Why Is There No Labour Party in the United States?* come close to this but ultimately concede that there was a large gap on such questions between Marx and those who regarded themselves as his followers in the US, which included Samuel Gompers.

[35] I have a brief discussion of the programmatic ideas of the SPD in 'Fin de Siècle: Socialism After the Crash', NLR 1/185, January–February 1991. For the party's positions on sexuality see David Fernbach, 'Biology and Gay Identity', NLR 1/228, March–April 1998, p. 51.

[36] 'Introduction to the Programme of the French Workers Party', in Marx, *Political Writings*, vol. 3, London 1974, p. 376.

mutually exclusive by supposedly Marxian US Socialists and trade unionists put them at odds with their mentor.

In 1887 Engels paid tribute to the giant strides being made by the
American workers' movement, embracing momentous class battles in
Illinois and Pennsylvania, the spread of the Eight-Hour Leagues, the
growth of the Knights of Labor, the sacrifices that had established May
1st as International Labour Day and the electoral achievements of the
first state-level labour parties.[37] But appreciative as he was, he insisted
that the whole movement would lose its way unless it could develop a
transformative programme: 'A new party must have a distinct platform',
one adapted to American conditions. Without this any 'new party would
have but a rudimentary existence'. However, beyond saying that the
kernel of this programme would have to be public ownership of 'land,
railways, mines, machinery etc', he did not speculate as to what problems that programme should address. Engels rebuked the doctrinaires
of the heavily German-American Socialist Labor Party for their hostility
to unions and failure to grapple with American reality. He urged them to
'doff off every remnant of their foreign garb', 'go to the Americans who
are the vast majority' and 'on all accounts learn English'.[38]

The advice Engels offered, though entirely justified, was also elementary
and even simplistic. Programmatic thinking was not entirely lacking in
the United States, but it was throttled by the given forms of the labour
movement. In many trade unions there was a formal ban on any political discussion, on the grounds that it would prove divisive. The largest
working-class organization, the Noble and Holy Order of the Knights of
Labor, had a similar ban. The Knights of Labor only emerged from clan-
destinity in 1881 and never entirely shook off its roots as a secret society.
Security threats—and its leaders' fears of foreign revolutionaries—
distracted it from public debate of its objectives. The unions and the
Knights made some efforts to organize black and female workers but
had no discussion of how, practically, to advance their rights.[39] Engels's
text was most likely to be read by the members of the Socialist Labor
Party, but he did not go far enough in pressing them to become relevant
to US conditions.

---

[37] Engels, 'Preface to the American Edition', *The Condition of the Working Class in England*, New York 1887.
[38] Engels, 'Preface to the American Edition', p. 14.
[39] Davis, *Prisoners of the American Dream*, pp. 30–1.

Engels's insistence that the US labour party would have to commit itself to nationalization of the railways and steel was timely—and if heeded by some Progressive coalition, public ownership might have averted the disaster awaiting these industries in the twentieth century. His brief list should have included the public ownership of banks, since they were critical to industry and agriculture. His call for the nationalization of land short-circuited the tangled problems of the country's three million farmers and four million tenants and labourers. By the time of the 1870 census there were 4.9 million wage earners, some of them white collar, but the agricultural sector was still very important. The spread of the Farmers' Alliance in the 1880s and 1890s showed the huge scope there was for mobilizing indebted farmers and rack-rented tenants or share-croppers, both black and white. Engels endorsed the idea that a US labour party should aim to win a majority in Congress and elect its candidate to the White House, but without an appeal to farmers, tenants and rural labourers—and much else besides—this was a pipe dream. While Marx and Engels were quite right to shun many of the 'sentimental reform-ers' with their patented cure-alls, some of these individuals focused on critical issues of taxation and banking, or security and democracy. The milieu of labour reformers had identified and skilfully exploited the issue of the eight-hour day, a programmatic demand that had a mobiliz-ing and universalist impulse (though enforcement was often difficult in US conditions). Quaker radicals were later to support Ida B. Wells's campaigns against segregation and lynching.

The London International had cordial relations with Richard Hinton, a labour reformer and organizer of the Washington, DC Section. When the German Marxist leader Friedrich Sorge sought to bring this section under his control, the General Council in London declared that this was going too far and that the Section should run its own affairs. Indeed, the Washington Section refused to back Sorge's expulsion of Section 12. The British-born Hinton was a former companion of John Brown and officer of the First Kansas Coloured Regiment and a man fascinated by Edward Kellogg's plan for a network of public banks and Osborne Ward's propos-als for cooperative agriculture and industry. In late nineteenth-century conditions the smallholder was on a hiding to nothing—cooperatives with some public support could have made a lot of sense. Hinton's Section included many civil servants who would actually have to imple-ment any massive programme of nationalization. They were probably aware that the country only had 60,000 civil servants and any socialist plan would have to stimulate local publicly or socially owned enterprise and bottom-up initiatives.[40] Hinton was later to be associated with Eugene Debs's Socialist Party, as editor of its magazine.

In his survey Engels developed a very polite critique of the ideas of Henry George, even conceding that the land tax might have some role. Another radical taxation proposal that merited examination was Schuyler Colfax's idea of a levy on all shareholding capital. Finally there was the issue of Lincoln's very unfinished revolution in the US South. Prior to the triumph of the ultra-racists in 1900 there were several movements which showed that white and black farmers and labourers could work together—they included the Readjusters, who gained power in Virginia in the late 1870s, the Farmers' Alliance, some branches of Populism and the fusion movement in North Carolina.[41]

In private correspondence Engels had a poor view of the theoretical grasp of the American Marxists and socialists. But within a little more or less than a decade of his death three outstanding works appeared that would very likely have changed his view: Louis Boudin, *The Theoretical System of Karl Marx* (1907); Thorstein Veblen, *The Theory of Business Civilization* (1904) and W. E. B. Du Bois, *The Souls of Black Folk* (1903). The eruption of titanic class struggles also had an impact on currents in US intellectual life far removed from Marxism. Eugene Debs's American Railway Union (ARU) broke with the caution of craft unionism and tried to organize the entire railroad industry. In 1894 the ARU forced major concessions from the Great Northern railroad, and its membership grew to 150,000. However, when the ARU showed that it could paralyse one half of the entire rail network, the Grover Cleveland Administration stepped in to break the strike through injunctions and imprisonment. A conversation with an ARU picket had an electrifying impact on the philosopher John Dewey:

> My nerves were more thrilled than they had been for years; I felt as if I had better resign my job teaching and follow him round til I got into life. One lost all sense of the right and wrong of things in admiration of his absolute almost fanatic sincerity and earnestness, and in admiration of the magnificent combination that was going on. Simply as an aesthetic matter, I don't believe the world has seen but few times such a spectacle of magnificent union of men about a common interest as this strike evinces . . . The govt is

[40] Montgomery, *Beyond Equality*, pp. 387–477.
[41] Evans, *Open Wound*, pp. 175–87.

evidently going to take a hand in it and the men will be beaten almost to a
certainty—but it's a great thing and the beginning of greater.[42]

Eugene Debs was arrested for defying the government injunction and
read Marx's work in jail. Marx's ideas were themselves beginning to
influence the culture of US radicalism just as they were also, in their
turn, shaped by the American experience of robber-baron capitalism and
desperate class struggle. Marx's dark vision clearly supplies the central
themes of Jack London's extraordinarily powerful novel *The Iron Heel*, a
book read by millions in a large number of languages—and a book which,
many claimed, changed their lives. The history of the United States in
the Gilded Age had resonated with such epic class struggles that they
fleshed out the social imaginary of socialists, and other radicals, not just
in North America but in Europe and far beyond—Latin America, Asia
and Africa. The New World had always tapped into European utopian
longings, sometimes accompanied by dystopian fears too. The United
States of the great capitalist trusts, and their Congressional marionettes,
offered an awesome spectacle—but so did the resistance of its workers
and farmers. The international day of the working class, May 1st, after
all memorializes the Haymarket martyrs of May 1886. So just as the US
capitalist, with top hat and cigar, typified the boss class, so the US work-
ingman, with his shirt and jeans or overalls, became the image of the
proletarian. The set-piece battles in industrial America between the two
were typically on a larger scale than European industrial disputes. There
is, of course, irony in the fact that, however iconic, the US worker was
ultimately defeated or contained, while organized labour in Europe and
the Antipodes secured representation and even some social gains.

A factor in the vulnerability of US labour was its failure to live up to
the anti-racial ideals that had been widely proclaimed in the period of
Reconstruction. Employers were often able to exploit and foster racial
antagonism. The more ideological wing of German-American socialism never recanted its commitment to human unity. Even a writer as
critical of the German-American Marxists as Messer-Kruse concedes that
they 'never renounced their devotion to the principle of racial equality',[43]
something which cannot be said of several traditions of Anglo-American

---

[42] Quoted in Louis Menand, *The Metaphysical Club*, New York 2001, p. 295; see also
David Montgomery's Epilogue in Richard Schneirov et al., eds, *The Pullman Strike
and the Crisis of the 1890s*, Urbana, IL 1999, pp. 233–50.
[43] Messer-Kruse, *Yankee International*, p. 188.

socialism. Indeed whatever their other failings, twentieth-century American Marxists, white as well as black, were to make an outstanding contribution to the battle against white racism and for civil rights. No other political current has such an honourable and courageous record.

It remains only to address a final problem. Marx's conception of history bequeathed a theoretical puzzle to later historical materialists—namely, what is the role of the individual in history? Such powerful writers and thinkers as Plekhanov, Deutscher, Sartre and Mandel debated the topic, drawing attention to the fact that even deep-laid historical processes often depend on highly personal capacities and decisions. Via the IWA, Marx had an impact on a generation of American workers and radicals but, despite heroic battles, it proved unable to build a political workers' movement to compare with those in Europe and the Antipodes. Engels was greatly invigorated by his visits to New York and Boston in 1888. This leads me to a final thought. If Marx or Engels had themselves sailed from England to make their home in New York or Chicago, might they have been able to educate their followers and find a more promising path of political development for the American Left?

There is no way of knowing. But if their conduct in Germany in 1848–49, or in the 1860s, is any guide, Marx and Engels might well have helped to consolidate the International's achievements. They would very likely have favoured opening the unions to the generality of workers and they would surely have given exceptional importance to curbing the freelance violence of the Southern 'rifle clubs' and Northern company goons. Marx would have urged workers to develop their own organizations. But, just as he saw the importance of the slavery issue at the start of the Civil War, so he would surely have focused on 'winning the battle of democracy', securing the basic rights of the producers—including the freedmen—in all sections as preparation for an ensuing social revolution. Eschewing reactionary socialism or the counterfeit anti-imperialism of some Southern slaveholders, they would have insisted that only the socialization of the great cartels and financial groups could enable the producers and their social allies to confront the challenges of modernity, and to aspire to a society in which the free development of all is the precondition for the free development of each.

ARENA *journal*

A twice-yearly, internationally oriented scholarly periodical, *Arena Journal* will continue a commitment of the first series of Arena to publishing material which reflects on a renewed left critical practice. It is a place for theoretically and ethically concerned discussion on the prospects for co-operation within contemporary life.

Arena Journal will respond to the challenges of the last twenty years to the 'classical' accounts of social life which have emerged from theories of subjectivity and the sign, challenges which have affected the status of figures such as Marx, Weber and Durkheim, as well as post-classical theorists such as Habermas and Giddens. A central focus of the Journal is upon the interpretive and technical intellectual practices and their relation to the reconstruction of social processes: class relations, forms of selfhood and community life.

ARENA *journal* No. 33/34, 2009
SPECIAL ISSUE: BEING ARAB

Subscribe to *Arena Journal*
Rates (in Australian dollars please)

	1 yr	2 yrs	3 yrs
Individuals	na	40	57
Organization	66	121	176

Overseas: add $14 (air only) per annum

Send to: **Arena Journal**
PO Box 18 North Carlton
Australia 3054
Telephone: 61-3-9416 0232
Fax: 61-3-9416 0684
Email glenise@arena.org.au

STUART HALL

LIFE AND TIMES

OF THE FIRST NEW LEFT

T
HE 'FIRST' NEW LEFT was born in 1956, a conjuncture—not just a year—bounded on one side by the suppression of the Hungarian Revolution by Soviet tanks and on the other by the British and French invasion of the Suez Canal zone.[1] These two events, whose dramatic impact was heightened by the fact that they occurred within days of each other, unmasked the underlying violence and aggression latent in the two systems that dominated political life at the time—Western imperialism and Stalinism—and sent a shock wave through the political world. In a deeper sense, they defined for people of my generation the boundaries and limits of the tolerable in politics. Socialists after 'Hungary', it seemed to us, must carry in their hearts the sense of tragedy which the degeneration of the Russian Revolution into Stalinism represented for the left in the twentieth century. 'Hungary' brought to an end a certain kind of socialist innocence. On the other hand, 'Suez' underlined the enormity of the error in believing that lowering the Union Jack in a few ex-colonies necessarily signalled the 'end of imperialism', or that the real gains of the welfare state and the widening of material affluence meant the end of inequality and exploitation. 'Hungary' and 'Suez' were thus liminal, boundary-marking experiences. They symbolized the break-up of the political Ice Age.

The New Left came into existence in the aftermath of these two events. It attempted to define a third political space somewhere between these two metaphors. Its rise signified for people on the left in my generation the end of the imposed silences and political impasses of the Cold War, and the possibility of a breakthrough into a new socialist project. It may be useful to begin with genealogy. The term 'New Left' is commonly associated with '1968', but to the '1956' New Left generation, '1968' was already a second, even perhaps a third, mutation. We had borrowed the phrase in the 1950s from the movement known as the *nouvelle gauche*, an independent tendency in French politics associated with the weekly newspaper *France Observateur* and its editor, Claude Bourdet. A leading figure in the French Resistance, Bourdet personified the attempt, after the war, to open a 'third way' in European politics, independent of the two dominant left positions of Stalinism and social democracy, beyond the military power blocs of NATO and the Warsaw Pact, and opposed to both the American and the Soviet presences in Europe.

This 'third position' paralleled the political aspirations of many of the people who came together to form the early British New Left. Some of us had met Bourdet in Paris, at a conference called to consider setting up an International Socialist Society, across the divisions of Western and Eastern Europe. The main protagonist of the idea in Britain was G. D. H. Cole, an austere and courageous veteran of the independent left, who was at that time still teaching politics at Oxford. Although he was a distinguished historian of European socialism and a student of Marxism, Cole's socialism was rooted in the cooperative and 'workers' control' traditions of Guild Socialism. His critique of bureaucratic 'Morrisonian'-style nationalization was enormously influential in shaping the attitude of many socialists of my generation towards statist forms of socialism.

The New Left represented the coming together of two related but different traditions—also of two political experiences or generations. One was the tradition I would call, for want of a better term, communist humanism, symbolized by the *New Reasoner* and its founders, John Saville and Edward and Dorothy Thompson. The second is perhaps best described as an independent socialist tradition, whose centre of gravity lay in the

---

[1] This essay is dedicated to the memory of Alan Hall, with whom I shared many of the experiences of those times. I first met Alan when he came to Balliol in 1952 from Aberdeen. He subsequently lectured in classics at Keele and was a passionate archaeologist of Graeco-Roman remains in Anatolia. He played a key role in the early New Left (including the passage from first to second generation) but died, tragically, in his fifties before he had the opportunity to put the New Left story on record himself. 'The First New Left: Life and Times' was originally presented as a paper at the 1988 'Out of Apathy' conference on the New Left, held in Oxford; a longer version appeared in the collection, *Out of Apathy: Voices of the New Left Thirty Years On*, London 1989, edited by Robin Archer and others.

left student generation of the 1950s and which maintained some distance from 'party' affiliations. It was people from this layer who, in the disintegration of those orthodoxies in 1956, first produced *Universities and Left Review*. I belong to this second tradition.

Arrivals

It may help to understand that moment better if I speak personally. I arrived in Oxford on a Rhodes scholarship, more or less straight from school in Jamaica, in 1951. I would say that my politics were principally 'anti-imperialist'. I was sympathetic to the left, had read Marx and been influenced by him while at school, but I would not, at the time, have called myself a Marxist in the European sense. In any event, I was troubled by the failure of orthodox Marxism to deal adequately with either 'Third World' issues of race and ethnicity, and questions of racism, or with literature and culture, which preoccupied me intellectually as an undergraduate. Retrospectively, I would identify myself as one of those described by Raymond Williams in *Culture and Society* who, following as a student of literature the engagement between the Leavisites and the Marxist critics, was obliged to acknowledge that '*Scrutiny* won'. Not because it was right—we were always critical of the conservative elitism of *Scrutiny*'s cultural programme—but because the alternative Marxist models were far too mechanical and reductive. (We did not yet have access to Lukács, Benjamin, Gramsci or Adorno.) On the wider political front, I was strongly critical of everything I knew about Stalinism, either as a political system or as a form of politics. I opposed it as a model for a democratic socialism and could not fathom the reluctance of the few Communists I met to acknowledge the truth of what was by then common knowledge about its disastrous consequences for Soviet society and Eastern Europe.

Like the rest of the small number of 'Third World' students at Oxford, my principal political concerns were with colonial questions. I became very involved in West Indian student politics. We debated and discussed, mainly, what was going on 'back home' in the expectation that before long we would all be there and involved in it. We argued about the West Indian Federation and the prospects for a new Caribbean economic order, the expulsion of the left from Manley's PNP Party in Jamaica under the pressures of the Cold War, the overthrow of the Jagan government in British Guiana, with the suspension of the constitution and the moving in of British troops. There was no 'black politics' in Britain; post-war migration had only just begun.

Later, as I began to take a wider interest in British politics, I came more into contact with the Oxford left. There was no 'mass' British political movement of the left or major popular political issue to which one could attach oneself. The choice seemed to be between a Labour Party which, at that moment, was deeply committed to an Atlanticist worldview, and the outer darkness of the far left. The first time I ventured into a Communist Group discussion meeting was to debate with the CP the application of Marx's concept of class to contemporary capitalist society. At the time, I felt that this was an extremely bold move—such was the climate of fear and suspicion which prevailed. After 1954, this climate began to change. There was a slow, hesitant revival of debate on the left and a group began to emerge around these discussions. Many of us attended the 'Cole Group' (as his seminar in politics was known), which, though formally an occasion for graduate students, doubled up as a wide-ranging discussion group of the broad left. Some of the earliest contacts and friendships, which were later to be cemented by the formation of the New Left, were forged there.

It is difficult now to conjure up the political climate of Oxford in the 1950s. The Cold War dominated the political horizon, positioning everyone and polarizing every topic by its remorseless binary logic. 'To recommend the admission of China to the UN was to invite the opprobrium of "fellow-traveller"; to say that the character of contemporary capitalism had changed was to be ranked as a "Keynesian liberal"', as the first ULR editorial put it.[2] The 'thaw' began as a debate about a range of contemporary issues: the future of Labour and the left in the wake of the Conservative revival, the nature of the welfare state and post-war capitalism, the impact of cultural change on British society in the early 'affluent' years of the decade. The pace of this debate was accelerated by the Khrushchev revelations at the Twentieth Congress of the CPSU. The response to '1956' and the formation of a New Left could not have occurred without this prior period of 'preparation', in which a number of people slowly gained the confidence to engage in a dialogue which questioned the terms of orthodox political argument and cut across existing organizational boundaries.

---

[2] Editorial, *Universities and Left Review* I, Spring 1957, p. i.

These strands were dramatically condensed by the events of '1956'. Soviet tanks in Budapest terminated any hope that a more human and democratic brand of communism would evolve in Eastern Europe without prolonged trauma and social convulsion. Suez punctured the cosy illusion that (to adapt Tawney's phrase) 'you could skin the capitalist-imperialist tiger stripe by stripe'. The Trafalgar Square Suez demonstration was the first mass political rally of its kind in the 1950s, and the first time I encountered police horses face to face, or heard Hugh Gaitskell and Nye Bevan speak in public. Bevan's fierce denunciation of Eden, I remember, scattered the startled pigeons into flight. One outcome of the ferment of '1956' was the publication of the two journals, *Universities and Left Review* and the *New Reasoner*, which, when they subsequently merged in 1960, formed the 'first' New Left Review.

A new student left

How and why did this happen then—and why, of all places, partly in Oxford? In the 1950s universities were not, as they later became, centres of revolutionary activity. A minority of privileged left-wing students, debating consumer capitalism and the embourgeoisement of working-class culture amidst the 'dreaming spires', may seem, in retrospect, a pretty marginal political phenomenon. Nevertheless, the debate was joined with a fierce intensity, self-consciously counterposed to the brittle, casual confidence of Oxford's dominant tone, set by the attempts of the 'Hooray Henries' of its time to relive *Brideshead Revisited*. In fact, Oxford also contained its rebel enclaves: demobbed young veterans and national servicemen, Ruskin College trade unionists, 'scholarship boys' and girls from home and abroad. Although they were unable to redefine its dominant culture, these outsiders did come to constitute an alternative—not to say beleaguered—intellectual minority culture. This was the 'ULR constituency'.

The Oxford left was very diverse. There was a small number of CP members—including Raphael Samuel, Peter Sedgwick, Gabriel Pearson—mainly in Balliol, where Christopher Hill was the tutor in Modern History. Next there was the great body of Labour Club supporters, the majority firmly attached to Fabian, labourist and reformist positions, and a few with their eyes fixed unswervingly on their coming parliamentary careers. Finally there were the 'independents', including some serious Labour people, who were intellectually aligned with neither of these two camps and shuttled somewhat uneasily between them. The latter group attracted more than its fair share of exiles and migrants, which reinforced its cosmopolitanism. Charles (Chuck) Taylor was a French-Canadian Rhodes scholar, as well as that even more perplexing phenomenon, a sort of Catholic Marxist; Dodd Alleyne was Trinidadian, I was Jamaican; Sadiq al-Mahdi was later to play a significant role in the Sudan; Clovis Maksoud was a founder member of the Syrian Ba'ath Party. Some, like Alan Lovell, a Welsh pacifist, Alan Hall, a Scots classicist, and Raphael Samuel, Gabriel Pearson, Stanley Mitchell and Robert Cassen, who were all Jewish, were what one might call internal émigrés.

The locus of our debate was the Socialist Club, a moribund organization left more or less abandoned since its thirties Popular Front days, which we resuscitated. It became clear that similar debates were developing in other universities and that there ought to be some common platform for this emerging student left. This explains the word 'Universities' in the title of the journal we eventually produced. The other half of its cumbersome and extremely uncommercial title signalled our concern with cultural questions, via a symbolic link with the *Left Review*, a wide-ranging and unorthodox literary and cultural journal of the 1930s and 1940s, more receptive to new cultural movements (for example, in its openness to Modernist currents) than any comparable 'party' journal of its time; Brecht was first published in England in its pages. The advent of 1956, however, destroyed the student-bound confines of this debate and catapulted us into the maelstrom of national and international left politics. The first issue of *Universities and Left Review*, which appeared in spring 1957, had four editors: Raphael Samuel and Gabriel Pearson, who left the CP after Hungary, and Charles Taylor and myself, representing 'the independents'. Its contents and contributors—Isaac Deutscher, Bourdet, Lindsay Anderson, Thompson, Cole, Eric Hobsbawm, Graeme Shankland on town planning, David Marquand on *Lucky Jim*, Joan Robinson, Basil Davidson—clearly demonstrate this translation to a wider stage.

English Marxist traditions

The New Left had equally important, though very different, roots in another tradition, represented by the *New Reasoner*. This tendency had its formation in Communist and Popular Front politics in Britain. Some of the 'Reasoners'—Edward Thompson, John Saville, Rodney Hilton, Christopher Hill, Victor Kiernan, Eric Hobsbawm—had belonged to that unique enclave, the Communist Party Historians Group which, under the inspiration of the little-known Dona Torr, developed a highly independent and original reading of British history, and a form of Marxist politics much more in touch with English popular radicalism, and quite distinct in style and inspiration from that sustained in the CP leadership by powerful but deeply sectarian figures like Palme Dutt.

The revelations of the Twentieth Congress stimulated inside the Party a painful reassessment of the whole Stalinist experience and the *Reasoner* first appeared in this context, as an internal opposition bulletin insisting on an open and public 'calling to account'. It was only after they lost their struggle for the right to express what were officially defined as 'factional' opinions, and the disciplines of democratic centralism were mobilized against them, that the majority of the 'Reasoners' either left the Party or were expelled and the *New Reasoner* appeared as an independent journal of the left. The final issue of the *Reasoner* was planned and produced before Suez and Hungary but, for it, these events were 'epochal':

> Even the urgency of the Egyptian crisis cannot disguise the fact that the events of Budapest represent a crucial turning-point for our Party. The aggression of British imperialism is uglier and more cynical than previous imperialist aggressions. But the crisis in world Communism is now different in kind.[3]

The New Left therefore represented the coming together of two different political traditions. How did this occur, and how well did it work? The organizational details of the amalgamation between the two journals can be quickly summarized. They continued to publish in tandem for a while, advertising and promoting each other. After a time the two editorial boards began to meet regularly around a broader political agenda, to appoint editorial board members in common and to recruit new ones. Both boards were increasingly preoccupied with the struggle to sustain the financial and commercial viability of two journals. Even more pressing was the cost in human capital. For many of us, normal life had more or less been suspended in 1956. Some had not stopped running round in circles since and were by then in a state of extreme political exhaustion. There were also, more positively, the opportunities we were missing to create a much wider, united political platform for our position. While we were aware of our differences, our perspectives had

---

[3] E. P. Thompson, 'Through the Smoke of Budapest', *Reasoner*, November 1956.

come closer together in the months of collaboration. Out of this variety of factors came the decision to merge and, with more suitable candidates like Thompson and others being unwilling to serve, I rashly agreed to become the first editor of New Left Review, with John Saville acting as chairman of the editorial board.

The first NLR

New Left Review in this form lasted two years. It was never, I think, as successful or distinctive a journal as either of its predecessors. The bimonthly rhythm and the pressures to connect with immediate political issues pushed us into becoming more of a left 'magazine' than a 'journal'. This required a shift of journalistic and editorial style which did not square with the original political intention and for which the board was unprepared. There were differences of emphasis and style of work between the board, which carried the main political weight and authority of the movement, and the small working editorial group that began to assemble around 7, Carlisle Street in Soho.

The 'New Reasoners'—Edward and Dorothy Thompson, John Saville, and others on the *Reasoner* board like Ronald Meek, Ken Alexander, Doris Lessing—belonged to a political generation formed by the experience of the Popular Front and the anti-Fascist movements of the thirties, the European Resistance movements during the War, the 'Second Front' campaigns for 'friendship with the Soviet Union' and the popular turn to the left reflected in the 1945 Labour victory. Although some younger Communists in the ULR tendency also belonged to this tradition, their relation to it was always different. In its overwhelming majority, the ULR generation's centre of gravity was irrevocably 'post-war'. This was a difference not of age but of formation—a question of political generations, within which the War constituted the symbolic dividing line. These differences did produce subtle tensions which surfaced around the new journal.

These differences of formation and political style of work were magnified by the location of the two tendencies in two quite distinct social and cultural milieus. The *New Reasoner*'s base was in Yorkshire and the industrial North. Although it had many readers elsewhere, it was organically rooted in a provincial political culture—not just that of the labour movement but also of organizations like the Yorkshire Peace Committee—and was intensely suspicious of 'London'. ULR also attracted support from many parts of the country; but it very much belonged to what the 'Reasoners' thought of as the 'cosmopolitan' or 'Oxford–London' axis. Although we did not consciously understand it at the time, the ULR-ers were modernists, if not actually 'rootless cosmopolitans'. As a colonial, I certainly felt instinctively more at home in the more socially anonymous metropolitan culture, though I regretted ULR's lack of organic connections to non-metropolitan working-class life.

It should by now be clear that, even within the editorial boards of the original journals, the New Left was far from monolithic and certainly never became culturally or politically homogeneous. The tensions were, for the most part, humanely and generously handled. But any careful reader of the journals will quickly be able to identify real points of difference and, on occasion, fiercely contended debates surfacing in their pages. It would therefore be quite wrong to attempt to reconstruct, retrospectively, some essential 'New Left', and to impose on it a political unity it never possessed. Nevertheless, although no two members would offer the same list, there was a set of linked themes which commanded wide enough assent to make it distinctive as a political formation.

In my reading, this centred on the argument that any prospect for the renewal of the left had to begin with a new conception of socialism and a radically new analysis of the social relations, dynamics and culture of post-war capitalism. Far from constituting a modest updating exercise, this was a far-reaching, ambitious and multifaceted intellectual project. So far as socialism was concerned, it meant coming to terms with the depressing experiences of both 'actual existing socialism' and 'actual existing social democracy' and transforming, in the light of those experiences, the very conception of 'the political'. So far as the latter was concerned, what we called modern 'corporate capitalism' had very different economic, organizational, social and cultural forms. It functioned according to a different 'logic' from that of entrepreneurial capitalism, described in Marx's classic theses or embedded in the language and theory of the left and inscribed in its agendas, its institutions and its revolutionary scenarios. For many of us (though not for everyone) this struggle to ground socialism in a new analysis of 'our times' was primary and originating—where the whole New Left project began.

The dominant account offered was that we were entering a 'post-capitalist' society in which the principal problems of social distribution had been solved by the post-war boom coupled to the expansion of the welfare state, Keynesian macroeconomic regulation and the 'human face' of the managerial revolution. All these were elements of what later came to be known as 'corporatism'—big capital, big state—or, from another point of view, the 'post-war consensus'. They had led to an erosion of traditional class cultures and the 'embourgeoisement' of the working class. Opposed to this scenario was the 'Old Left' argument that since the system was still patently capitalist, nothing of any significance had changed. The classes and the class struggle were exactly what and where they had always been, and to question this was to betray the revolutionary cause.

The majority of the New Left, however, refused this binary logic. The new forms of property, corporate organization and the dynamics of modern accumulation and consumption required a new analysis. These processes had had effects on social structure and political consciousness. More broadly, the spread of consumerism had disarticulated many traditional cultural attitudes and social hierarchies, and this had consequences for politics, the constituencies for change and the institutions and agendas of the left, with which socialism must come to terms. Lacking much indigenous material to go on, the American analysts—Riesman, Galbraith, Wright Mills—who were at the cutting edge of these developments provided us with our main purchase on these arguments.

Culture and politics

Closely linked to this was the argument about the contradictory and politically indeterminate 'drift' of social and cultural change. These changes fell short of a transformation of society, yet clearly but ambiguously dismantled many of the old relations and formations on which the whole edifice of the left and the project of socialism had historically been constructed. Again, there were at least two competing versions of this. One was that since the fundamental class structure of British society remained intact, 'change' could be only of the most superficial 'sociological' kind. It picked up incidental and mainly stylistic differences in such marginal areas as new attitudes and lifestyles amongst young people, new patterns of urban life, the movement out of the inner cities, the growing importance of consumption in everyday life, the 'weakening' of older social identities, and so on, which did not touch 'the fundamentals'. This fundamentalist account was matched, on the other side, by a relentless celebration of change for its own sake in which the new mass media had acquired a massive investment. With the expansion of the 'new journalism' and the rise of commercial television, society seemed bewitched by images of itself in motion, reflecting off its shiny consumer surfaces.

Again, the New Left insisted on occupying neither of these simple alternatives, choosing instead a more complex 'third' description. We were not necessarily at one in terms of how we understood these shifts (the exchange between Edward Thompson, Raphael Samuel and myself on my speculative piece, 'A Sense of Classlessness', in the pages of *ULR* is one *locus classicus* of this debate), but we were agreed about their significance. In my view, much that was creative, albeit chaotic and impressionistic, about the 'picture of the world' which came from the pages of New Left writing owed its freshness and vitality (as well as its utopianism) to the effort to sketch the meanings of these rapidly shifting contours of change. That is indeed one place where the New Left investment in the debate about culture first arose. First, because it was in the cultural and ideological domain that social change appeared to be making itself most dramatically visible. Second, because the cultural dimension seemed to us not a secondary, but a constitutive dimension of society. (This reflects part of the New Left's long-standing quarrel with the reductionism and economism of the base–superstructure metaphor.) Third, because the discourse of culture seemed to us fundamentally necessary to any language in which socialism could be redescribed. The New Left therefore took the first faltering steps of putting questions of cultural analysis and cultural politics at the centre of its politics.

In these different ways, the New Left launched an assault on the narrow definition of 'politics' and tried to project in its place an 'expanded conception of the political'. If it did not move so far as the feminist principle that 'the personal is political', it certainly opened itself up to the critical dialectic between 'private troubles' and 'public issues', which blew the conventional conception of politics apart. The logic implied by our position was that these 'hidden dimensions' had to be represented within the discourses of 'the political' and that ordinary people could and should organize where they were, around issues of immediate experience; begin to articulate their dissatisfactions in an existential language and build an agitation from that point. (This was the source of our much-debated 'socialist humanism'.) The expanded definition of the political also entailed a recognition of the proliferation of potential sites of social conflict and constituencies for change. Although we were in favour of a strong trade unionism, we contested the idea that only those at the 'point of production' could make the revolution.

The critique of reformism and its singularly British representative, 'Labourism', was entailed in this enlarged discourse of 'the political'. We looked for a more radical and structural transformation of society: partly because we were committed to many of the fundamental perspectives of the classical socialist programme; partly because we saw in modern capitalism a greater, not a lesser concentration of social power and could trace the impact of 'commodification' in areas of life far removed from the immediate sites of wage-labour exploitation; but above all because of the much broader critique we had of 'capitalist civilization and culture'. No one expressed the fundamental and constitutive character of this argument for and within the New Left more profoundly than Raymond Williams. It was in this sense that we remained 'revolutionaries', though few retained any faith in a vanguardist seizure of state power. The opposition between 'reform' and 'revolution' seemed to many of us outdated: more a way of swearing at and anathematizing others than having any real analytic-historical value in its own right. We sought, in different ways, to bypass it.

In these and other significant ways, the dominant tendency of the New Left was 'revisionist' with respect both to Labourism and to Marxism. We had come into existence and now lived in the age of 'many Marxisms'. Few, if any, of us could have been described, after 1956, as 'orthodox'— principally because, though we held different positions about how much of Marxism could be transposed without 'revision' to the second half of the twentieth century, all of us refused to regard it as a fixed and finished doctrine or sacred text. For example, of considerable importance to some of us was the rediscovery, through Chuck Taylor, of Marx's early *Economic and Philosophical Manuscripts*, with their themes of alienation, species being and 'new needs', which he brought over from Paris in 1958 in French and which only shortly thereafter became available to us in an English translation.

New Left Clubs

There were many other themes which any comprehensive account would be obliged to discuss: the debate around 'socialist humanism', the analyses of the Third World and, in connection with the Campaign for

Nuclear Disarmament, 'neutralism', NATO and disarmament; popular culture and the media. However, since the New Left is so often tagged as mainly an intellectual formation, it may be more appropriate to remind readers that the 'first' New Left, however mistakenly, thought of itself as a movement rather than simply a journal. Shortly after the publication of the first issue, ULR called its first 'readers' meeting' on an inauspicious Sunday afternoon, which was followed by the foundation of the London ULR Club. In the early years the Club (later the London New Left Club) attracted to its weekly meetings audiences of three or four hundred, drawn from the whole spectrum of the left. For a time it provided an extremely important, lively, often contentious focal point for people with no other formal political commitment. It differed from the typical left organization or sect in that its purpose was not to recruit members but to engage with the political culture of the left on a very broad front, through argument, debate, discussion and education.

The Club became an important independent centre for left politics in London, particularly after it found a permanent home—through another of Raphael Samuel's nerve-rackingly risky but brilliantly innovative ventures—in the Partisan Café in Carlisle Street. This was the first left 'coffee bar' in London, with a clubhouse and library on the floors above. On the fourth floor it housed the offices of ULR, later to become those of NLR. Following the merger, a number of New Left clubs sprang up around the country. The last issue of NLR which I edited, number 12, listed thirty-nine in various stages of political health. The clubs reflected, in programme and composition, the cultural and political character of their localities: the Manchester and Hull Left Clubs were close to the local labour movement; the Fife Socialist League was linked, through Lawrence Daly, to an independent socialist movement amongst miners in Scotland; the Croydon and Hemel Hempstead Clubs had a more 'cross-class' or even 'déclassé-new-town' feel to them.

Very early on, the London New Left Club pioneered the propaganda and leafleting for the first CND Aldermaston March, which the club membership supported en masse. This was the beginning of close links between the New Left, the modern peace movement in Britain and the birth of CND as a mass political organization. Among its other activities, the New Left Club in London became deeply involved in 1958 with the race riots in Notting Hill and with the anti-racist struggles of the period around North Kensington. We participated in the efforts to establish tenants' associations in the area, helped to protect black people who, at the height of the 'troubles', were molested and harassed by white crowds in an ugly mood between Notting Hill station and their homes, and picketed Mosley and other far-right meetings. In the course of this work we first stumbled across the powerful traces of racism inside the local Labour Party itself, and Rachel Powell, an active club member, unearthed the scandal of 'Rachmanism' and white landlord exploitation in Notting Hill.

Peter Sedgwick once acutely observed that the New Left was less a movement than a 'milieu'. He was noting the lack of tight organizational structure, the loose conception of leadership, the flat hierarchies, the absence of membership, rules, regulations, party programme or 'line' which characterized the New Left, in sharp contrast with other political tendencies and sects on the far left. These features were the product of our critique of Leninist and democratic-centralist forms of organization and emphasis on self-organization and participatory politics, which we can now see retrospectively as 'prefigurative' of so much that was to come afterwards. Sedgwick may also have been obliquely commenting on the low level of working-class participation—or, to be more accurate, the 'cross-class competition' of many, though by no means all, of the New Left clubs. This could be seen as—and indeed was—a serious weakness, but oddly enough, it also had some compensations. Where the clubs were particularly strong was in those social strata emerging within and across the rapidly shifting, recomposing-decomposing class landscapes of post-war Britain. This separated us, not from ordinary working people, for we had many of those as active supporters, but from the political cultures of the traditional labour movement and the revolutionary cadres of the sects. Nevertheless, it gave the New Left a privileged access to the grinding, grating processes of contradictory social change.

Prefigurative practice

With all their weaknesses, the clubs signified the project of the New Left to be a new kind of socialist entity: not a party but a 'movement of ideas'. They were a sign that, for us and for the left, the 'question of agency' had become deeply problematic. We adopted this approach partly out of conviction, partly because we thought the movement of ordinary people into politics—breaking with the crust of conventional opinions and orthodox alignments in their own lives, on a concrete issue, and beginning to 'take action for themselves'—was more politically significant than the most correct of 'correct lines'. Another reason was that we saw in embryo in CND a new kind of political mobilization—beyond, so to speak, the big party battalions—which reflected certain emergent social forces and aspirations characteristic of their time, in relation to which it was necessary for the left to develop a new political practice.

CND was one of the first of this type of 'social movement' to appear in post-war politics—a popular movement with an unambiguously radical thrust and an implicit 'anti-capitalist' content, formed through self-activity in civil society around a concrete issue, but lacking a clear class composition and appealing to people across the strongly drawn lines of traditional class identity or organizational loyalties. It was already possible to recognize in these new movements features of modern society and points of social antagonism which—like the civil-rights movement at the time, and feminist and sexual questions, ecological and environmental issues, community politics, welfare rights and anti-racist struggles in the 1970s and 1980s—have proved difficult to construct within the organizational agendas of the traditional left. Without these social movements, however, no contemporary mass political mobilization or movement for radical change in modern times is now conceivable.

Ultimately what CND posed for the New Left—as the new social movements always do—was the problem of how to articulate these new impulses and social forces with the more traditional class politics of the left; and how, through this articulation, the project of the left could be transformed. The fact that we had no greater success than the left has had since in trying to construct a 'historical bloc' out of such heterogeneous social interests, political movements and agendas, in building a hegemonic political practice out of, and with, these differences, does not negate the urgency of the task. What we can learn from the 'first' New Left here is what questions to ask, not which answers work.

As far as the Labour Party was concerned, many people in and around the New Left were members of it. Many were not. As a movement, our attitude to the Labour Party was quite clear. Our independence from organizational links, controls, party routines and discipline was essential for our political project. The majority vote for unilateralism at the Labour Party Conference, for which many of us campaigned, was a clear example to us of 'defeat-in-victory', as a result of mistaking a platform victory for the winning of new popular political positions. Inside the machine, CND withered and shrivelled into a talisman, a fetish of party conference resolutions, plaything of the manoeuvres of the block vote, without touching ground in the political consciousness or activity of many actual people.

At the same time we recognized that the fate of socialism in Britain was inextricably bound up with the fate and fortunes of Labour. We recognized Labour as, for good or ill, the Party which had hegemonized the vast majority of the organized working class with a reformist politics. We honoured its historic links to the trade-union movement. We acknowledged it as the engine of the 'welfare state' revolution of 1945 which we never underestimated because it represented a reform, rather than an overthrow, of the system. We remained deeply critical of the Fabian and labourist cultures of the Party, of its 'statism', its lack of popular roots in the political and cultural life of ordinary people, its bureaucratic suspicion of any independent action or 'movement' outside its limits, and its profound anti-intellectualism. We opposed the deeply undemocratic procedures of the block vote and the Party's empty 'constitutionalism'. Yet we knew the Labour Party represented, whether we liked it or not, the strategic stake in British politics, which no one could ignore.

We therefore developed an open and polemical politics in relation to the Gaitskell leadership, on the one hand, and the 'nothing-has-changed, reaffirm-Clause-4' perspective of the traditional left on the other; taking up—here as elsewhere—a third position, opening a 'third front'. In the revisionist debates of the 1950s and 1960s we opposed the post-capitalist, 'human face of corporate capitalism' theses proposed in Crosland's *The Future of Socialism*, while recognizing him as a formidable and intelligent opponent. We insisted—against the doctrinal immobilism of much of the Labour and trade-union left—on the necessity of grounding the perspectives of the left in a new analysis of the novel conditions of postwar capitalism and social change. Some people would continue to work for this inside the Labour Party; others worked outside. We did not see how there could be a 'correct' line on this issue when there was so little relationship between what people wanted politically and the vehicle for achieving it. Our strategy was therefore to sidestep it and instead to involve people, whatever their affiliations, in independent political activity and debate.

This 'parallel' strategy required, as its necessary condition, the maintenance of journals, clubs, a network of contacts and forms of demonstration, argument and propaganda to articulate this 'third position', which were not subject to the routines of the Labour HQ at Transport House but were nevertheless designed to break back into and have an effect on the internal politics of the Labour Party and the labour movement. We called this the strategy of 'one foot in, one foot out'.

Going to the people

What type of organizational leadership did these strategies presuppose? The metaphor to which we constantly returned was that of 'the socialist propaganda'. As Edward Thompson put it in the *New Reasoner*:

> The New Left does not propose itself as an alternative organization to those already in the field; rather, it offers two things to those within and without the existing organizations—a specific propaganda of ideas, and certain practical services (journals, clubs, schools, etc).[4]

The notion of a 'socialist propaganda of ideas' was, of course, borrowed directly and explicitly from William Morris and the relationships forged in the Socialist League between intellectuals, struggling to make themselves what Gramsci called 'organic', and the working class. We had all read and been inspired by the 'Making Socialists' chapter of Thompson's *William Morris: Romantic to Revolutionary*. Indeed, the first editorial of NLR was framed at either end by a quote from Morris's *Commonweal* article of July 1885: 'The Labour movement is not in its insurrectionary phase.' I added: 'we are in our missionary phase'.[5]

Although it was not fully theorized, this conception of leadership was based on certain clear presuppositions. The first was the necessity of challenging the conventional anti-intellectualism of the British labour movement and overcoming the traditional division between intellectuals and the working class. The second was the repudiation of three alternative models: 'vanguardist' and 'democratic-centralist' conceptions of revolutionary leadership; Fabian notions of the middle-class 'experts' within the state machine giving socialism to the working classes; and the

---

[4] Thompson, 'The New Left', *New Reasoner* 9, Summer 1959, p. 16.
[5] Hall, 'Introducing NLR', NLR 1/1, Jan–Feb 1960, p. 2.

traditional Labour left faith in constitutional mechanisms, conference resolutions, winning the block votes and 'electoral contests with slightly more "left" candidates'.[6] Third, our view was that changes in British society had brought a large number of the new, post-war social strata within reach of socialist education and propaganda. Fourth, we had a deep conviction that against the economism of the Stalinist, Trotskyist and Labourist left alike, socialism was a *conscious* democratic movement and socialists were *made*, not born or given by the inevitable laws of history or the objective processes of the mode of production alone.

We also challenged the prevailing view that the so-called affluent society would of itself erode the appeal of socialist propaganda—that socialism could arise only out of immiseration and degradation. Our emphasis on people taking action for themselves, 'building socialism from below' and 'in the here and now', not waiting for some abstract Revolution to transform everything in the twinkling of an eye, proved, in the light of the re-emergence of these themes after 1968, strikingly prefigurative. As we put it in the first issue of NLR:

> We have to go into towns and cities, universities and technical colleges, youth clubs and Trade Union branches and—as Morris said—make socialists there. We have come through 200 years of capitalism and 100 years of imperialism. Why should people—naturally—turn to socialism? There is no law which says that the Labour Movement, like a great inhuman engine, is going to throb its way into socialism or that we can, any longer . . . rely upon poverty and exploitation to drive people, like blind animals, towards socialism. Socialism is, and will remain, an active faith in a new society, to which we turn as conscious, thinking human beings. People have to be confronted with experience, called to the 'society of equals', not because they have never had it so bad, but because the 'society of equals' is better than the best soft-selling consumer capitalist society, and life is something lived, not something one passes through like tea through a strainer.[7]

This position may seem naive and has certainly been dubbed 'utopian' and 'populist' since. But it was populist in the Narodnik sense of 'going to the people' and in terms of what they/we might become, rather than in the sense of massaging popular consent by cynical appeals to what the people are said by their betters to want. We had an instinctive, if not well-formulated, notion that the socialist project had to be rooted in the here

[6] Thompson, 'The New Left', p. 16.
[7] Hall, 'Introducing NLR', p. 3.

and now and connect with lived experience: with what we have since learned to call 'the national-popular'. 'The people' is, of course, always a discursive construction and the blurring of a precise social referent in the populism of the early New Left was certainly significant. But there is more than one kind of populism and it can, despite all its problems, be articulated either to the right or the left, and serve either to short-circuit or to develop popular antagonisms. The 'populism' of the early New Left was certainly of the latter sort, as Edward Thompson, its main architect, put it in the *New Reasoner*:

> What will distinguish the New Left will be its rupture with the tradition of inner-party factionalism, and its renewal of the tradition of open association, socialist education and activity directed towards the people as a whole . . . It will insist that the Labour Movement is not a thing, but an association of men and women; that working people are not the passive recipients of economic and cultural conditioning, but are intellectual and moral beings . . . It will appeal to people by rational argument and moral challenge. It will counter the philistine materialism and anti-intellectualism of the Old Left by appealing to the totality of human interests and potentialities, and by constructing new channels of communication between industrial workers and experts in the sciences and arts. It will cease to postpone the satisfactions of Socialism to an hypothetic period 'after the Revolution', but will seek to promote in the present, and in particular in the great centres of working-class life, a richer sense of community.[8]

The tensions and contradictions implicit in this 'populism' were never wholly resolved. The rapid shifts in social structure of the post-war period, which we constantly tried to characterize without pinning them down precisely, cut unevenly into the New Left; we failed to build these differences into a new 'historical bloc', though that was our implicit aim. The tensions already alluded to between the provincial North and cosmopolitan London, like later versions of the North/South divide, were much more complex than this simple opposition suggests. Nevertheless, they shadowed some critical differences in the pace and character of class recomposition and social decomposition in post-war British society and came to stand metonymically for the diversifying ground of politics, without providing a principle of articulation. The tensions between intellectuals and activists were a continuing, if largely unspoken, problem connected to the much wider issue of the uncertain status of intellectuals in English cultural life generally and the disabling philistinism of

---

[8] Thompson, 'The New Left', pp. 16–7.

the left. Cutting across all these tensions from another direction was the almost totally hidden question of gender—the fact that the great majority of the editorial-board leadership were men and that many of those on whom the actual work of keeping the whole enterprise going fell were women: the usual sexual division of labour, reproduced so often in the left. About this last question the New Left preserved—as did the rest of the left—a profound unconsciousness.

We hoped that the clubs would develop their own independent organization, leadership and channels of communication (perhaps their own news-sheet or bulletin), leaving the journal free to develop its own project. But we lacked the resources to bring this about, which exacerbated in the clubs feelings that they had no control over the journal, and in the editorial board the fear that a journal of ideas could not be effectively run by committees. It was, in effect, this last issue and the cross-pressures associated with it which finally precipitated my own resignation from the editorship of New Left Review in 1961.

It is not for me to attempt any overall assessment of the 'first' New Left, which I see as only a first stage in the constitution of a new kind of left politics. It seems absurd to attempt to defend its record in detail or to impose, retrospectively, a consistency it did not possess. Its strengths and weaknesses, errors and mistakes, remain and are unanswerable—to be learned from rather than repudiated. Nevertheless I would make the sharpest distinction between what we did and how we did it, and the wider project. I remain as committed to the latter as I was then. The 'third space' which the 'first' New Left defined and tried to prise open still seems to me the only hope for the renewal of the democratic and socialist project in our new and bewildering times.

REVIEWS

Susan Buck-Morss, *Hegel, Haiti and Universal History*
University of Pittsburgh Press: Pittsburgh 2009, $16.95, paperback
164 pp, 978 0 822 95978 6

ANDERS STEPHANSON

THE PHILOSOPHER'S ISLAND

Hegel mentioned Haiti exactly once, as far as we know, in a life not marked by taciturnity; but it was a great idea to put the two together. The pairing here makes for a stirring polemic. Buck-Morss insists that Hegel knew the Haitian Revolution for what it was, a profoundly modern event on the cutting edge of world history; that the Revolution played a central role in his articulation of the master–slave dialectic; and, finally, that there is a lesson to be learnt from this regarding the 'unapologetically humanist project' she thinks politically necessary for our present moment. She is right that Hegel knew about Haiti, but she is wrong about the master–slave dialectic. Her appeal to some syncretic universalism, meanwhile, is a matter of opinion. I myself remain unconvinced. To reduce the opus to a few propositions, however, is to misrepresent it. There are lots of other allusive and elusive arguments, a series of points on a graph, or constellation of flashes in the sky, connected by the 'pathways' that are meant to explain what's going on.

The form itself is important: two main essays, of which the second, 'Universal History', is an expansive commentary on the first, 'Hegel and Haiti'; both being framed by introductions which in turn constitute self-reflective commentaries, chiefly on the first intervention. Written in the self-professed spirit of a fragmentary philosophical and political history, 'Hegel and Haiti' itself is conceived as a 'mystery story', in which illustrations provide the clues. Summary is hard. This is a book that advertises its adventurousness. It must be held to that standard.

'Hegel and Haiti' first appeared in 2001 as a controversial article in *Critical Inquiry* and is reproduced virtually as was. Buck-Morss now describes it, a bit extravagantly, as 'something of an intellectual event'. The world(s) of Hegel scholarship paid scant attention but others certainly found the argument an eye-opener; not least because it restored the Haitian Revolution to its rightful place among the monumental transformations of its epoch, having been largely ignored in standard Eurocentric accounts. Buck-Morss's linking it to Hegel, supreme philosopher of the world-historical, brought the point home with the greatest polemical verve and power. One must begin, therefore, with that connexion. Hegel's concern with Haiti, obscured but really quite obvious in her view, provides the central drama of the proceedings. Lots of people have of course thought about the Haitian Revolution, as well as slavery, in Hegelian terms. It has been hard, indeed, to think of slavery in any other way, as it has been hard to think of identity and difference outside of that dialectic, certainly until Gilles Deleuze's frontal assault on the dialectic itself in the name of (Nietzschean) frontal assault. In the Caribbean context, specifically the Francophone one, there is a distinguished lineage of engagement with Hegel going back at least to Aimé Césaire in the early 1940s. We are always already in Hegel, as the staunchly anti-Hegelian Michel Foucault once implied. What's new in Buck-Morss's account, then, is not that one might profitably read the Haitian master–slave relationship in Hegelian terms but that Hegel himself read that relation in Haitian terms, in his first great publication, the *Phenomenology of Spirit* (or *Mind* if you prefer) in 1807.

To have Hegel not only reading Haitian events but drawing precise philosophical conclusions from them is not an easy proposition, since he said nothing about them until 1830, the year before his death, when he commended the Haitians for having created a real, legal state and a Christian one at that. So on this matter, Buck-Morss needs to present a more sustained argument than on any other. It is not enough to be suggestive; what is at issue in her account overall is the relation, the connexion, not the finer points of Hegelian philosophy or the particularities of Haitian history. This is a prudent but problematic move. Lifetimes have been spent on Hegel (often productively); there is a library and a half about the master–slave dialectic alone. What Buck-Morss wants to establish is that the form and content of that dialectic is derived from Haiti. She tends, accordingly, to be more precise about Hegel than about Haitian events, which she typically presents in extended footnotes, the genre of the ever-present caveat. She knows the Revolution is no single event and that the historiography is fraught with controversies and difficult matters. No synopsis or 'take' is provided.

The empirical argument is set up by means of a gloss on David Brion Davis's epochal work from the 1960s and 70s: the massive conceptual presence of 'slavery' in the Enlightenment, as the antithesis of 'freedom' on the part of the properly autonomous, free-willing Self, is contrasted with the astonishing lack of interest in actually existing slavery; a supreme case of ideological misrecognition, so to speak, which fails egregiously to see that the institution of slavery was integral to the whole operation of 'Europe', that indeed it was an economic condition of possibility for the very emergence of the enlightened bourgeoisie itself. In the French Revolution this paradox (is it a paradox?) came to its sharpest possible expression, courtesy of the slave revolt in Saint-Domingue that broke out in August 1791. Saint-Domingue, on the eve of the Revolution in 1789, was less the jewel in the crown than an enormous chunk of the bank accounts of the expansive French bourgeoisie. The island was the supreme envy of every rapacious maritime entrepreneur in Europe: by far the greatest money-machine in the colonial world. Five hundred thousand slaves, a majority born in Africa and imported at accelerating pace in the 1780s, produced half of all the sugar and coffee consumed in Europe and the Americas. Mercantilist policies ensured that the metropolitan French made enormous profits in the re-exporting business. Upwards of a million people in France probably depended for their wherewithal on the colony, but the trade was also strategic, the surpluses underwriting naval expansion. It made some sense for France to concede its Canadian possessions in the 1760s to secure Saint-Domingue and the smaller colonies in the Caribbean. It was this prized possession, then, that was lost after an exceedingly bloody war, or series of wars, beginning in 1791 and ending with the declaration of independence on 1 January 1804, when Saint-Domingue was renamed Haiti/Hayti in accordance with an ancient Amerindian designation.

The moment of Haitian independence—the first and, as it turned out, the only politically successful slave revolt in the New World—occurred when Hegel was at Jena, thinking about reciprocity and the struggle for recognition within the conventional context of Smithian property, exchange and the division of labour. What interests Buck-Morss here is the decisive ways in which the problem of recognition escalates in Hegel, as it were, from the Smithian frame into a potentially lethal struggle between master and slave; revolving, indeed, around the stark contrast between 'liberty or death' much beloved by Western revolutionary liberals. This is what takes place in Haiti, as the astounding end product of a struggle that saw, in essence, the defeat of three of the most eminent European powers—Spain, Britain and France. There is, then, a certain *correspondence* between Hegel's reconceptualized struggle for recognition and the unfolding Haitian events, grasped as a successful struggle to the death in the name of liberty.

Hegel was an ardent reader of news about current events and always considered thought, Philosophy, in some essential way a condensation of the present. Given that Haiti was news, Hegel cannot not have paid attention to it; once we realize that, the *Phenomenology* must be read in a new way. Exhibit A in Buck-Morss's account is *Minerva,* a German journal of public affairs which Hegel read. Politically sympathetic to the Girondists in France, it happened to take an early interest in Saint-Domingue. Its very first issue in 1792 contained a relatively informed article about the uprising; the journal returned to the subject consistently and incisively from late 1804 onwards, a period which thus coincides with the genesis of the *Phenomenology.* (Readers may wish to brush up on their German *Frakturschrift* by examining this for themselves, as *Minerva* is now conveniently online in facsimile.) Once again, 'the eyes of the world are now directed towards St. Domingo', the publication noted, following the 1804 Declaration of Independence; adding, condescendingly, that one could not call this agglomeration of resident blacks a real republic. That verdict introduced what was actually a vicious propaganda tract, originally ordered up by Napoleon himself. The tone changed markedly a year later when *Minerva* published an excerpt from Marcus Rainsford's highly flattering portrait—C. L. R. James called it a hagiography—of Toussaint Louverture, the pre-eminent black leader. 'The Negroes', *Minerva*'s editor now said, 'appear here in a very different light' and Toussaint Louverture is 'an admirable, really great man' whose sad fate was most regrettable. Essentially, the point was that whereas the French themselves had regressed into barbarism and terror, Toussaint's regime indicated moderation, civility and humanity. With less enthusiasm, *Minerva* also published documents and analyses pertaining to Toussaint's successor, the rather more drastic and brutal Jean-Jacques Dessalines.

Why, then, Hegel's silence? One would think that there would be some textual residue somewhere, some snippet; *something.* There is nothing. Buck-Morss's response to the issue of silence is, first, to suggest that such materials might have been edited out from the *Nachlass* and, second, to say that the absence of Haiti is no stranger than the absence of the French Revolution which everyone (well, almost everyone) agrees is in there. Both omissions can be explained by the combination of censorship and Hegel's precarious situation in 1806. He was then rather an obscure thinker in a German principality, still struggling at the age of 36 to find a proper academic job and to escape from being Friedrich Schelling's philosophical sidekick: a figure, in short, with reasons to be careful and very far from the magisterial, national renown he would later achieve. The coded nature of his account may also have had something to do with his Masonic connexions. As far as Buck-Morss is concerned, then, it is a no-brainer: how could Hegel have written about masters and slaves and the dialectical reversal without having the monumental fact of the Haitian overturn in mind? She is incensed that

Hegel Scholarship has ignored this obvious feature for two centuries; but she is not surprised.

It is indeed true that Hegel followed current events and must have been aware of the Haitian Revolution. What he made of it is another matter. Here it must be said: not only is there no positive evidence that he had Haiti in mind in the master–slave dialectic, such a notion actually makes no sense within the philosophical argument of the *Phenomenology*. Moreover, Hegel lived in an era when things happened. The Revolution in France broke out when he was an impressionable 19-year-old in Tübingen across the Rhine, rooming with Friedrich Hölderlin; the two soon to be joined by the boy-wonder Schelling, in what must have been one of the most stimulating flatshares of all time. Not surprisingly, Hegel considered the French Revolution and its aftermath the central, world-historical event of his epoch. Though sharply critical, in an almost Burkean way, of the tendency to abstraction, immediacy and terror, he always saw the validity of the Revolution as a historical break, as something qualitatively new shining through in the unfolding process of the *Weltgeist* towards Freedom. Every 14 July, year in and year out, he would toast the Revolution. All in all, there was a good deal to contemplate in current affairs between 1789 and 1806, the year Hegel finished the *Phenomenology* in Jena, on the evening before the grand Battle began. It was at Jena, too, that Hegel had occasion famously to witness the invading *Weltseele* himself riding by on his horse, the enhancer and enlarger of the New, 'der Grosse Staatsrechtslehrer' doing away with piddling German inwardness. If Napoleon, the embodiment of World History, had been soundly trumped by the black revolutionaries, there must have been reason for him to consider their place in History. Or?

Hegel's silence says nothing in itself, so to speak. The thinker was not in the habit of naming things. What one gets in Hegel is very largely Hegel: pages and pages without a proper name in sight. Masters and slaves, or bondsmen—yes, indeed; but no real examples of how they worked. (The lectures, published posthumously, are another matter.) Considering Hegel's often mind-numbing abstraction, his nigh-on private philosophical language and what one might call his circumspection about saying anything explicit about anything, his silence on Haiti might just have been par for the course. Or? Here it must be said that the section on 'Absolute Freedom and Terror' in the *Phenomenology* is about as loud as it can be in referring critically to France, and to Rousseau's unmediated General Will. If Hegel could be that explicit about France, why could he not have been a little more forthcoming about the events in Haiti, remote indeed as they must have been from any German view? *Minerva*, read by the Prussian monarch, obviously felt no restraint in that regard. A more suggestive explanation is that Hegel's profound fascination with Napoleon and his historical significance rendered the Haitian rupture indigestible, or at any rate less remarkable than it actually was.

Hegel scholars, it is true, pay no attention to the Haitian Revolution (an exception is the Franco-African scholar Pierre-Franklin Tavares); but then again most of them do not pay much attention to the French Revolution either, or indeed to any other than purely intellectual 'history'. 'Context', when it matters, is typically grasped as having to do with the development from Kant to Fichte to Schelling to Hegel, perhaps with some trips off the beaten track into Herder and Schiller. This, as far as it goes, is of course quite proper: the shadow of Kant towers over the proceedings, and Fichte invented the whole problematic of recognition. Buck-Morss's passion gets the better of her here: the Haitian reference is not 'obvious'; it is counterproductive to argue that, because of its 'obviousness', it is also wrong to invoke, say, Aristotle, or the classics, or Fichte. How could the classically steeped Hegel have been able to disassociate his thinking from the Aristotelean baggage, the taxonomical point of reference for any Western argument about mastery and slavery? Lots of things, potentially, could have gone into Hegel's theorization; what in fact did?

One can argue more or less plausibly about silences and absences; it is another matter to argue on the basis of what is actually in the *Phenomenology*. Given the difficulties of that text, this is anything but straightforward; but one decisive thing seems plainly wrong in Buck-Morss's account. Hegel's master–slave dialectic does not end, notoriously, in anything distinct, certainly not in any struggle to the death or actual reversal, along the lines of Haiti, however one construes it. The master–slave dialectic, it will be recalled, appears in a sequence of configurations, or 'figures', having to do with the development of 'self-consciousness', the new stage after the immediacy of 'consciousness' as such; and it is derived specifically from a posited struggle for recognition. The struggle to the death, potential or actual, appears not in the master–slave relationship but in the preceding structure of erstwhile equality between two figures which, in the absence of community and overarching authority, are moving into self-consciousness: desiring, indeed requiring, recognition of the other to achieve certainty of self and doing so by staking their lives. They recognize each other as mutually recognizing one another, but need to struggle to prove that they are above and beyond mere life, mere existence. Actual death, as opposed to the risk of death, would however short-circuit the dialectic; and so the value of mere life returns when the weaker of the two chooses, rationally, to become the slave or servant of the other.

This next stage or moment, the resultant master–slave dialectic, then generates the famous irony whereby the master, the essential, dominant person, in being totally recognized by his slave (Hegel usually refers to a neutral 'it' but the translation is gendered) actually finds himself devoid of real recognition, dissatisfied in his desire for it, at the same time as he is in truth dependent for his wherewithal on the slave; who, because of his labour, because of the things he produces for the master, begins to recognize his inessential position as truthfully valid, genuine and actually essential. The apparently stable, 'recognized' relationship, then, turns out to be false. Yet no struggle to the death is entailed here. The slave does not 'win' by killing the master or taking his place; either solution would halt dialectical development. He wins instead by achieving a certain autonomy. Indeed, what emerges in the next section is not revolution but, tellingly, the Stoic figure, suggestive of some stoical slave who *retreats* from the world and, in supreme philosophical autonomy, finds a way of thinking his world that way. This is followed, in turn, first by the advent of 'scepticism' and, second, by 'the unhappy consciousness', the dualistic sensibility constitutive of early Christianity.

Whether Hegel had anything concretely historical in mind with this sequence, or whether he was being entirely abstract, is subject to intense and polarized debate. I myself think Michael Forster is right here to say that, yes, Hegel, probably under the influence of the ancient historian J. F. Reitemeier, is referring to the world-historical unfolding which classical antiquity—Athens, chiefly—goes through up to the moment of Roman Christianity; the proviso being that he also thinks this process, or logic, can be present in other epochs; and that history, in a way, is about the progressive attenuation of that possible relation, understood more generally as one of domination and servitude, *Herrschaft und Knechtschaft*. Hegel, in that sense, is being at once diachronic and synchronic. A related but distinct alternative, proposed by Fredric Jameson in *The Hegel Variations*, his forthcoming commentary on the *Phenomenology*, is that the master–slave dialectic has the character of myth, along the lines of Rousseau's Social Contract: neither strictly historical, nor strictly abstract. In either case, arguably, the configuration would be available as an inspiration for, or a model 'applied' to, current events and so to Haiti. The trouble even with that weaker form of the argument, however, is that those events do not in fact correspond to the structure of Hegel's account, either diachronically or synchronically. The revolution in Haiti was not a retreat into stoical self-awareness: it was a case of pure substitution if ever there was one—no recognition involved.

Buck-Morss is not interested in the stoic follow-up and does not see the difficulty. She quotes Hegel's defining statement that only in staking one's life in struggle does one become 'a person', which would seem to fit hand in glove Dessalines's concise charge that death is in every way preferrable to slavery. Yet that statement is not in fact part of the master–slave section. It is part of the earlier moment of the emergent self-consciousness and mutual recognition which, after said struggle to the death, *results* in the new relationship of subjugation. Haiti does not fit. One wishes that it had. The revolution in Saint-Domingue was indeed a struggle about liberty or death: the issue throughout was slavery and it only became a struggle about national independence in 1802 when Napoleon made the fatal mistake of trying to reintroduce slavery, an attempt that 're-racialized' the conflict. It was thus a struggle about the most radically dehumanizing way of extracting surplus labour in existence. Hegel's interest in slave labour, however 'material', is ultimately idealist in the sense that the driving force is the need for recognition, a notion of inter-subjectivity, spasmodically developing in the unfolding of freedom in history. Franz Fanon, in the 1950s, had a peremptory response to this philosophical idealism. The master, says Fanon, needs and desires no recognition, genuine or hollow, from the slave. What the master needs and desires is labour and production, full stop. There is no reciprocity in Hegel's idealist terms and none ever develops. Fanon of Martinique, where slavery, contrary to law, was never abolished after 1794, proposes a zero-sum game much more in tune with actual Haitian events than Hegel's. Later, in the context of French North Africa, Fanon would develop for the specifically colonial situation a notion of a spatially stunted dialectic, where segregation thwarts any real interaction and the struggle becomes one of occupation, replacement or substitution.

What, indeed, of the actual Haitian events? The rich plantation economy in Saint-Domingue was, first of all, not a *simple* system. Sugar production required resources, infrastructure, intensive and extensive production methods—capital, in short—combined with variable slave labour. More than thirty thousand slaves were imported every year during the 1780s, from different places and linguistic cultures. Given the complexity of sugar-cane production and handling, slave labour was used for a range of tasks. The resultant social and racial structure was not clearly divided into free and slave, white and black. There were thirty to forty thousand whites, mostly resident in towns, a good number of them fairly poor and eking out an existence in the interstices of the colonial economy. There were also almost thirty thousand *gens de couleur*, often referred to as 'mulattoes' but actually a legal rather than a social group, defined internally according to a bewilderingly extensive scale of putatively precise mixture. Some of them owned plantations, predominantly in coffee rather than sugar, and slaves; about a hundred thousand slaves, or a fifth of the total. There were also free blacks such as the central figure of the 1790s, Toussaint Louverture, himself an owner of slaves when the revolt initially broke out. Add to this social map, by no means exhaustive, three highly separate topographical regions and the overall picture is anything but transparent. Only the centrality of slave labour and plantation production is clear.

Enter the French Revolution in 1789 and, two years later, the Saint-Dominguan Revolution, which would end with independent Haiti: two monumental sequences of events whose relationship is not transparent either. The Haitian Revolution was in no way a *function* of the French. It had its own dynamic and was not mired in the same ideological arguments. Rights of Man notwithstanding, the French revolutionaries had a hard time with colonial slavery, as the nature of the empire itself. From the varied perspective of black Saint-Domingue, it was not apparent in the early stages how to relate to the metropolitan events. Thus, for example, it was rumoured that the King had been thwarted by the Revolution in his benevolent intention to grant slaves three days to work on their own plots. Toussaint, subsequent to the slave uprising, allied himself with the Spanish Crown and only switched sides after the French Emancipation Decree in early 1794; that decree would not have happened had not a similar one been issued six months earlier in Saint-Domingue. At the same time, neither 'France' nor 'Saint-Domingue' was a self-enclosed entity. In French terms, Saint-Domingue was a structural element of the metropolitan bourgeoisie itself, without which no Revolution. Hence it was not so farfetched for slaves in Saint-Domingue to be sceptical of the metropolitan revolutionaries. Still, revolutionary French commissioners on the island played an important role in initiating emancipation, though one can debate if they were pushed or actually triggered it. Léger-Félicité Sonthonax was about as radical as any slave insurrectionist.

A decisive factor throughout, moreover, was geopolitics and war. Allied with the white planter class, Britain intervened and occupied Saint-Domingue, as did Spain. France, with permanent revolution at home and European war abroad, had no real capacity to control events in its principal colony. Thus, by default, Paris came to rely on the extraordinary Toussaint Louverture as well as such mulatto commanders as André Rigaud. It was their forces that, in the name of France, repelled and eventually, in 1798, ejected the British, who suffered immense losses. Resident white planters, *French* planters, had been willing to go for 'independence' under British auspices, not the black ex-slaves or free *gens de couleur*. This earned Toussaint some metropolitan recognition: he became deputy governor and commander-in-chief. C. L. R. James has left us an unforgettable portrait of him in the still riveting *The Black Jacobins* (1938); but it must be said that Toussaint was scarcely a Jacobin. He genuflected, if anything, towards the Girondists; but arguably remained very much a figure of the *ancien régime*. When the uprising began in 1791 he was 48 and had been a free man for fifteen years. Sympathetic accounts of the time tend to make him into some prototypical Nelson Mandela, conciliatory towards whites, capable of farsighted restraint in dealing with defeated enemies and so forth. He was in fact an astonishing

REVIEW

and brilliant practitioner of 18th-century power politics, with the keenest grasp of the whole panoply of military and political means at his disposal.

Toussaint's secret betrayal of the plan to incite a slave revolt in Jamaica, a stone's throw away from Saint-Domingue, could be used in any textbook on classical realism: preserving working relations with the powerful British naval forces was more important than any racial or political solidarity with slaves in Jamaica. The ruthless elimination of Rigaud and his autonomous forces in the South is another case; as, in a different vein, the clever manner by which Toussaint sent allied white officials back to Paris so as to get them out of the way, having turned on them or convinced them that they should represent him in the metropole. What he did not grasp (by the same token?) was perhaps the autonomous workings of ideology. C. L. R. James takes him to task for being silent, for not arousing the masses, for keeping his cards obsessively close to his chest. This is true, descriptively, but assumes, not quite convincingly, that Toussaint had some full-fledged ideology of liberation to convey in the first place. He was certainly clear about the abolition of slavery and said so. Still, when he occupied for strategic reasons neighbouring Santo Domingo in 1801, he did not de facto do anything fundamental to eliminate actually existing slavery.

The decision to invade what was then technically a French possession but still essentially Spanish and the announcement of a constitution for Saint-Domingue later the same year proved to be miscalculations. Both acts certainly angered Napoleon, now in power, who was also secretly privy to the sundry deals Toussaint had made with Britain and the United States. What caused Napoleon to make the final decision to attempt the reconquest of Saint-Domingue and eventually the reintroduction of slavery—a much greater miscalculation as it turned out—is subject to debate. A tremendous force, the greatest French army ever to be sent overseas, was assembled in 1802; the temporary Peace of Amiens with Britain had opened up for the operation. Initially successful, it was ultimately an unmitigated disaster. Toussaint himself, to be sure, was soon imprisoned in France; but his second-in-command, Dessalines (who had actually betrayed him), in conjunction with disease and lack of logistical support, destroyed the French forces. On 1 January 1804, Dessalines declared independence, in a remarkable symbolic gesture calling the new country by the old Amerindian name 'Haiti'. Toussaint himself remained loyal to France till his wretched death, starved and cold to the bone, in a remote Alpine prison in 1803. Napoleon, languishing far less wretchedly out in the South Atlantic some years hence, regretted the whole military operation, realizing that his erstwhile idea to put his money on Toussaint instead had been right.

This potted history—my own concoction, but much indebted to David Geggus and others in the burgeoning field of Haitian history—skips over much of the 'material' aspect. Saint-Domingue had two 'values' here, one potential and the other real. The former was geopolitical. In the age of sails and winds, it sat at the central entry passage to the inner Caribbean. This is the reason Britain's deals with Toussaint prohibited him from creating any navy. Autonomous black power was not something London relished; it was to be contained on land or, if a convenient way presented itself, eliminated altogether. Its very existence was a threat to every slave regime in the region. The second 'value', apart from the slave trade itself, was the immense profitability of sugar and coffee cultivation, in turn necessitating the importation of foodstuffs. The upheavals and the abolition of slavery did not destroy production altogether; but it never recovered, for the very simple reason that no regime, white, black or mulatto, could make people work to maintain it. Every government tried, chiefly by means of repressive, proto-military labour regulations. Ex-slaves chose subsistence farming instead. No one could make them do otherwise. In the best of all possible worlds, some genuinely cooperative system would have been preferable, along with a transition to more diversified agriculture; but the Revolution eliminated slavery, not property as such, or the existence of a ruling class. Haiti, contained and isolated, was thus overtaken in the capitalist world-market by such slave regimes as Cuba, Jamaica and Brazil. In Haiti, 'the last instance' arrived with the utmost clarity.

What would Hegel have made of this, or whatever he could glean of it? How would he have grasped, in particular, the specifically world-historical aspect? Buck-Morss thinks Hegel saw the novelty of Haiti, and its significance for his reworked notion of the struggle for recognition, and he used it. My own hunch, nothing more, is that, if pressed on the matter in 1806, he would rather have said the same thing he was to say in the 1820s about slavery and Africa. Hegel considered slavery an absolute wrong, a transhistorical wrong; but as with many such phenomena, it had appeared for a retrospectively rational reason, the movement from consciousness to life, in accordance with its potential and concept. Slavery should be abolished, but gradually (Hegel, as Tavares emphasizes, was a follower of the French abolitionists Raynal and Grégoire). The dialectical 'good' in this 'bad' thing, however, was to have removed Africans from the static and childish immediacy of their essentially ahistorical life at home to modern conditions across the ocean; brutally dehumanizing and horrible conditions, to be sure, but modern nonetheless, which then rendered possible the eventual reversal, as he said in 1830, into a modern state with laws and Christianity. The transhistorical lesson, so to speak, is the necessity of exposure to History and to disciplining: wrong now that the owl has flown but right in retrospect. When Hegel does mention Haiti, then, it is in terms not of master–slave relations, or their abolition or sublation, but of blacks being capable of constituting a State.

Arguments of this kind would reappear forcefully in Hegel's dialectical followers Marx and Engels: colonialism is absolutely bad but, relatively, it serves to remove the peasantry from their rural idiocy and to recast them into a class for itself. The dangers with such a progressive yardstick are apparent. On the more immediate point, it should be emphasized that Hegel, in setting forth developmental progression, was eschewing biological racism, as in fact he had already done in the *Phenomenology* with his attack on phrenology. What interested him was not race as such but place and History. At the same time, however, he was being coarse, crude and wrong about Africa. Here he did not merely reflect the ignorance of his times. Hegel had access, immediate access in Berlin, to much better knowledge that demonstrated that the 'real Africa' was certainly nothing like his patronizing and silly image of *das eigentliche Afrika* south of the Sahara, where the Truth of Africa resided, as it were. Buck-Morss, rightly following Robert Bernasconi, castigates Hegel for these shortcomings but interprets them, logically in her own terms, as a regression from the erstwhile insights of the *Phenomenology*. My own view is that the philosopher of the world-historical was always apt to think this way.

Thinking the world-historical herself, Buck-Morss attempts a radical departure from Hegel. She rejects his historical schema, the synthetic transcendence and the progressive unfolding. From the perspective of another kind of universal history, she wants to preserve (or illuminate) some of the more surprising connexions of Hegel and Haiti. Her central 'finds' here, pursued grippingly, are Freemasonry and Voudou. It turns out that everyone in this story is a Mason or might well have been one: Toussaint, along with many others in the black and mulatto elite, Napoleon, Rainsford, many French abolitionists, Hegel himself, or at least lots of his philosophical and political chums. *Minerva* itself was a Masonic organ. No particular politics, alas, actually followed from membership. As Buck-Morss points out, it all depended on the individual lodges. She describes Masonry in the end as 'the paranoid's empty signifier'. Nevertheless, what excites her about it is that it offered a non-verbal, open and indeed syncretic mode of inclusion across vast spaces, additive and mutating rather than synthesizing. Prompted by the work of Alfred Métraux and Joan Dayan, she sees correspondences with Haitian Voudou, the similarly syncretic practice of open, additive and non-dogmatic inclusion of strangers in a fictive but real collectivity in which difference coexists and is never transcended in the name of any totality; superior to Masonry, indeed, because it does not seek eternal knowledge and eternal symbols. It is, to use her favourite image, porous; without sharp edges.

These models offer her an opening to move beyond both Hegel and Haiti to the idea of a universal humanism. Hegel is a synthesizing totalizer with an imposing schema of history. Haiti, meanwhile, is no redemption story. In fact, she says on reflection, 'no clear historical narrative of any kind emerges'. Nevertheless, what the Haitian Revolution does signify, along with some moments of clarifying flashes in the rupture, is the principle of universal emancipation, the unequivocal destruction of slavery, racial and otherwise. Thus Haiti breaks the limits of the Enlightenment and this crucial moment belongs to everyone. 'Common humanity', she says, 'exists in spite of culture and its differences'—we just have not been able to see that humanity 'inclusively enough'. Moreover, such humanism in the spirit of universal history breaks both with the old victim–avenger model of history and the notion of a vanguard 'in possession of the overarching truth'; a vanguard she represents, interestingly, by the motley crew of Dessalines, bin Laden, Lenin and W. Bush. The friendly fire, so to speak, is ultimately directed at postmodernism and its Marxist counterpoint which, both in their different ways, are taken to task for being incapable of transcending the particularity of the given.

We need to think differently, then, and see the sparks when they appear. The book ends in a crescendo of exhortation: 'The limits of our imagination need to be taken down brick by brick, chipping away at the cultural embeddedness that predetermines the meaning of the past in ways that hold us captive in the present. We exist behind cultural borders, the defence of which is a boon to politicians.' What is one to say to that? No doubt we are lacking in imaginative power and locked up in our restricted cultures; but is this really our fundamental problem? Buck-Morss's voluntarism is in every way idealist. It is also devoid of strategic content, since none can appear within her undifferentiated 'humanity'. One might posit a universal interest along the lines of 'everyone has an interest in the earth not being destroyed in a nuclear war', or 'everyone has an interest in the climate not being fouled up to the point where we all drown'. The universality of anti-slavery, however, is of a different order. That principle was established, or illuminated, after a lethal struggle by slaves and ex-slaves against forces which tried to preserve or reimpose the system, chiefly because it was immensely profitable. It was a class issue, imbricated in race. The system was replaced by 'free labour' which Marx, suggestively, called wage slavery. This is the system that now reigns supreme in our own epoch, an epoch in which, as Hegel would put it, the negation is missing and the pages of History are empty. What the Haitian events reveal, then, in the starkest possible way is not the significance of 'humanity' as such but the persistence of class and class contradiction. For two centuries after slavery the wretched Haitian peasantry has been oppressed and exploited, but this is not a problem that can be resolved by opening the imagination to the sparks of our common humanity.

Buck-Morss might well object that the point of universal history is that it is not about interests. Indeed, she says that universal history is not 'history grasped as a process', in the Hegelian way; it is, rather, a 'method'. She also offers some generalities about globalization and hints at rhizomes and multitudes, never followed up. So the world-historical, syncretic or synthetic, remains elusive amidst the humanist project. In fact, the Haitian Revolution turned out to be world-historical in rather an unexpected and oddly dialectical sense. For in thwarting Napoleon, it allowed the United States to buy very cheaply indeed that vast and amorphous territory known as 'Louisiana' and so to launch in earnest its move to become a truly transcontinental power; one that Hegel, in a different context, pondered as a possible future locus of world history, though he refused to predict. Economically, the expansion of the United States was transformed by a very profitable commodity, produced in novel ways, which also drove a good deal of industrialization in Britain and, by extension, Europe: cotton. The massive growth of cotton production, the engine of 'modernization' together with steam and railroads, gave slavery a second wind, and opened up the way not only for territorial expansion but also for the struggle to the death in the United States known as the Civil War.

One of the great ifs, meanwhile, is what would have happened had Napoleon elected to join forces with Toussaint in 1802, propelling French multiracial power in the region together with what then amounted to the best army in North America. Hegel, the philosopher of 'necessity', rejected such idle speculation; but it is hard not to relish the image of the great liberal slaveowner in the White House having to face that salutary nightmare. Meanwhile, Guadeloupe and Martinique, where slavery was not finally abolished until 1848, are still under French rule. These Caribbean islands are thus, curiously, part of 'Europe'; more precisely, part of that supremely ideological construct known as the European Union, which likes to parade itself as *das eigentliche Europa*. Courtesy of subsidies and metropolitan tourism, they are doing fairly well in their subaltern place, replete with euros and MEPs. Hegel's truth, however, resides elsewhere.

Reinhold Niebuhr, *The Irony of American History*
University of Chicago Press: Chicago 2008, £11.50, paperback
174 pp, 978 0 226 58398 3

GOPAL BALAKRISHNAN

SERMONS ON THE PRESENT AGE

Deliverance from Republican rule in 2008 was heralded at home and abroad as the end of America's darkest hour of reaction. In one respect, the change was undeniable. As the face of US power, it might be hard to imagine a more striking contrast to Bush and his Vulcans than the serene and visionary Obama, personifying in the eyes of many a moral heritage squandered by the outrages of unilateralism. Once again, the city on a hill had adjusted to a new historical situation, earning the credit of a world that had recently been blown off course by the arrogance and greed of 'the other America'. In *Servius et la Fortune*, Georges Dumézil claimed that in archaic Rome and Vedic India such reversals were scripted according to a fixed mythological formula in which a barely legitimate 'regime-changer' is deposed by a providentially elected outsider, a mediator who magically restores the façades of civic tradition, but otherwise sticks to the course. America, of course, looks elsewhere for its constitutional parables. Liberal pundits were inclined to see the result in nearly providential terms, as a sign of the country's untapped capacities to ward off imperial decline, financial catastrophe and the inherited racial divisions of the body politic. Naturally, a change of this magnitude would be accompanied by a realignment of policy ideals and precepts, to set the tone for the advent of a more introspective, less strident brand of leadership.

Where did American liberalism's intellectual centre of gravity now lie? After a long season on the defensive, its leading minds had come to chalk up some of their political misfortunes in Middle America to the off-putting secularism of their 'core values'. Finally, in o8, they were able to fight back and win with celebrity ministers of their own. On the campaign trail, Obama let it be known that he was a great admirer of the once-renowned Protestant theologian Reinhold Niebuhr. The imprimatur was widely noted and educated opinion, from public radio's *Democracy Now* to the *Wall Street Journal*, was inundated with profiles of this pastor, a luminary of America's early Cold War middlebrow intellectual scene. Reviewers concurred that Niebuhr was an eloquent critic of Manichean worldviews, while also a steadfast proponent of vigilance in the face of a global nemesis. Most agreed that his writings from the Truman era offered a tonic remedy for post 9/11 hangover; thoughtful reflections on the national penchant for crusades. Of course, the influence attributed to such intellectual favourites can mislead, as with the more fabulous accounts of Leo Strauss's impact on the circle around the younger Bush. But candidate Obama's distillation of Niebuhr indicated an actual familiarity with the writer, from whom, he explained, we can get 'the compelling idea that there's serious evil in the world', and the sense that 'we have to make these efforts knowing they are hard, and not swinging from naive idealism to bitter realism'.

What light can a German-American theologian of the mid-20th century shed on the current predicaments of US foreign and domestic politics, at the onset of a period of downsized capacities and ambitions? After all, Niebuhr's 1948 appearance on the cover of *Time* magazine occurred at the all-time peak of American power, when it enjoyed nearly half the world's GDP, and openly brandished its nuclear supremacy before a clearly defined international enemy. Reflections on the moral ambiguity of such unprecedented wealth and power were meant to prompt a sense of responsibility and measure amongst the rulers of the free world. Beneath the portrait of the brooding clergyman, *Time*'s caption read 'Man's Story is not a Success Story'; within, a feature interview conducted by Whittaker Chambers, 'Faith for a Lenten Age', presented the ex-pacifist as a prophet for a new age of atomic anxiety. Niebuhr's path from founder of the Fellowship of Socialist Christians in America in 1928 to ardent Cold Warrior had brought him into the midst of what C. Wright Mills called 'the power elite', whose outlook he now essentially shared, albeit with the sort of troubled afterthoughts that one might expect from those who minister to the great and good.

It was his regional ethnic background, as with many Americans of the time, that had once predisposed him to socialism, although thereafter he showed no special attachment to these roots. Born in Wright City, Missouri in 1892, he was the son of a first-generation German immigrant from Lippe-Detmold, southwest of Hanover, who had carved a place for himself within the Deutsche Evangelische Synode von Nord-Amerika, then numbering some 200,000 Mid-Western souls. The young Niebuhr followed in his father's footsteps: after a mainly German-language schooling and seminary, topped off by a short stint at Yale Divinity School, he was posted by the Synod to a small church in the leafy northwestern suburbs of Detroit. An ambitious, hard-up 25-year-old, Niebuhr was frustrated at being limited to his own tiny denomination, and leapt at the chance to do war work in 1917—'American entrance into the war has given the conflict new meaning'. In an *Atlantic* article, he denounced the German-American community for a neutralism just then coming under broad attack, as Wilson mobilized for a campaign to turn back the Hun and bring democracy to the Old World. Through the 20s Niebuhr poured out muscular, social-gospel op-eds on issues of the day for the *Evangelical Herald* and *Christian Century*, occasionally for the *Atlantic*, *Nation* and *New Republic* as well. He was soon a keynote speaker on student Christian circuits, cultivating, according to his biographer Richard Wightman Fox, a charismatic-preacherly style: shouts, whispers, flailing arms; pacing the platform under the influence of God. His youthful notion of Christianity as the religion of the individual was replaced by sonorous rejection of liberal-rationalist claims for man's perfectibility—'the evil in man is at the centre of the self, and involves all his unique capacities of freedom'—and insistence on Biblical ontology: 'The human self can only be understood in a dramatic-historical environment.'

The British Labour Party had become his model for 'the successful application of Christianity to politics' after hearing Ramsay MacDonald lecturing at Toynbee Hall, on a 1923 trip to Europe with the YMCA's Sherwood Eddy. Back home, the Princetonian Norman Thomas, a former Presbyterian minister, struck him as a plausible American MacDonald, 'radical and responsible'. Niebuhr joined Thomas's Socialist Party in 1929, shortly after taking up a chair at the Union Theological Seminary in Manhattan, part-funded by Eddy. In 1931 *Time* magazine judged him 'one of socialism's ablest, most trustworthy advocates'. Two years later, *Moral Man and Immoral Society* struck a more apocalyptic note: faith-based proletarian mobilization was necessary to overcome—by violence if necessary—the social inertia of consumer society; this brought castigation from his Socialist Party comrades, and in the later 30s Niebuhr shifted to the safer ground of the Christian interpretation of history.

His political positions adjusted to the changing moods of the country: strongly for Prohibition in 1916, downgrading it in 1928; enthusiastic about the 'vigour' of the Soviet experiment after a YMCA trip to Moscow in 1930, but always anti-Marxist. He launched a well-informed attack on Henry Ford's philanthropic humanitarianism, but only after the *Nation* and *New Republic* had already done so. In 1925 he joined with other German-American pastors in helping the Mayor of Detroit fight off a KKK-backed electoral challenger but took a dim view of African-American prospects, noting that 'urban industrial life has so devastated the spirit of black Americans that they can hardly be approached as allies in the rebuilding of American society'. A *de facto* recruiting sergeant among German-Americans in 1917, he was a pacifist in the 20s and a military-interventionist in 1940, who later justified the atom-bombing of Hiroshima and Nagasaki. He was a militant Zionist, arguing in 1946 before the Anglo-American Committee of Inquiry on Palestine, and in his syndicated columns, for the forcible relocation of the Arab population from their 'pathetic pastoral economy', to make way for the 'Jewish energy and skill' that would dynamize the region.

It was in the post-war period that Niebuhr—valued not least for his handy, if Missouri-accented, command of German—emerged as an unofficial advisor, then official consultant to Truman's State Department on stemming the Communist tide in Europe, having briefly participated in Kennan's Policy Planning Group as well. A 1946 *Life* article, 'Fighting for Germany', set the tone, and was reprinted in *Time* and the *Reader's Digest*. He had no quarrel with Yalta, but strongly supported military aid to the Greek and Turkish Right. Niebuhr was a moving force in Americans for Democratic Action, and in 1948 penned a vicious attack on Henry Wallace as the Communists' candidate. This was the context for the *Time* cover and soubriquet of 'Establishment theologian'; Niebuhr was the man of the hour when it came to reconciling New Dealers to the hard realities of the Cold War. He did not flinch at the necessity of the H-bomb; the US was not only right to 'defend' Korea but must summon the fortitude to protect other 'soft spots' for decades to come. From 1952 until his death nearly twenty years later, Niebuhr was cruelly disabled by strokes and depression; his public presence became more shadowy. The pious Carter would later claim him as an inspiration for a presidency that in a long ensuing period of resurgent conservatism would become a byword for indecision and drift. Some might see this as a bad omen.

Until its recent return, Niebuhrism suffered from the loss of both executive sponsorship and any apparent utility in America's culture wars. *The Irony of American History* was reissued last year with a ringing endorsement from Obama amidst a widespread sense of its renewed relevance for a country that was moving beyond divisive partisanship. Originally supposed to be titled 'This Nation Under God', the book was based on two lecture series: the first from May 1949, on the eve of the final collapse of the KMT regime on the Chinese mainland, and the second from 1951, a year into a fully fledged, US-led hot war against Communist forces on the Korean peninsula. Though saturated with religiosity, the book's language makes clear that it was addressed to an educated, liberal milieu that had some familiarity with Marxism: Americans outside of this demographic were not in the habit of referring to their country as a 'bourgeois society', as this work repeatedly does. Its tone marks it off as an artefact of an occasionally apocalyptic post-war America, *The Naked and the Dead*'s world of guns-and-butter Fordism, in the years before it became more obvious that the happy days of white picket fences and rock music were here to stay.

It begins by affirming what all his readers were expected already to understand: 'we', Americans, are defending freedom against a 'demonic tyranny' that claims to represent the cause of justice. But, he added, this obvious moral difference partly conceals the whole meaning, because it does not clarify our responsibility for the situation in which we now find ourselves. In order to pursue this war effectively, Americans must bring into focus the appropriate means of attaining our obviously legitimate goals. But this relation of means to ends is not entirely within our control, because it unfolds in specific contexts that thwart human purposes to varying degrees. The coefficient of this resistance gives rise to unique patterns of history. Niebuhr went on to propose that particular historical situations could be seen as structured according to distinct modes of emplotment: the main ones being pathos, tragedy and irony, with each entailing its own understanding of the meaning of evil and adversity, and the appropriate stance to take towards them.

But determining which mode of emplotment best coheres with the essential meaning of the contemporary struggle against Communism is not easy, because each one might capture some aspect of it. The pathetic understanding sees the way of the world as beyond the limited scope of human comprehension and action; it typifies the fatalistic worldview of 'the sleep-walking cultures of the Orient', and arguably has the least purchase on the contemporary experience of the Occident. From antiquity, Western Man has, by contrast, inclined towards seeing destiny in tragic terms, and acted accordingly. For Niebuhr, the struggle against a demonic Communism has some of the elements of a tragedy, in that 'our' efforts to save the world now threaten to destroy it in a nuclear holocaust. A modern version of this view held that America's statesmen should be willing to tempt fate, however more likely this would be to bring it on, in the uncompromising pursuit of liberty. This attitude of *pereat mundus* ends in a sort of atomic existentialism, posing the extreme question of to be or not to be. Niebuhr argues that this view, happily, does not illuminate the inner meaning of our historical situation. For alongside tragic hubris, post-classical Christian traditions allow us to explore less self-destructive relations to our finitude. If not all denominations of this faith, then at least a certain modern Christian realism recognizes man's situation as ironic—unfolding within a dialectic of unintended consequences and reversals that enables us to stand aside from our own convictions with humility and a knowing smile. The chief irony of the historical moment is that though we find ourselves, in 1949, at the pinnacle of power, in abandoning our isolation we have less influence on our environment than ever before.

The contemporary experience of the end of ideology—of a disillusionment with all secular theodicies—heightens Americans' awareness of the contingency of our own political commitments, marking us off from radical dogmatists. But not everyone is able to see the ironies of history: 'the critical, but not hostile detachment which is required for their detection, is only infrequently attained.' Moreover, irony tends to be self-undermining. Without it we become like our enemies, yet an awareness of the contingency of our commitments 'tends to an abatement of the pretensions that led to the ironic situation' in the first place. Irony takes the form of a recurring realization that our commitments, while sound, are far from self-evident to others. The problem is then that the waning of naive belief can lead either to a retreat from politics or to an embittered and heedless resolution. The politically engaged ironic consciousness that is opposed to fanatic ideology keeps itself from devolving into a more literal-minded relativism—or in the worst cases, a cynical zealotry—by upholding a place for the transcendent, for unimpeachable truths. This post-secular feeling for the sacred serves as a mere ballast for a socially responsible reflexivity.

Irony, for Niebuhr, best captures the meaning of our struggle with a secular world religion that has radicalized an older bourgeois faith in progress. An earlier Yankee vision of Manifest Destiny has been refuted by recent history, but Communism has taken it up with its hyperbolic claim to be making history through the collectivization of all life. On his trip to Moscow in 1930 Niebuhr had observed the new materialist society with a mixture of admiration and disgust, marvelling that never before could one witness the spectacle of 'a generation sacrificing and being sacrificed for the welfare of future generations.' By the time he gave the lectures that went into *The Irony of American History* he had come to see Communism as a greater evil than Nazism. The latter was a moral nihilism that openly rejected justice and equality. The fact that its infamies are exceeded by Communism speaks to 'how much more plausible and dangerous the corruption of the good can be in human history than explicit evil.' But this judgement was attenuated by another comparison, of Communism to Islam. Modern civilization has inherited from medieval times a lust for military adventures to aid the helpless. In lines that speak to today's broad-based post-terror fatigue, Niebuhr gestures towards the futility of any crusade, and the advantages of waiting it out over a long, coming period of defeats in the non-European world, in the calm hope that the great foe will eventually succumb to our spiritual and material superiority.

The Irony of American History argues that, for all these advantages, the US was now on the defensive in the realm of ideological warfare, saddled with a self-righteous Yankee mentality repellent to educated opinion in both Europe and Asia. Niebuhr's plea for irony was clearly pitched as an attempt not just to console and instruct a disoriented liberal elite, but to clarify what distinguished 'us' from 'them' in a context in which Communism's promise of an emancipation from material want seemed quite plausible to many. In what way then were we essentially different from our radical brother? Niebuhr could not assume that ironic reflexivity could stand guard over the Republic's destiny, for its constituency would be small in a polity divided between a paranoiac conservatism and a liberalism whose optimistic pragmatism was now mutating into a wide-eyed faith in social engineering. American social science and behavioural psychology were as deterministic as Soviet Marxism, and led to the same deadening, bureaucratic voluntarism. Deweyan pragmatism was one of the main local variants of an insidious modern drive to abolish suffering, finitude and the need for spiritual consolation. Niebuhr was well aware of a European sentiment captured in Heidegger's claim that Bolshevism and Americanism were two sides of the same spiritual coin: 'In its most pessimistic moods European neutralism charges, in the words of *Le Monde*, that we are a "technocracy" not too sharply distinguished from the Russian attempt to bring all of life under technical control.'

Irony is often seen to be one of the many distinguishing spiritual characteristics of the West, going back to Socrates and Quintilian. From the 19th century, when it became identified with a form of consciousness attuned to the contingent, paradoxical and ephemeral, Europeans of various persuasions were wont to note its absence amongst their counterparts across the ocean. Like its sponsorship of Abstract Expressionism, the belated embrace of the ironic ideology by the more enlightened wing of the US establishment had its advantages in the context of a world culture war. From Lionel Trilling to Leo Strauss, something like irony was being promoted during this period as a way for intellectuals to reconcile themselves to the new mass society. What were the historical precedents for this mid-20th-century ideologization of irony? The early 19th-century political romantics were without exception ironists on behalf of an *ancien régime* mortally threatened by Revolutionary and Napoleonic forces. (Kierkegaard wrote: 'they want the established order to continue, but they have the more or less certain reflexive knowledge that it no longer exists.') This was a legacy that Thomas Mann could look back to in his *Reflections of an Unpolitical Man*, his defence of Imperial Germany's war aims, whose last chapter 'Irony and Radicalism' placed the two terms in diametric opposition. For Mann, romantic irony was the intellectual recognition of the primacy of concrete life over the abstract intellect.

Perhaps aware of its rather different meaning for Schlegel, Kierkegaard or Mann, Niebuhr passed over these earlier conjunctions of irony and romanticism without comment. The reason why is that he chose to see this same affirmation of concrete life against a quasi-transcendental rationalism, in diametrically opposed terms, as the quintessentially radical doctrine. In their own ways, Marx, Nietzsche and Freud, that is to say, Communism, fascism and, in the heart of postwar American culture, a demoralizing psychologism, could all be subsumed under this capacious figure. However implausible this act of force was, in his 1941 *The Nature and Destiny of Man: a Christian Interpretation* Niebuhr used 'romanticism' to designate the outlook of those forces pitted against the American way of life, although curiously in this work the historical perspective of the enemy has no name, for it is neither pathetic, tragic nor ironic.

Anticipating its current, looser meaning, irony was understood as an appreciation of ambiguity in opposition to a simplifying, good-and-evil worldview. Whether the United States traced its origins backed to Virginian deism or Massachusetts Calvinism, its self-conception as a people chosen by providence made it especially resilient to the charms of understatement and double meanings. In *Democracy in America*, Tocqueville wrote of his conversations with them: 'It is impossible to conceive of a more troublesome and garrulous patriotism.' Niebuhr felt that Americans could learn a lesson in the political meaning of irony from considering the evolution of the British monarchy, an aristocratic old regime hollowed out and transformed into a modern welfare-state democracy. Of the happier ironies of American history he noted, the most important is the conversion of its Democrats, who once upheld the Jeffersonian standard of yeoman small government, to a seemingly opposed programme of using the Federal Government and industrial unions to curb the power of big business. We do not often see the degree to which New Deal prudence has reshaped our actual political practice because we cling to a Painean individualism that has become, in yet another ironic reversal, the credo of recalcitrant plutocrats and their henchmen: 'our businessmen talk endlessly of liberty in accents which Europeans . . . associate with a decayed liberalism transmuted into a vexatious conservatism.'

These reversals and mismatches of party labels to socio-historical content have made it difficult for our allies to understand what we represent. US statesmen needed to learn that the cause of liberty was being set back by the widespread misperception that America is a pure laissez-faire society relying on the motive power of the individual. Niebuhr's concern that these hypocrisies and anachronisms exposed the US to enemy propaganda in the public opinion of both Europe and Asia occasioned some reflections on how the US should proceed at the United Nations. His earlier pacifism never went so far as to rule out military force. By the mid-30s he had come to support sanctions to hold the Axis in check, until the failure of the League of Nations led him to look at international bodies with a scepticism that matched Acheson's or Morgenthau's. He would thereafter define his political outlook in stark opposition to Wilsonian illusions. But unlike his realist acquaintances, he saw advantages in the UN as a public forum where the US might attain a better understanding of the perspectives of friends and neutrals in order to respond more effectively to the charges of the enemy. The problem was that the republic's insular past had not prepared it for international hegemony:

> We can understand the neat logic of either economic reciprocity or the show of pure power. But we are mystified by the endless complexities of human motives and the varied compounds of ethnic loyalties, cultural traditions, social hopes, envies and fears which enter into the policies of nations, and which lie at the foundation of their political cohesion.

Historically, Yankee foreign policy had been limited to opening markets and conquering backward peoples. Niebuhr quoted a speech from Senator Beveridge of Indiana to convey how this continental power conceived of its civilizing mission after its turn-of-the-century conversion to Empire:

> God has not been preparing the English-speaking and Teutonic peoples for a thousand years for nothing but vain and idle self-contemplation and self-admiration. He has made us the master organizers of the world to establish system where chaos reigns . . . He has made us adept in government that we may administer government among savage and senile peoples. Were it not for such a force this world would relapse into barbarism and night. And of all our race he has marked the American people as his chosen nation to finally lead in the regeneration of the world.

Niebuhr cited the passage without commenting on its now obvious proximity to another, less philanthropic vision of international white supremacy. With the defeat of fascism and the onset of decolonization, all such language soon disappeared from the official discourse of the West. He had never subscribed to any version of it, but in this book neither the elimination of the country's original inhabitants nor its centuries of slavery and later variant of apartheid are considered under the otherwise expansive rubric of the ironies of America's history.

In sorting out the claims and counterclaims of today's international struggle, the Christian realist reminds his readers how important it is to remember that the world's have-nots have no monopoly on the truth. In fact, their utopianism is often more delusional than the various ideologies that legitimate the advantages of the rich and powerful. By the time Niebuhr published *The Irony of American History*, decolonization was in full swing and turning into an international class struggle: 'a doctrine of class war originally designed for industrial society and aborted there, has become the dominant pattern of international relations.' Although the Communist interpretation of international inequality is even less plausible than its account of domestic inequality, the material distance between core and periphery is far greater and now more conspicuous. Communism is attractive in lands of despotic and feudal backwardness, because it fuses the promise of scientific mastery with millenarian hopes for a restoration of community. It sees the poverty and squalor around it as the product of 'imperialism', of which Americans are now the chief practitioners. 'We are thus in danger . . . of facing the international "class struggle" with uncomprehending fury.'

The fatalistic 'pathos' of the Orient has allowed its masses to be subject to the 'romantic' voluntarism of a steely new elite. It now confronts an America whose older political culture is threatening to dissolve into, at one pole, a liberal version of this same 'romantic' belief in the technocratic mastery of fate, and at the other, an extremist liberty-ism that threatens the world with nuclear 'tragedy'. America was in urgent need of post-secular irony to comprehend and overcome these warring perspectives. Despite its apparent fragility, it expressed the highest cultural potentials of late modernity, a vantage point of transcendence in an age of the contending dogmas of mass society. But what lay beyond the horizon of this epoch of world civil war? Maybe Oswald Spengler had been right after all that the universalization of the West, in whatever form of modernity prevailed, inexorably spelled its cultural decline. Television, Niebuhr mused, 'may represent a threat to our culture analogous to the threat of atomic weapons to our civilization.' In due course, as the atmosphere of exterminism began to break, responsible ironists shifted their attention to the cultural contradictions of an affluent and permissive capitalism.

More recently, its current economic predicament has generated a historical situation whose ironies have yet to be appreciated. At a time when it was widely believed that Keynesianism had solved the economic contradictions of capitalism, Niebuhr expressed a note of sceptical dissent:

> The lip service which the whole culture pays to the principles of laissez-faire makes for tardiness in dealing with the instability of a free economy, when the perils of inflation or deflation arise. They are finally dealt with pragmatically; but not before the consequences of inaction have become very apparent. Some believe that the lessons taught in the great depression of 1929 have been so well learned that a recurrence of such a catastrophe is impossible; but it is not altogether certain that this is true.

This was not simply a matter of prudent regulation, for it appeared obvious to this ex-socialist that 'we have thus far sought to solve all our problems by the expansion of our economy. This expansion cannot go on forever and ultimately we must face some vexatious issues of social justice'. For a half-century, thoughts along these lines have been more or less buried in the mainstream, and even amongst those far to its left, who seem, even as another great depression begins, to believe without question in the coming resurrection of capital. After all, it was not so long ago that our way of life seemed to be sweeping away all obstacles in its path. Today's convoluted, slow-motion meltdown has only begun to undermine the vast edifice of fictitious capital by which the existing world is sustained. Whatever difficulties lie ahead, surely this order of things will outlast the present century, for today, unlike in Niebuhr's time, no adversary appears to call its existence into question. For the time being the prevailing attitude seems to be that, after a rough patch, today's world system of capital and states will continue down a familiar path, except that the US will now have to share the leadership of the world with China and Europe, and gamely accept the necessity of curbing the excesses of financialization. Reforming the status quo presupposes its continued existence, and since these reforms are now so urgently needed, who could doubt the perdurance of the system that underwrites them? The nearly ubiquitous acceptance of this syllogism suggests that even as the vitality of capital 'objectively' falters, 'subjectively' its writ still runs further and deeper than ever. Although the now immeasurable excess of the latter over the former is not indefinitely sustainable, everyone who matters at home and abroad clearly has a strong interest in forestalling a coming devaluation of values. The prime directive of 'post-hegemonic' politics will be, perforce, the keeping up of financial and geo-political appearances.

Less than a year after its triumph, American liberalism finds itself in disarray. In Schmittian terms, it thought it had voted in the restrainer, but instead it may have installed the accelerator. Whatever form of emplotment best captures the current predicament of the United States, its new leader looks to the political theologian of Cold War liberalism to cohere its essential meaning, telling the Nobel Peace Prize committee: 'As a man of faith, I wish the world was otherwise. As President, I must face the world as it is.' Commentators have rhapsodized over this government's stately rhetoric of moral realism, but there are reasons to suspect that America's power elite no longer occupies the vantage point from which the pattern of world history might come into view. Niebuhr noted a certain limited convergence of West and East during the Cold War but, like so many of his admirers today, would probably have been unable to face its latest, most unexpected phase with 'laughter and a knowing smile'.

Jan Breman, *The Poverty Regime in Village India*
Oxford University Press: New Delhi 2007, Rs 795, hardback
458 pp, 978 0 195 69083 5

REVIEW

AARON BENANAV

LANDSCAPES OF LABOUR

Contemporary research on poverty tends to adopt one of two approaches. The first, based in political economy, is policy-driven, in line with the latest World Bank prescriptions; it operates a closed shop of mutual references and rarely admits dissenting views. The second, rooted in anthropology, consists of micro-level village studies. While quantitative analyses—even where they are informed by a more critical outlook—convey very little about the actual people concerned, field notes, conversely, generally lack a sense of the broader social, political and—above all—historical determinants of the contexts within which their subjects operate. The sociology of Jan Breman stands out for its combination of closely specified accounts of the real conditions in which people live and work with analysis of the structural forces that shape their trajectories. Famous for his field studies in India, he has also written on Indonesia, Pakistan and now China. Breman is an unparalleled storyteller. His careful descriptions of individual lives capture a totality of human relations in a single instance: the precarity of life at the bottom of the village economy; the lucky accidents that propel one or another out of the morass of poverty, and the churning of an informal economy that inevitably causes them all to slide back down. These realities tend to disappear behind reams of numbers showing healthy GDP growth and even declining poverty in India. As Breman writes, such figures do not accord with what he has seen with his own eyes in Gujarat, one of the most 'dynamic' states in India. His work in the country's lower depths tells a different story, in which vast inequalities and crushing deprivation persist.

Born in Amsterdam in 1936 to a working-class family—his father was a mailman, his mother a domestic servant; both came from families of bargemen—Breman grew up in a society savaged by the Depression and then the Second World War. The first of his family to attend college, he was initially held back from pursuing an academic career, in part by fears over its effect on his awareness of his own class origins, but also—until he won a scholarship at the end of the 1950s—by the sheer cost of studying. Childhood visits to Amsterdam's Colonial Institute had introduced him to Java's *wajang* puppetry and *gamelan* music, and Breman's studies initially focused on Southeast Asia: his MA thesis, eventually published in 1963, was on Javanese demography. But tense relations between the Dutch and their former colony prevented him from pursuing fieldwork there. The Netherlands had refused to relinquish control of West New Guinea in 1949, and by 1958, Indonesia had broken off diplomatic relations; in the early sixties military conflict had become a possibility. Breman reoriented himself towards India, conducting his first fieldwork in south Gujarat in 1962, where he was immediately drawn to the 'agrarian proletariat of tribal origin': called Dublas, they were renamed 'Halpatis' or 'people of the plough' by Gandhi, himself a Gujarati.

The doctorate based on this research, gained in 1970, was published in English in 1974 as *Of Patronage and Exploitation*; several more works centred on Gujarat have followed—*Beyond Patronage and Exploitation* (1993), *Wage Hunters and Gatherers* (1994), a study of the 'making and unmaking' of Ahmedabad's industrial working class (2004)—as well as more general volumes on Indian labour, such as *Footloose Labour* (1996), *The Labouring Poor in India* (2003) and, most recently, *India's Unfree Workforce* (2009). He has also returned to Javanese themes, notably in *Good Times and Bad Times in Rural Java* (2002), and has now begun investigations into the experience of migrant workers in China.

The Poverty Regime in Village India is based on fieldwork covering four villages in south Gujarat between 2004 and 2006; a companion volume published at the same time, *Labour Bondage in West India: Past and Present*, covers the colonial and immediate post-Independence periods, providing the historical backdrop to the work Breman has done in the region since the 60s. In response to criticisms that his previous village studies focus on exceptional, rather than exemplary cases—and that what is true of south Gujarat does not necessarily hold for all of India, let alone for the world's billion-strong informal proletariat—Breman has somewhat altered his methodology in *The Poverty Regime*: expanding his fieldwork to include more villages, located in different relations to processes of de-agrarianization and industrialization; and, after forty years of investigations, placing increased emphasis on the 'longitudinal' dimension. The text is perhaps odd in its rhythms of self-reference: almost every indented quotation comes from a previous work by Breman himself, and the researcher figures in his own account at various stages; fragments of an intellectual autobiography are scattered throughout.

The body of the book consists of four case studies, framed by introductory and concluding chapters that set Breman's findings in a wider political and social context. Scores of photographs accompany the text, depicting everyday life and labour in the villages in question, and fleshing out one's sense of the world Breman is describing. The first case study centres on a small village by the Ambika River, some 35 miles south of Surat—its pseudonym here is Gandevigam—and looks back to some of Breman's early work in *Of Patronage and Exploitation*. When he first arrived in south Gujarat in the 1960s, an extensive caste-based system of debt-bondage still operated, tying landless Halpatis to Anavil Brahman landowners. Halpatis often had to borrow money to pay for wedding ceremonies. To repay this debt, the *hali* would work on the master's farm and his wife would work in the master's house; while bonded, the *hali* would receive grain rations in the off-season. But the debt was never repaid, instead serving to ensure the continuation of the relationship: the landowners were assured of a supply of labour, and the landless provided with a minimal food security.

By the 60s, the *halipratha* debt-bondage system was disappearing, and agriculture in south Gujarat changing rapidly, with the contractualization and monetization of social relations—that is, the commodification of labour. The Brahmans themselves, especially the younger generation, began to leave the villages, no longer wanting to dirty themselves with farming. With the breakdown of patronage, Brahmans no longer felt obliged to grow labour-intensive crops, such as sugar cane, which provided work for the landless. They began to plant orchards instead, since these could be tended and harvested with minimal labour inputs—mango trees could be tended year-round by a single farm servant. There was thus progressively less work in agriculture for the local Halpatis. The landless had been excluded from Nehruite land-reform programmes in the 1950s, on the pretext that they would find work in industrializing cities. But industry failed to supply enough jobs; the result was a massive oversupply of labour.

The Poverty Regime retraces a Smithian story here, in which the attraction of baubles from the towns enticed landowners to rationalize production. But Breman also implies that the landless played some part in their liberation from *halipratha* bondage. After Independence, landless Halpatis were increasingly unwilling to subordinate themselves to their masters, leaving one for another without paying debts, or else choosing the insecure life of the casual day labourer over the secure but demeaning life of the farm servant. Breman has from the start been wary of any idealization of pre-capitalist relations of personal domination, which were in reality degrading and often violent. But with the decline of the bonded-labour system, the landless had lost not only security of income, but also a range of traditional rights, such as gleaning from the master's land. They still lived in poverty, but now, with their labour commodified, were more insecure.

Breman's work is central to current debates on the character of the informal sector, which has grown to employ more than 90 per cent of the Indian labour force. The term originated in the early 1970s, to describe a part of the urban labour force outside the organized labour market, with its statutory regulations. The World Bank had at first maintained that this informal labour force would disappear automatically, with rising growth; migrants streaming in from the countryside simply needed time to acclimatize to the rhythms of industrial labour. In the meantime, there was no need to be concerned by abysmally low wages, since informal workers could draw on traditional networks to mitigate their insecurity. As the informal sector grew, however—boosted not least by the fiscal austerity and structural adjustments imposed by the IMF and World Bank itself—it became clear that informal workers were never going to matriculate into the relative security of formal employment. The World Bank now declared that the formal sector itself was the problem—unions had built too strong a base there—and called for further flexibilization. So was born the myth of the informal worker as entrepreneur.

Mike Davis has written an extensive critique of this myth in *Planet of Slums*, drawing material from Breman's work. According to Breman, many of those in the urban informal sector do indeed work on their own account. But those familiar with the political economy of an earlier age of Western capitalism will recognize this own-account work for what it is: not entrepreneurship, but piece-work. From workshops that double as living quarters, these workers are in fact selling nothing but their labour power; they are proletarians. Piece or job work is a form of disguised wage dependency, which reduces both the direct risk to the employer and the bargaining power of the worker. Davis summarizes these points neatly in his own work. Yet in focusing on the urban slum as the dwelling place of the new informal proletariat, he misses an important aspect of Breman's recent interventions. When Breman returned to Gujarat in the late 70s, a new labour regime was beginning to stabilize. Increasingly, the rural economy was dominated by rhythms of migration, linking villages to one another and to the growing urban economy. However, this migration was not permanent, but rather circulatory, and was not only or even predominantly rural-to-urban, but also between rural areas.

This migration pattern had been wholly ignored by research at the time, which tended to assume that when people left the village, they left for good. The same surveys overlooked the influx of labour in rural areas. In fact, local landless Halpatis left their villages to work in brickfields further south only

REVIEW

to return home seven months later. Migrants from deep in the hinterland of south Gujarat, and even from other states—particularly Maharashtra—arrived in the same villages to fill local labour demand, only to leave again. A purely economic interpretation of this migration is, according to Breman, woefully inadequate. It assumes that migration is an effect of supply and demand disequilibria across linked labour markets: workers leave areas of low labour demand for areas of high demand, where wages are better. This cannot be true, because there are already underemployed workers in the areas of labour influx. Why do employers choose migrant workers, when local landless are already available and for the same price? This question orients Breman's investigations. In order to answer it, *The Poverty Regime* sets out to trace the networks that linked migrant workforces to their places of work, looking in depth at the changing experiences in two more villages: one, dubbed Chikhligam, just east of Gandevigam, and another near Bardoli, in south Gujarat's fertile central plain.

Breman is confident that the great circular migration is a consequence rather than cause of the change in agrarian employment patterns. Migrants started streaming into the villages and cities of south Gujarat because deeper inland, and not only in Gujarat, labour relations had changed fundamentally. As across much of the global South, population growth pulverized land holdings and outpaced food production, as well as contributing to ecological destruction: deforestation and overuse of other resources has led to soil erosion in areas that already suffered from low fertility. State actions have also had a profound impact: the Ukai dam that fed the Green Revolution in south Gujarat flooded out the landless and land-poor living upstream, while the construction of surfaced roads allowed displaced labour to move into the towns and villages. Breman does not entirely neglect the draw of clothes or even basic consumer goods—modernity's lures—which have trickled into villages as second-hand commodities, purchased on minimal credit. But again: once migrants started arriving, how did they outcompete local labour?

When Breman took his question to employers, they responded that local Halpatis were too lazy or not particularly suited to work in the fields—even though Halpatis had worked in the fields for years and were supposedly chosen for the brickfields further south because of their hard work. In the absence of any reasonable economic basis for the choice, *The Poverty Regime* suggests that employers prefer the migrants because they are easier to control: they have no home to return to, no family business to attend to, and no community on which they can depend; they tend to stay away from the local landless and often speak a different language. Caste and kin are still active bases of identification, counteracting horizontal class alliances.

The Poverty Regime emphasizes that the system based on circulatory migration is neither haphazard nor chaotic. Landless migrants do not wander the countryside or cities, looking for work. On the contrary, this is a stable labour regime that, however inefficiently, allocates work among the landless. Central to this process is the *mukadam*, or jobber, a figure roundly ignored by institutional surveys. *Mukadams* appear in villages during the rainy season when there is little work and offer the landless an advance on future wages to tide them over. Then, when the time comes, the *mukadams* return to collect workers and lead them to a job site. Only the men and their wives are taken, as well as some older children; the young and old, except children still nursing, are left behind in the village. The migrants stop along the way, taking up work in various villages, but they have a definite trajectory. Once they arrive at the designated job site, the *mukadam* becomes a 'gang boss'. He interacts with the employer, manages the workers, gives them a meagre grain ration while they are working, and pays them when they are done. The *mukadams* are usually from the villages themselves, though not from among the landless castes. They have to know how to read and write, keeping accounts of how much each worker owes or is owed. At the end of the job, the migrants receive the balance, if there is one. If a worker has borrowed a large sum—usually to pay for a wedding, since *mukadams* have taken over from landowners in filling this role—it may take two or three seasons before the worker pays back what he owes.

The consolidation of this labour regime has led to a new debate among researchers: is this 'neo-bondage' merely a continuation of *halipratha*, a quasi-feudal throw-back, or is it something new, a capitalist wage-labour relation? Breman sets himself firmly in the latter camp. Drawing on his own working-class background for experiential support, Breman tries to measure the dawning 'proletarian consciousness' of workers, which separates them from *halis* of previous generations. *Halipratha* was a debt-bondage system akin to Western feudalism: neither contractualized nor monetized, it was a personal form of domination. *Halis* were kept in check by relations of deference, supported by the everyday violence of masters to servants. Not that ill-treatment as such has disappeared: Breman notes that violence of men against women remains a permanent feature of everyday life. Indeed, among the migrants, the 'double shift' is omnipresent. But now, aggression flows somewhat more in the opposite direction, from landless to Brahmans, especially when the latter attempt to further restrict the freedom of the former. Riots broke out when the farmers started hiring private bodyguards to protect their crops from theft. Such episodes are part of a larger, structural change in labour relations.

Unlike under *halipratha*—where relations began informally when the *hali* was engaged and then continued throughout his life—contracts with *mukadams* are temporary, lasting only until the completion of a job or for a few years thereafter if wedding expenses have to be repaid. *Mukadams*, furthermore, are not employers but rather intermediaries. Deference, while still expected, is no longer on offer to the same extent. The landless give their children names formerly reserved for the higher castes, wear better clothing and buy consumer goods: cigarettes replace *bidis,* and so on. The landless have also come to abhor working in agriculture. If they have to take farm-ing jobs (when and where they are available), Halpatis prefer the freedom of casual labour to the bondage of the farm servant, even if they pay dearly in security of employment. These perhaps minor transformations are for Breman a barometer of proletarianization, following a change in the form of labour itself—its commodification. This is indicated above all by the fact that the employers care little how their workers survive when not employed. Indeed, one of the main reasons, according to Breman, why Brahmans pre-fer to employ migrants is that they are never faced with this question.

The new labour regime in India is based on a blurring of the urban and rural workforce into a general designation of 'wage hunters and gatherers', as the title of Breman's 1994 book has it. *Mukadams* recruit the landless for manual labour of whatever kind, in whatever location. Breman gives a vivid description of the labourers' situation:

> These working men, women and children are sometimes needed in the towns and sometimes in the countryside. Sometimes they are put to work in the obscure and degraded landscape in between these two extremes: along-side the highways and railway lines, in agro-industrial enclaves, brick kilns, quarries and saltpans, gathered together in temporary camps that arise where rivers are dammed, where earth has to be moved to dig canals or lay pipe-lines, where roads have to be laid or bridges and viaducts built, and so on. They live and work at these sites as long as the job lasts. The rest of the time they are confined in slum-like, sprawling settlements on the fringes of vil-lages, squatting with no legal title, waiting until the call comes for them to leave again.

This is not, however, to discount the importance of urbanization. Surat, for example, is one of the fastest growing cities on India's west coast. But the ine-qualities of the countryside accompany the landless into the cities, where the best jobs even in the informal sector are reserved for higher castes. Halpatis, lacking basic education, find themselves relegated to the most unskilled urban work: in construction, for example, or as 'helpers' in factories. When the construction job is finished, excess workers are simply dispersed. This of course assumes that the landless even make it to the cities. Breman argues that they have largely been shut out of the urbanizing trend. Halpatis cur-rently living in cities migrated there long ago, perhaps following former masters. The problem is not one of transportation, but rather income: living day to day with no savings, they cannot afford time without work, searching for employment. Nor can they afford to set up permanent residence, even in the slums. The latter are not open to all comers—indeed, they are filled with petty slumlords, racketeers and rubbish mongers of all kinds.

How do the poor but not destitute find a foothold in the urban milieu? Breman's fourth case study covers a village some 65 miles south of Surat, an urbanizing area in the shadow of an industrial complex built alongside the Bombay–Ahmedabad railway line. Here he finds the services of *mukadams* supplemented by a system of informal recommendations. Employers ask 'loyal'—that is, docile—labourers if members of their families or villages are looking for work; those available are then fetched from the countryside. The result is that, here too, local proletarians are shut out of industries staffed with a migrant labour force, which tends to self-segregate, both at work and in the slums, according to caste and kinship relations. Though somewhat better paid, migrant workers in diamond-cutting and artificial-silk production are no more secure.

Here, the massive oversupply of labour is only half the story. Against those who claim that a wall exists between the informal and formal sectors, Breman maintains that the two are deeply imbricated. In his 1996 *Footloose Labour* he memorably depicted 'the landscape of labour' as a vast plain, broken by many larger and smaller hills:

> These hills are zones of industrial activities whose top is made up of workplaces that are related to, or which even completely satisfy, the criteria of formal sector employment, while from lower down attempts are made to gain access to the secure but fenced-off positions . . . Great mobility and fluidity prevail at the foot of the hills. There are many candidates for whatever chance is made available. Those who qualify in the first instance are then interested in prolonging their employment for an indefinite period in the hope of, finally, gaining access to the privileged corps that enjoys more permanent tenure with all the advantages this entails.

Breman suggests that trade unions may be largely indifferent to the plight of casual workers, who are supposedly too numerous to organize. Instead, unions busy themselves fighting rearguard actions to preserve what formality remains, thereby falling prey to a logic Marx described in *Capital*: dividing the employed against the precariously employed, both lose.

Throughout *The Poverty Regime*, Breman reflects on the changes that have occurred since his previous rounds of fieldwork. In the 80s, he thought he saw signs of progress: the agrarian economy of south Gujarat was largely stagnant, but the non-agrarian sector was expanding—opening up new opportunities for the landless. But employment peaked at the end of the 80s, in part due to the completion of infrastructural and other building projects, both public and private. The spectre of 'absolute redundancy' haunts the present volume: work is becoming harder and harder to find; three quarters of Halpatis live beneath the poverty line and spend up to 75 per cent of their income on food.

REVIEW

Today, Breman argues, this destitution afflicts the land-poor as well as the landless. In the 1970s, he had suggested that the Dhodhia—another tribal caste, who own some land, but not much—were able to use income earned from migration to improve their farms or educate their children. Migration was, for them, only a temporary necessity. This was an argument against the exclusion of the landless from land reform: even a smallish plot could help reduce poverty among the land-poor. Here he concedes that the Dhodhia were not a vanguard but an exception. For the bulk of this caste, landholdings were fragmented by patterns of inheritance, amid rising population growth. They are now no better off than their Halpati counterparts.

Among the other trends Breman records is the breakdown of traditional bonds, including those within the family. The landless milieu is full of broken homes, often because one or both parents lean a little too hard on local varietals of moonshine. Members of the same family in many cases do not know where others work, or what they earn. Young men leaving for the cities often arrive unattached, bonding with others from their village or region, but these bonds too break down. Landless labourers often tell Breman that what they need are leaders. He proposes that they have to get organized, and notes that when informal workers have done so, as in the Communist-run state of Kerala, they have won improvements. To be sure, the informal sector workers are not complacent as to their plight. They make use of the weapons of the weak: stealing, breaking equipment, feigning ignorance, working slowly and carelessly. Breman stresses their defiant insistence on 'their right to live and work in dignity'. He concludes that 'there is no evidence at all of internalization of dependence and subordination, or a docile acceptance of deprivation'.

On occasions when the workers have risen together to press their interests, the Indian state—invoking a Gandhian rhetoric of resisting change imposed through force—tends to step in against them. Breman's concluding chapter contains a sharply critical account of the role of the Indian state in the perpetuation of the 'village poverty regime'—noting that when Prime Minister Singh 'went on record saying that the days of the "licence raj" were over for good, he basically confirmed that cheap labour would continue to be the cornerstone of economic policy.' Breman voices deep scepticism about government schemes such as those envisaged by the National Rural Employment Guarantee Act and the Unorganized Sector Workers' Social Security Bill, both passed in 2005. This is not merely because of practical considerations—though objections can and have been made about the geographical targeting and overall feasibility of the schemes—but for more fundamental reasons:

> To undo the vulnerability and insecurity that are the logical outcomes of the informalization doctrine, attempts to establish a floor of minimal well-being

have to rely on arrangements that are essentially formal in nature. Such initiatives stand no chance in an economic policy frame that remains firmly based on cheap labour.

Pointing to the 'enormous gap between the logic of the proposals and the economic policy currently being pursued in India', Breman considers 'the prospects for a New Deal targeting the working poor of India to be very meagre'.

But might it be possible for their situation to get even worse? Breman fears that opposition to internal 'enemies' (Muslim or otherwise) could easily be directed against the poor as such. Variants of social Darwinism are already common among elites: the poor, they say, are incapable of raising themselves up, even with state aid, and are only a burden. This growing hatred of the poor has found its way into the statistical record, source of claims that poverty in India is falling. In Gujarat itself—under the watchful eye of Narendra Modi, BJP chief minister of the state since 2001—the state's official 2004 Human Development Report claimed that the poverty rate had fallen to under 13 per cent; a miracle produced by simply omitting scores of cases of deprivation. As Breman observes, villages like Gandevigam hand out 'Below Poverty Line' (BPL) cards to almost all landless households.

Such wishful thinking is, however, not only intended to make the poor disappear, but also to make sure they keep up the good work. Gujarat depends on its super-exploited strata to deliver high rates of growth, advertising its easy labour laws in the national media. It was an early site of India's neoliberal transformation since 1980, and in its use of targeted public investment to support the development of high-tech industries on an East Asian model, sees itself as a beacon of what the country might become. Breman modestly suggests that his findings undermine the claims of India's neoliberals, by indicating how much of Gujarat's population has remained untouched by its growth. But in fact his analysis achieves much more: other states cannot emulate Gujarat's uneven growth, since this has depended in large part on its ability to draw migrant labour from poorer states into its informal labour force. Poor states are meanwhile getting poorer, as public investment declines, and rich states, possessing better infrastructure, have drawn a large share of rising private investment. Uneven growth on the 'South Asian model' is self-reinforcing.

Since the end of the 1990s, India has increasingly been ranked with China as one of the twin economic giants of the twenty-first century. Yet it is arguably India, with its talk of 'leapfrogging the industrial revolution', that presents the model for most of the rest of the world: growth will be based on industrial parks providing IT services for a global market, while manufacturing stagnates. This is a pattern of development that provides

REVIEW

jobs only for the educated, and for very few among them. It is a model in which the agricultural surplus population is no longer a weapon of development, but rather an unemployable, superfluous mass. Rather than China's labour-intensive manufacturing, India's trajectory more closely approximates that of Sub-Saharan Africa, Latin America, the Caribbean, the Middle East and North Africa, where manufacturing employment has stagnated or even declined. Could the stark disparities Breman depicts, then, represent the future of capitalism? In 2003, he wrote:

> The fight against poverty seems to have been transformed into a fight against the poor. A point of no return is reached when a reserve army waiting to be incorporated into the labour process becomes stigmatized as a permanently redundant mass, an excessive burden that cannot be included now or in the future, in economy and society. This metamorphosis is, in my opinion at least, the real crisis of world capitalism.

He is one of the few researchers sounding the alarm of this other crisis, raging on beneath the financial turmoil of today's headlines.